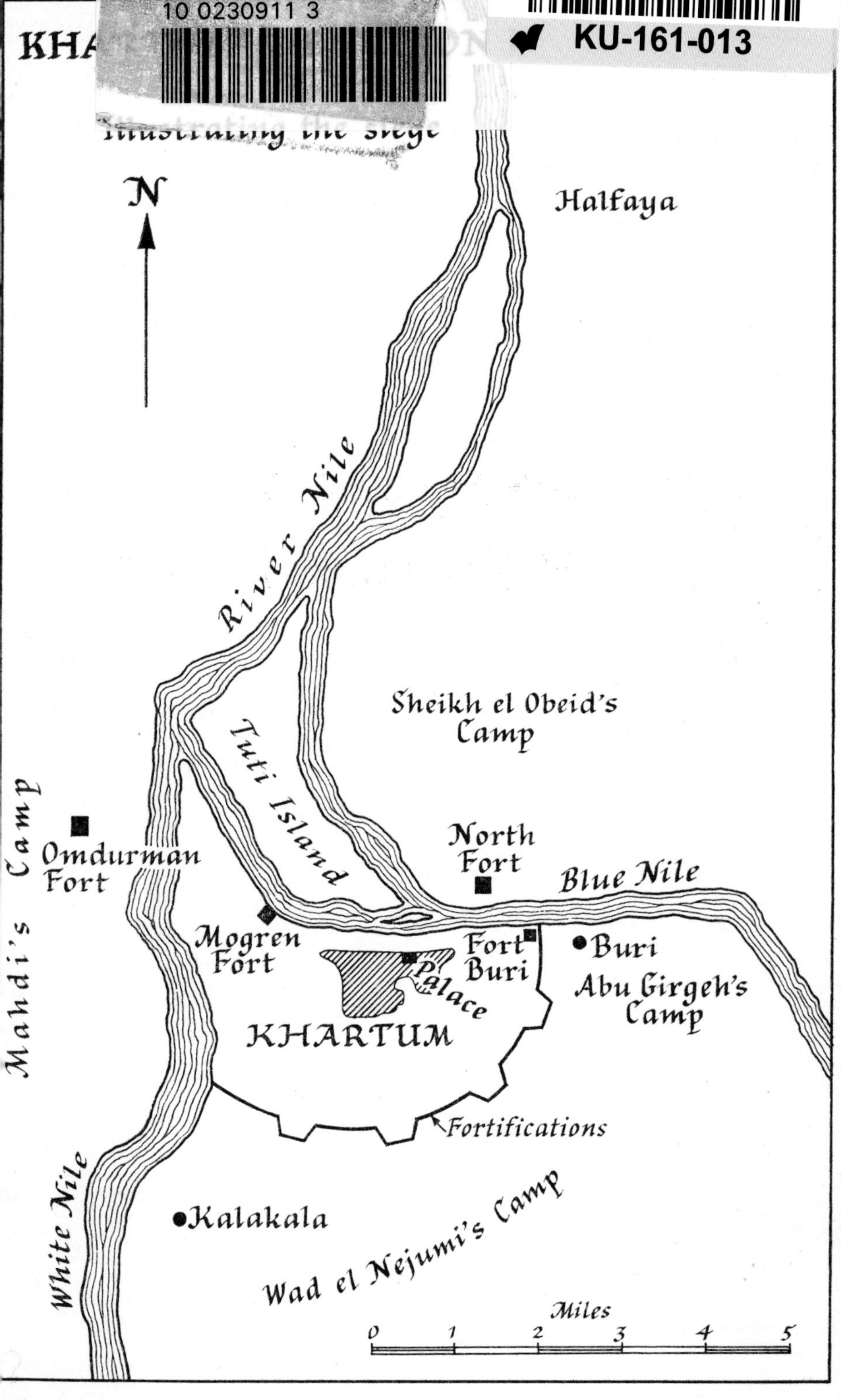
Illustrating the siege
N
Halfaya
River Nile
Sheikh el Obeid's Camp
Tuti Island
North Fort
Blue Nile
Omdurman Fort
Mahdi's Camp
Mogren Fort
Fort Buri
Buri
Palace
Abu Girgeh's Camp
KHARTUM
Fortifications
White Nile
Kalakala
Wad el Nejumi's Camp
Miles
0
1
2
3
4
5

MISSION TO KHARTUM

By the same author

REBELLION IN PALESTINE

ANGLO-EGYPTIAN RELATIONS 1800–1953

THE PURITAN TRADITION IN ENGLISH LIFE

THE SEAT OF PILATE

ARAB NATIONALISM AND BRITISH IMPERIALISM

THE PERSIAN GULF IN THE TWENTIETH CENTURY

IRAN: A SHORT POLITICAL GUIDE

THE MAKING OF THE SUEZ CANAL

FOUR ASPECTS OF EGYPT

LATE VICTORIAN: THE LIFE OF SIR ARNOLD TALBOT WILSON

Fiction

TROUBLE IN MURISTAN

MISSION TO KHARTUM

The Apotheosis of General Gordon

JOHN MARLOWE

HISTORY BOOK CLUB

This edition published in 1969 by
arrangement with Victor Gollancz Ltd.
by The History Book Club Ltd.
4 Fitzroy Square, London W.1

To

Desmond & Mary Graves

Printed in Great Britain by
The Camelot Press Ltd., London and Southampton

CONTENTS

INTRODUCTION

THE GORDON LITERATURE AND LEGEND

THERE IS IN existence an immense amount of published material about Gordon. First, there are numerous biographies, extracts from Gordon's own writings, reminiscences about Gordon, etc. Secondly, there are the biographies and memoirs of contemporary public men who had dealings with Gordon. Thirdly, there are numerous historical works dealing, in part, with the public events in which Gordon was involved.

Behind all these publications are first, the immense mass of Gordon's unpublished correspondence, and second, the official and demi-official diplomatic correspondence, the reports of Parliamentary debates, and the Press reports and commentaries concerning the public events of Gordon's career.

But for the final tragedy of Khartum, which popular sentiment, roused by the Jingo Press, by Gordon's personal admirers and by Gladstone's political enemies, elevated into a kind of contemporary Passion Play, Gordon would have been remembered in the by-ways of nineteenth-century history as a colourful eccentric—a soldier of fortune, a skilled guerrilla leader, a religious crank, a minor philanthropist, a gadfly buzzing about on the outskirts of public life. Because of his mission to Khartum in January 1884, and the manner of his death in Khartum a year later, he became a legend and a cult—a Christian martyr and the *beau idéal* of a British soldier and Imperial administrator. The Dean of Lichfield, preaching at a memorial service to Gordon, stated that, if he had been a Roman Catholic, he would have been canonised. In fact, he became, in the England of the 1880's, a popular saint, worshipped by a cult and commemorated by a growing legend, in a way which was less typical of England than of the land where Gordon died. The cult was served, and the growth of the legend nourished, by a spate of publications. Carefully edited extracts from Gordon's voluminous correspondence, mostly consisting of religious speculations and meditations, found a ready market, as did reminiscences of

Gordon by those who had known him, accounts of Gordon's career, published sermons about Gordon, poems about Gordon, fiction based on Gordon, and boys' adventure stories with Gordon as the hero. The tone of virtually everything that was published was one of uncritical adulation. Every recorded saying was a pearl of wisdom. Every recorded action was characterised by bravery, purity or unselfishness. The fact that Gordon's highly individual religious beliefs had kept him detached from any particular Church gave to his religious views a popularity which only heresy can achieve and which orthodox religious leaders can only challenge at their peril. Virtually the only dissentient note was voiced by an agnostic, Annie Besant, who, in a pamphlet entitled "Gordon Judged Out of His Own Mouth", dared to subject his words and actions to a critical analysis. Others, and particularly the public men who were being misrepresented and traduced by the makers of the Gordon legend, followed the example of Gladstone who, for the remaining ten years of his life, refused to defend himself by making any adverse public comment about Gordon.

Gordon had gained some ephemeral fame in 1863–4, when he was a young R.E. officer of 30, as a result of his exploits as a guerrilla leader in China. But he had received no recognition, apart from a C.B., from the British Government, and was relegated to an obscure military assignment, building forts in the mouth of the Thames. "Chinese Gordon", as he was dubbed by the Press, was soon forgotten. Two books were published in England about his Chinese exploits during the next few years, but neither created much stir. He only started to rub shoulders with the great world of politics and public affairs in 1874, when he took service with the Khedive of Egypt, first as Governor of Equatoria province (1874–6) and then as Governor-General of the Sudan (1877–9). From then on he became increasingly a public figure, simultaneously seeking and shunning publicity, gaining a popular reputation as a quasi-miracle-working knight-errant and an official reputation as a mischievous and tiresome eccentric. In the eyes of the British people he came to be regarded as a reincarnation of St George; in the eyes of British officialdom he was seen as a meddlesome Don Quixote.

In 1881 a selection of Gordon's correspondence while in the

Sudan—*Colonel Gordon in Central Africa 1874–79*, edited by Dr G. B. Hill—was published; in December 1883, A. Egmont Hake, a relative of Gordon's, published a biography entitled *The Story of Chinese Gordon*. This, apart from the two forgotten books about his China exploits, and numerous letters to the Press, articles in Service magazines, and pamphlets printed for private circulation by Gordon himself, represented the extent of the "Gordon literature" at the time of his departure on his last mission to Khartum. But Gordon was a voluminous letter-writer and, in spite of his frequently-expressed objections to sociability, a man with a wide and influential circle of friends. There was plenty of material in the pipeline. The searchlight of publicity which was directed on Gordon in Khartum during the whole of 1884 started a premonitory trickle of "Gordon literature" which was later to become a spate. In 1885, after Gordon's death, the cult really got under way and the legend began to take shape. During the next few years were published innumerable volumes of biography, reminiscence, anecdote, etc., about Gordon. The three really important publications, which were all published under the auspices of Gordon's family, were: (1) an edition of Gordon's Khartum Journals by A. Egmont Hake, who contributed a somewhat tendentious Introduction, which was published in July 1885; (2) *Events in the Life of General Gordon* by his brother, Sir Henry Gordon, published in 1886; and (3) A selection of Gordon's letters to his sister Augusta, covering most of his adult life, and dealing principally with his religious speculations and meditations, published in 1888.

The flow of biography, reminiscence and anecdote continued almost unabated until 1896, in which year was published the best full-length biography of Gordon up to that time—by D. C. Boulger, who seems to have been a sort of public relations officer to Gordon during his lifetime.

The reconquest of the Sudan, starting in 1896 and culminating in the battle of Omdurman in 1898, was popularly regarded in England as wiping out the stain left by Gordon's death. The creation of the Anglo-Egyptian Sudan and its administration, to all intents and purposes, as a British colony, was seen as a posthumous justification of Gordon's sacrifice. In a limited sense Gordon was commemorated in the Gordon College, later to become the first University of the Sudan, and by a statue on camel-back erected in the main square of Khartum. But his real memorial was the Anglo-Egyptian Sudan itself, of which an etherialised and idealised Gordon became, in some sort, the patron saint. A "Gordon Sunday" was kept each year at the end of January to commemorate his death; the example of Gordon was set before young British administrators as the ideal of what a British administrator should be; Gordon's "muscular Christianity" and ascetic mode of life probably influenced the ethic of the British administration; his views about Egyptian rule and the necessity of protecting the pagan south from the Moslem north certainly influenced British policy in its attitude towards Egypt and in its tendency to segregate the south from the north.

From about the turn of the century onwards, there began to be published the biographies and memoirs of those public men who had been closely concerned with Gordon's mission to Khartum. These continued to be published at intervals over the next twenty years or so. The most interesting and important of them, as far as the student of Gordon is concerned, was Lord Cromer's *Modern Egypt*, published in 1908. Lord Cromer, as Sir Evelyn Baring, had been British Agent in Egypt at the time of Gordon's Khartum mission and had been very closely concerned with it. Some 200 pages of *Modern Egypt* are devoted to a detailed account of it. This account, naturally in the circumstances, was an apologia for Cromer's own part in the affair. It was not ungenerous to Gordon, extremely critical of the British Government, and did not entirely exculpate Cromer himself. But it concluded that Gordon was "wanting in some of the qualities which were essential to the successful accomplishment of his mission", that "one of the leading features of General Gordon's strange character was his total absence of self-control" and that he "took a mistaken view of his duty".

Cromer, after twenty-five years of successful administration in Egypt, had acquired a reputation for infallibility in that broad spectrum of British middle-class opinion which formerly had idolised Gordon. In spite of a certain amount of published protest about his assessment of Gordon, the legend, although it was later to be refurbished by some scholarly, and some less scholarly, writers, was never quite the same again, although Gordon's reputation for goodness and courage, neither of which Cromer had impugned, remained unimpaired.

By 1930 it seemed likely that the sum of available first-hand information about Gordon, whether in published or unpublished form, was complete. There must have been few people still alive who had had any dealings with Gordon. Almost all those who had, had either committed the details to paper or would remain for ever silent. There was a formidable mass of published literature about Gordon. There was an even more formidable mass of Gordon's own writings, only extracts from which had been published, but most of which had been preserved. Those who had inherited this unpublished literature, whether public bodies or private individuals, were generally prepared to make them available in their entirety to serious researchers. Official and demi-official correspondence concerning Gordon in the Public Record Office had just become available to the public. The personal and political passions which had raged at the time of Gordon's death had died down. All the principal protagonists, and most of their immediate relatives, were dead. The time for evaluation had arrived, coinciding neatly with the approaching centenary of Gordon's birth in 1933.

Meanwhile, in 1918, controversy about Gordon's personal character had been instigated by Lytton Strachey's publication of a volume of essays entitled *Eminent Victorians*, containing short biographical sketches of four representative Victorian characters, of whom Gordon was one. Lytton Strachey was a member of the "Bloomsbury group", at that time regarded as the *avant-garde* in English literature and art. The four essays, based as to fact on a cursory inspection of not always reliable secondary sources, did not pretend to be scholarly biographies but represented the literary vanguard of that reaction against Victorian standards and attitudes which was to dominate the intellectual atmosphere in England during the 1920's. *Eminent Victorians* was a protest against the inherited attitudes of the middle-aged middle class, which included an uncritical admiration for the public images of such Victorian figures as General Gordon. Strachey made no attempt to correct these attitudes by objective criticism. Instead, he used, with wit, and with great literary skill, the weapons of irony and mockery. These qualities gave *Eminent Victorians* a *succès de scandale* in the eyes of a public to whom a little iconoclasm did not come amiss. Some of the *succès de scandale* was due to allegations about drunkenness contained in the essay on Gordon. These were based on a spiteful and, as was later demonstrated,[1] inaccurate account of an incident in the Sudan described in a little-known book by Colonel Chaillé-Long, an American who had been a subordinate of Gordon's in Equatoria, and who appears to have nursed a grudge against him as a result of some uncomplimentary remarks about him contained in some published extracts from Gordon's letters. (But there is evidence—see *inter alia* W. S. Blunt's *Gordon at Khartum*, p. 94, and Roy Jenkins' *Sir Charles Dilke*, p. 183 n.—about Gordon's drinking habits, quite apart from the Chaillé-Long story which was the basis of Strachey's allegation.)

This rather unimportant facet of Strachey's essay on Gordon received quite disproportionate prominence and, together with the changing popular climate towards Victorians in general, and the cumulative effect of the disclosures in the various political biographies and memoirs which had been published, contributed towards a progressive tarnishing of the Gordon image in the public mind. It was perhaps an inevitable reaction from the previous near-idolatry. By the end of the 1920's therefore, not only was his career due for objective appraisal; his character was also due for rehabilitation.

In 1931 Dr Bernard M. Allen published a well-documented and scholarly account of Gordon's career in the Sudan using, for the first time, the unpublished diplomatic correspondence in the Public Record Office, as well as other relevant unpublished material. This book, although rather unduly weighted in Gordon's favour, was the first, and a very successful, attempt at an objective appraisal of the most important part of Gordon's career. Dr Allen followed this up in 1933 by an account of Gordon's career in China (*Gordon in China*) which was distinguished by similar scholarship and only less important because the material available was less voluminous and the events described less controversial and less central to the mainstream of British Imperial history. In 1935 Dr Allen published a "popular" biography of Gordon consisting essentially of an abridged version of his two earlier works.

In 1933 a biography of quite another kind was published—*Gordon: An Intimate Portrait* by H. E. Wortham. The chief interest and value of this work lies in the author's sensitive and perceptive appraisal of Gordon's character, and particularly his religious beliefs. This appraisal is mainly based on Gordon's own letters which, as the author states in his Preface, were his "principal source".

The combination of Dr Allen and Mr Wortham gave to the world, for the first time, a rounded and objective picture of Gordon's character and career.

Also in 1933 was published, in French, an account by an Egyptian writer (M. Sabry: *L'Empire Egyptien sous Ismail et l'Ingerence Anglo-Française*, Livre 3 (1873–1879)) of Gordon's mission in Equatoria, which developed the theme, generally believed in France, and in Egypt, that Gordon, in his career as a servant of the Egyptian Government in the Sudan, had acted as a British agent, devoting himself, at the expense of the Egyptian Government, to the furthering of British Imperial designs in Central Africa.

During the first twenty years after the Second World War, when the reaction against Victorianism characteristic of the inter-war period had been succeeded by a feeling of almost reluctant respect, no fewer than six new biographies of Gordon were published in English. The most notable of these is Lord Elton's *General Gordon* published in 1954. Like H. E. Wortham's biography, this book is more concerned with Gordon's character and religious beliefs than with the events of his career, and is principally interesting from that point of view. Like Wortham, Elton made a particular study of Gordon's unpublished letters. In 1961 Lord Elton published an abridged version of Gordon's Khartum Journals, the first since Egmont Hake's rush job to catch the market in 1885.

There have also been published during the last twenty years a number of works in English by Arabic scholars which throw much light on Anglo-Egyptian policy in the Sudan during Gordon's time there. These include: *The Mahdiya: A History of the Anglo-Egyptian Sudan, 1881–1899*, by A. B. Theobald (1951); *British Policy in the Sudan, 1882–1902*, by Mekki Shibeika (1952); *The Mahdist State in the Sudan*, by P. M. Holt (1958); *Egypt and the Sudan, 1820–1881*, by R. L. Hill (1959); and *A Modern History of the Sudan*, by P. M. Holt (1961). There has also recently been published an apparently unexpurgated edition of Wolseley's private Journal written during the course of the relief expedition which he commanded—*Lord Wolseley's Campaign Journal of the Khartum Relief Expedition, 1884–85*, edited by Adrian Preston (1967).

It may well seem that there is nothing more which can be usefully written about Gordon. Commemoration, information, evaluation; all seem adequately and admirably to have been achieved. But the subject of General Gordon, like that of another great Victorian—Cardinal Newman—seems to be virtually inexhaustible. There are similarities between the two men. Both were addicted to self-explanation and self-justification on paper, the results of which have proved a rich quarry for biographers. The loyalty, the ability and the reputation of both were simultaneously derided and exploited by the respective Establishments which they served, and which employed them on impossible missions, issued them with vague instructions, and hampered them with unreasonable prohibitions. Both men were strangely compounded of arrogance and humility, of toughness and sensibility, of reasoning power and superstition. Both were submissive to Divine and rebellious against human authority. Both lacked that essential hypocrisy which can achieve a working compromise between the spirit and the flesh, between the ideal and the real, between the demands of the conscience and the promptings of the will. For Gordon, as for Newman, the frustration of his outward career was a reflection of the contradictions of his inner life.

The strangeness of Gordon's character, the exciting and bizarre events of his life, the controversial and still uncertain part which he played in an episode which has passed into the mainstream of English history, are sufficient to explain the fascination which he still excites, even after the potency of the legend created by the manner of his death—the hero betrayed, the victim sacrificed—has evaporated.

My own intensive interest in Gordon started as a by-product of a study which I was making of British policy in Egypt during the early days of the British occupation. During the course of that study, I found myself seeking an answer to three questions concerning Gordon's mission to Khartum. Why was Gordon chosen? What was he expected to do? Did he disobey his instructions? The search for an answer to these questions led to a long digression, of which this book is the result.

I hope that it may throw some additional light, both on Gordon himself, and on that tangled maze of political rivalry, military intrigue, Jingo sentiment and financial interest in which Gordon became involved as a result of his connection with Egypt and the Sudan.

Denham,
September 1968

JOHN MARLOWE

CHAPTER ONE

THE MISSIONARY

THE DEPARTING TRAVELLER was evidently a person of some importance. On the Continental departure platform at Charing Cross railway station, at about a quarter to eight of a winter's evening in January 1884, stood three very distinguished gentlemen who had come to see him off. One, who opened the carriage door for him and his companion, was H.R.H. the Duke of Cambridge, first cousin to the Queen and Commander-in-Chief of the British Army. The second, who handed him his ticket, was the Earl of Granville, the Foreign Secretary. The third, who carried the small hand-bag which appeared to be his only luggage, was Viscount Wolseley, the Adjutant-General, and England's best-known and most successful soldier.

The centre of all this deferential and distinguished attention was a small, slight, active-looking man, about fifty years of age, with fair, slightly grizzled hair and moustache and the reddish complexion imparted to fair skins by exposure to a tropical sun. There was nothing very remarkable about him in appearance except for his eyes which, somebody had once noted, "sparkled like blue diamonds". Accompanying him was a younger man, tall and spare, a Lieut.-Colonel in an English cavalry regiment. He seemed to appreciate that he only had a walking-on part in the scene which was being enacted and soon disappeared inside the railway carriage.

The little man with the blue eyes appeared either to be a careless traveller or else anxious to emphasise the hurried nature of his departure. A few minutes before the train was due to start, a young man dashed on to the platform with a black metal uniform-case which had been nearly left behind. When this had been stowed in the carriage, and while whistles were being blown and green flags waved, it was discovered that the traveller had forgotten to bring any money, or his watch, with him. Hurriedly Lord Wolseley pressed upon him a handful of sovereigns and his own watch and chain. Then, after farewell handshakes all round, the traveller, with the quick, agile movements which were habitual to him, leapt into the carriage, and the train snorted its way into the winter darkness towards Dover and the English Channel.

The traveller was Major-General Charles George Gordon, C.B., generally known to the public as "Chinese Gordon" as the result of his exploits as a guerrilla leader in China some twenty years before. His companion was Lieut.-Colonel J. D. H. Stewart of the 11th Hussars. Only that afternoon General Gordon had been taken by Lord Wolseley to an interview with four members of the Cabinet at the War Office, where he had received some rather ill-defined instructions to proceed to the Sudan and deal with a rebellion which was raging in that region. Characteristically, Gordon had insisted on starting that very night. Colonel Stewart, an officer who had spent some months in the Sudan on an official mission only a year before, and who happened to be in London at the time, was instructed to accompany Gordon as his Military Secretary and had, perforce, to accommodate himself to Gordon's precipitate travelling arrangements.

Who was this "Chinese Gordon" and what was the mission on which he had been speeded by such a distinguished company?

Charles George Gordon was born on 28 January 1833 at Woolwich, where his father, an officer in the R.A., was stationed at the time. He was the fourth of five sons in a family of eleven children. His eldest sister, Augusta, who never married, and who was some twelve years his senior, was to be his principal confidante throughout his adult life, particularly in religious matters. His eldest brother, Henry (later Sir Henry), born in 1818, who, like most male members of the Gordon family, became an Army officer, seems to have acted as a kind of family lawyer to his unworldly younger brother. Charlie Gordon's early childhood was spent at a variety of military stations, at home and overseas, according to his father's various postings. But, by the time he was ten years of age, the family had settled in the West of England, and Charlie went to Taunton Grammar School, where he spent five years. Then, after a year's special coaching at a "crammer's" establishment at Shooter's Hill, he passed into the Royal Military Academy at

Woolwich in 1848 just before his sixteenth birthday. He passed out of the R.M.A. in June 1852, into the R.E.'s, at the age of 19. One of his biographers[1] writes that he left the R.M.A. "with few regrets, little general education, a marked proficiency in surveying, and a life-long horror of examinations". He seems to have been a fairly normal officer-cadet, except that he had shown occasional signs of that ungovernable temper which was later to affect his career. From Woolwich he went to the R.E. Depot at Chatham for nineteen months and then, in February 1854, to Pembroke Docks to assist in constructing fortifications. Here, under the influence of "a very religious Captain of the name of Drew", he seems for the first time to have turned his mind towards those religious speculations which were later to dominate his life.

From Pembroke, Gordon "wangled" his way out to the Crimea, where he arrived at the beginning of 1855. He served as an R.E. subaltern throughout the siege of Sebastopol, conducting himself both bravely and efficiently. He then served on boundary commissions, first in Moldavia and then in Armenia, helping to delimit the frontier between Turkey and Russia.

He returned to England at the end of 1858 and, in April 1859, was promoted to Captain and became Field-Work Instructor and Adjutant at the R.E. Depot at Chatham. A year later, he volunteered for active service and, in July 1860, was posted to China where an Anglo-French force was engaged in trying to force on the Manchu Empire observance of treaties for opening Chinese ports to European commerce. By the time Gordon arrived at Tientsin in September 1860, the war had ended with the capture of the Taku forts covering Peking, the Chinese capital. He took part in the burning of the Summer Palace at Peking, undertaken by the British force as a reprisal for the death by torture of some British and Indian hostages in Chinese hands, and described it as "wretchedly demoralising work for an army".

He spent the next eighteen months on garrison duties at Tientsin. During that time he made opportunities to see as much of the country as possible, making one journey to the Great Wall, a distance of several hundred miles, and paying several visits to Peking, about forty miles away, where he made a professional study of the Taku forts and made himself known to Sir Frederick Bruce, the British Minister. In March 1862 the British force of about 3,000 at Tientsin, under the command of Major-General Staveley (who was a brother of one of Gordon's sisters-in-law), was transferred to the international treaty port of Shanghai, threatened by the Taiping rebellion which had for some years been waged against the Chinese Government. Gordon was transferred with the rest of the force and soon found himself once more in the firing line.

Up to this point his career had been that of an efficient, ambitious junior officer of the R.E.'s. He was now about to demonstrate his capacity as one of the greatest masters of irregular warfare that the British Army has ever produced, and to lay the foundations of that remarkable subsequent career, in which frustration warred with achievement, ambition with humility, and Christian resignation with rebellious self-assertion. He was also about to experience a first taste of fame, the conscious desire for which, contending against self-contempt for the unworthiness of such a desire, was to become such a beguiling temptation to one for whom the grosser lusts of the flesh seem to have made no appeal.

The Taiping rebellion was, in its origins, a religious movement directed against the Manchu dynasty and the traditional Chinese Confucian culture. Its leader was Hung Seu Tsien, a native of southern China who, after having failed as a young man in the competitive examinations for Chinese Government service, and after having learned something about Christianity from American missionaries, proclaimed himself as the younger brother of Jesus, commanded by God to establish his authority upon earth. He preached, practised austerities, surrounded himself with faithful disciples, and, eventually, rose in rebellion against the Government. By 1853 the Tien Wang, as he was by that time known, had established his capital at Nanking and he and his adherents were in control of much of central China. It appeared possible that he would eventually overthrow the Manchu dynasty and establish himself as Emperor in Peking. The supposed influence of Christianity on the Taipings earned them a certain popular esteem in Europe and there was some tendency to regard them as oppressed people struggling against the corruptions of Chinese Imperial rule. The European Powers, intent only on opening China to trade and on preserving the privileges which they had extorted at the treaty ports, remained neutral, prepared to recognise both sides impartially in accordance with the ebb and flow of the fortunes of civil war.

Established in Nanking, the Tien Wang retired into his palace where he devoted himself to meditation and to more carnal enjoyments, leaving the conduct of the rebellion to his generals, or Wangs. In the winter of 1860–1 the Taipings advanced westwards from Nanking down the Yangtse valley into the province of Kiangsu. This province, on the south bank of the Yangtse between Nanking and the sea, was one of the richest in China. It consisted of an alluvial plain intersected with rivers and canals, which were the principal means of transport—a flat land of cultivated fields, innumerable villages, many walled towns and a large population. At the eastward, seaward end of the province was the great international settlement of Shanghai. In the centre, situated on the Grand Canal which ran north and south through the province, was the important city of Soochow, centre of the Chinese silk trade, about 100 miles west of Shanghai.

The British attitude towards the civil war, like that of the other European Powers, was one of neutrality. Their only interest in China was the opening of the ports and waterways to European trade in accordance with those treaty "rights", for the observance of which they were fighting in the north. In pursuance of this interest, Admiral Hope, commanding the small British naval force in Chinese waters, sailed up the Yangtse in January 1861 and secured an undertaking from the Tien Wang that his forces would not come within thirty miles of Shanghai. This agreement was observed by the Taipings for nearly a year but, in December 1861, they crossed the thirty-mile limit and advanced into the immediate vicinity of Shanghai. The forces defending the town consisted of 1,000 Indian troops, 1,000 French troops, a British naval squadron and half a battery of artillery. (Units of the Chinese Imperial Army, such as it was, were engaging the rebels elsewhere in the Yangtse valley.) A defence committee of European merchants was set up under the direction of Admiral Hope, who called for British reinforcements from Tientsin and Hong Kong and arranged for the raising of a small force of Chinese under European officers and commanded by an American soldier of fortune named Ward. This force, which was stationed at Sungkiang, about twenty miles outside Shanghai, was at first maintained by the European merchants and was a new version of a similar force, also commanded by Ward, which had been raised earlier for the defence of Shanghai and disbanded the previous May.

In January 1862 the British naval squadron, in co-operation with Ward's force, moved into action against the rebels, with the object of driving them beyond the thirty-mile radius. Several successes were won and several towns captured. Ward's force, about 1,500 strong, acquitted itself well and, in order to encourage recruiting, was given the sobriquet of "The Ever Victorious Army".

In April 1862 General Staveley arrived at Shanghai from Tientsin with the advance guard of the British force. He had agreed with Bruce, the British Minister at Peking, that his force should be used to keep the rebels outside the thirty-mile perimeter around Shanghai. The British Minister was adamant that it should not be employed outside this perimeter and that its objective should be confined to the defence of Shanghai and not extended to an attempt to crush the rebellion.

During the course of operations during the summer and autumn of 1862 it became apparent to Staveley that a purely defensive policy of keeping the rebels outside the thirty-mile perimeter was inadequate to defend Shanghai and that it would be necessary at least to capture Soochow and force the rebels back on to the other side of the Grand Canal. To accomplish this, much more co-operation with the local Chinese authorities, and a stiffening and strengthening of the European-officered Ever Victorious Army, would be necessary. Co-operation with the Chinese authorities was assisted by the appointment of Li Hung Chang, a capable and energetic official, who had command of all Chinese military forces in the area, as Governor of Kiangsu in place of his incapable predecessor. But the forces under his command were incompetent and the Ever Victorious Army became progressively demoralised, first by the death of their commander, Ward, who was killed in a skirmish in September, and then by a quarrel between Burgevine, Ward's American successor, and the new Chinese Governor, which resulted in Burgevine's dismissal. The nadir in its fortunes was reached in February 1863 when, under the temporary command of Captain Holland, of the Royal Marines, it was defeated in an attempt to capture the town of Taitsan, north-west of Shanghai and just outside the thirty-mile perimeter.

Meanwhile, Staveley had been in consultation with Li Hung Chang and in correspondence with Bruce in Peking and with the War Office in London, about the future role and leadership of Ward's force. Li was prepared to take over the responsibility of paying it provided that he was given control of it. Staveley wanted to appoint a serving British officer to command it in order to provide for effective British liaison with and effective British control over the offensive operations which he considered necessary. He already had in mind for the job his relative Charles Gordon who, as an R.E. captain, had played a distinguished part in offensive operations against the rebels during the summer and autumn. But Bruce was adamant against any extension of British responsibility for operations against the rebels and, supported both by the American Minister and by Admiral Hope, was in favour of reinstating Burgevine in the command.

As the result of a fortuitous delay, due to a cyclone, in the arrival of Bruce's recommendations to the Foreign Office, Staveley's recommendations to the War Office got to London first, and approval was given for the secondment of serving British officers to the Chinese forces. On the strength of this approval, which he received in February 1863, Staveley informed the War Office that he was appointing "Brevet Major Gordon, R.E., to the command of the Ward Force". The terms of his appointment, which was made in March 1863, had been agreed between Staveley and Li in January. The British commander was to be under the orders of the Governor, who would be responsible for paying and equipping the force, which was not to be employed outside the thirty-mile perimeter without previous consultation with the British and French commands in Shanghai.

Gordon took over just after the defeat of the force at Taitsan which has already been mentioned. He had known from Staveley about the possibility for some time and had been keen to get an appointment which, at first sight, did not seem to afford any very promising opportunities for an ambitious officer. He had prepared himself for it during January and February by an intensive survey of the country around Shanghai. The Ever Victorious Army at that time consisted of about 2,000 Chinese soldiers and eighty European officers. The officers were mostly soldiers of fortune, a tough lot, undisciplined, disloyal, and quite capable of deserting to the enemy if it were made worth their while financially. Few of them were English and many of them were disgruntled at Burgevine's dismissal. The men had been demoralised as a result of the recent defeat at Taitsan. There were obvious possibilities of friction with the Chinese Governor and probable difficulties about pay and supplies. It seemed likely that any attempt to operate outside the thirty-mile perimeter would be attended with difficulties and delays imposed by the Allied command.

The primary object of the campaign undertaken by the Ever Victorious Army under Gordon's command was the capture of Soochow and the driving of the rebels beyond the line of the Grand Canal. It was a campaign in which Gordon's peculiar genius flowered as naturally as the talents of a conventional British Army officer would have wilted—a campaign of swift, darting movements, mostly by water and under cover of night, in which battle fronts were as fluid and as rapidly changing as the allegiances of most of the participants. There were no long lines of communication, no heavy siege or baggage trains, no meticulously written orders, no complicated problems of supply. It was a campaign in which flair was more important than organisation, and in which the will and personality of the commander had to take the place of any recognised chain of command.

There were endless difficulties. With his officers over discipline. With Li over the payment of his troops. With Bruce, who wanted Burgevine reinstated. Gordon overcame the first, partly by force of his own personality, partly with the assistance of General Brown, Staveley's successor, who permitted the secondment of British officers to serve under Gordon's command. He overcame the second by reason of the intimate, if rather stormy, relationship he established with Li, who came greatly to admire Gordon's personality and military genius, although he was frequently exasperated both by his outspokenness and by his persistent demands for money for his troops. On one occasion Gordon actually resigned his command as a result of difficulties over the pay of his troops and over trouble which arose between him and General Ching, the Chinese commander of the Imperial troops in the province. But these and other difficulties with Li were smoothed over, mainly, it appears, owing to the tactful mediation of Halliday Macartney, an Englishman in Li's service, and it was Li who successfully opposed Bruce's demand for Burgevine's reinstatement and insisted on Gordon's retention.

A serious crisis arose at the beginning of August when Burgevine, after his application for reinstatement had finally been turned down, seized an armed river steamer near Shanghai and, accompanied by several European freebooters, sailed it to Soochow to join the rebels. This occurred just after Gordon had tendered his resignation and was one of the factors which induced him to withdraw it and press on towards the capture of Soochow.

Soochow surrendered at the beginning of December, a few weeks after Burgevine had surrendered to Gordon and been given a safe-conduct back to Shanghai. One of the terms of the surrender was that the lives of the Taiping Wangs, or chiefs, in Soochow should be spared. In spite of this, several of them were beheaded on Li's orders after the surrender. This caused a serious crisis in the relations between Gordon and Li, and had wider repercussions affecting the whole future of the campaign against the rebels. Gordon was furiously indignant at Li's action, which he regarded as having compromised his own honour and that of his force. He reported the matter to General Brown, who, at Gordon's request, took the Ever Victorious Army under his own command and away from that of Li, and ordered Gordon to take no further part in operations against the rebels. Bruce approved of Brown's action and wrote to Gordon asking him to remain in command of the force under General Brown's orders and to "avoid collisions with the Chinese".

Bruce had always been dubious about the offensive role of the Ever Victorious Army and reluctant to see any British officers employed against the rebels outside the thirty-mile perimeter. He disliked anything in the nature of a British commitment to assist the Chinese Government against the rebels and wished to preserve an attitude of neutrality, subject to the security of the treaty ports. He had recently written to General Brown expressing the opinion that any British officer commanding a Chinese force "will speedily find himself in a position which is neither compatible with his professional reputation nor with what is due to the character of a British officer". On more general grounds he had warned Brown that "the situation in Europe is very critical and H.M.G. wants to keep clear of complications in China". The Soochow incident must have seemed to him as both a confirmation of his views and as an opportunity to revert to the old defensive policy of securing Shanghai and leaving the Government and rebels to fight it out between themselves.

But he had reckoned without Gordon himself. In the first flush of his indignation, Gordon had not only recommended the removal of his force from Li's command and its disengagement from the rebels; he had threatened Li with handing Soochow back to the rebels. He had rejected Li's attempts at reconciliation, refused a present of money, and returned a letter of congratulation from the Emperor which Li had caused to be sent. But, during the course of the campaign, Gordon had been greatly impressed with the misery inflicted by the Taipings on the wretched inhabitants, and he was reluctant to do anything leading to a Taiping reoccupation of the country which he had won from them. When he realised that his withdrawal from the campaign might well lead to this, he decided, without consulting Bruce or Brown, to reconcile himself with Li and to resume the campaign against the rebels. So, in February 1864, after Li had issued a public proclamation exonerating Gordon from all responsibility for the execution of the Wangs, he again took the field, telling Bruce that he realised that he was "open to very grave censure" and expressing confidence that, with his assistance, the rebellion could be defeated in six months, while without him it would take six years.

The incident had aroused very strong feelings, both among

the British community in China and in England, where there was a certain amount of rather ill-informed sympathy for the Taipings. People found difficulty in reconciling Gordon's first violent reaction to Li's behaviour with his subsequent condonation of it. Markham, the British Consul in Shanghai, protested. But Hart (afterwards Sir Robert Hart), the Inspector of Customs, who, with Macartney, had acted as a mediator between Li and Gordon, supported Gordon's attitude and wrote a letter to Bruce in praise of it. Bruce, although he could not have approved, accepted the *fait accompli* with a good grace and told Gordon that he had informed the Chinese Government that he approved of his action provided it was understood that "in future operations in which a foreign officer is concerned the rules of warfare, as practised among foreign nations, are to be observed". Nevertheless, the impression had been created that Gordon, however high-minded in character, and however brilliant as a leader of troops, was inclined to be flighty in his judgements and unamenable to discipline. It was he who had raised all the fuss about Li's treachery in the first place. And then, having created a diplomatic incident over it, he had disobeyed the orders he himself had solicited, and ignored the indignation he himself had excited against Li, by making friends with him again as though nothing whatever had happened in deference to a sentimental feeling which took more account of Chinese than of British interests. It seems probable that this impression, percolating through the corridors of Whitehall, explains the moderate official enthusiasm shown for Gordon's extraordinary feats in China, and helps to explain the subsequent official reluctance to give him any important employment.

Gordon's return to the field against the rebels in February had the effect which he expected. His own campaign, aided by a much closer co-operation with Li than had ever existed before the Soochow incident, ended in May with the capture of Changchow, an important town on the Grand Canal some fifty miles north-west of Soochow. Two months later the Imperial forces captured Nanking and the Tien Wang committed suicide. The Taiping rebellion was at an end. The Ever Victorious Army, which had returned to its headquarters at

Quinsan, between Soochow and Shanghai, after the capture of Changchow, was disbanded. Gordon, in recognition of his services, was promoted by the Emperor to the rank of Ti-tu, or Field-Marshal, invested with the rare and high dignity of the Yellow Jacket, and presented with a large gold medal. He refused all the monetary rewards which were offered him. The British Government promoted him to Lieut.-Colonel and invested him with the Companionship of the Order of the Bath, a reward, as Lytton Strachey remarked, "usually reserved for industrious clerks".

After the disbandment of his force in June, Gordon remained in Shanghai until November 1864, at the request of the British Minister and the Chinese Government, assisting in the organisation and training of an all-Chinese force for internal security duties. He then sailed for England, where his exploits had gained him a certain popular notoriety as "Chinese Gordon".

He was entitled to two years' leave under the generous Army regulations of those days, but only took eight months. During this time, spent mostly at his parents' home at Southampton, he seems to have had something like a nervous breakdown after the strain and responsibility of the past two years. He behaved with great eccentricity. He shunned his friends and rebuffed those who had taken an interest in his Chinese exploits and who might have helped him in his future career. He shrank from the publicity which he had earned as a result of these exploits. So his friends and well-wishers desisted from their efforts and the public soon forgot all about him.

Soon after his return home his father died and he described himself as spending most of his time acting as A.D.C. to his mother. He had long religious conversations with his sister Augusta, by then an austere maiden lady of 45, and appears to have undergone something in the nature of a religious conversion. Up to this time he had been an apparently normal, if unusually successful, young man of an evangelical piety not unusual in his class and background. It might have been expected that, with an assured career and two years of leisure in front of him, he would have started looking for a suitable young woman with whom to share his life. But then something happened. Afterwards—and this is probably retrospective simplification—he described it as a revelation inspired by 1 John 4:15, "Whosoever shall confess that Jesus is the Son of God, God dwelleth in him and he in God." From this foundation he developed over the years, through constant reading of the Bible, and through constant study of his favourite work other than the Bible—Thomas à Kempis' *Imitation of Christ*—a personal theology, akin to Gnosticism, in which the spirit was seen as perpetually at war against the flesh, and the indwelling of Christ as the subjugation of the flesh by the spirit. He found support for this theology in innumerable texts from the Bible which, as was not uncommon at the time among Evangelical Protestants, he regarded as having been literally inspired by God.

Gordon was incapable of repose or relaxation. He had little interest in nature, none at all in the arts. The dislike of social occasions and the general faroucheness imposed on him by his nervous condition after his return from China grew into a habit and became equated in his mind with that renunciation of the flesh which his religious beliefs imposed on him with increasing persistence. At the centre of his being there was a void which religious meditation could not fill and which could only be filled by a life of action. He soon found idleness intolerable and applied for re-employment. He was posted to Gravesend as R.E. Officer Commanding that station with the principal duty of superintending the erection of forts in the mouth of the Thames.

He remained at Gravesend, a professional backwater, for the next six years. By the time he went there he seems to have recovered his nervous poise and was once more ready and anxious for achievement and for advance in his profession. He was only thirty-two years of age and already a Lieut.-Colonel. With his ability, his ambition and his record, he might well have considered himself earmarked for higher things before long. But, as the years went by, he began slowly to realise that he lacked favour in high places. In 1867, when the expedition to Abyssinia against King Theodore was being prepared, he applied unsuccessfully to the War Office to be employed on it, and was much mortified at being refused. He attributed the refusal to the prejudice against R.E.s in Whitehall. But it was more likely due to his near-insubordination in China and to his eccentric behaviour after his return to England.

At Gravesend he divided his time between prayer in the early morning, his military duties from eight until two, and good works for the rest of the afternoon and evening. He was an excellent military engineer and soon found fault with the plans for the fortifications, which were in fact quite useless. He pointed this out to the War Office and a lively official correspondence ensued. But no notice was taken of his views and he probably only succeeded in confirming in the eyes of officialdom his reputation for being difficult.

He was a hard taskmaster towards his subordinates. When being rowed about the Thames inspecting construction works he insisted on his oarsmen rowing "flat out", a symptom of that neurotic urge for restless and impatient movement from place to place which was afterwards to grow on him. He seems to have seen little of his military colleagues outside working hours. In his ample spare time his religious feelings found an outlet in social and charitable work among the poor of Gravesend. He visited the sick, he threw open the grounds of his official residence, he taught in Sunday schools, he befriended homeless boys, taking some of them into his home, providing food and clothing and finding jobs for them. He lived with austerity and frugality. With a great earnestness, and a total lack of self-consciousness, he preached the Gospel of the indwelling of Christ to all those with whom he came into contact.

In all this charitable work he was driven, partly by the necessity for crucifying the flesh which his religious beliefs enjoined upon him, partly by a lively compassion for human suffering which had been awakened by the miseries he had seen in China and which made him more sensitive than most Englishmen of his class to the miseries of the English poor. He was also driven by loneliness, by the emotional void at the centre of his being which neither sacred nor profane love were ever able to fill, and by that ever-present, restless craving for activity which could never be assuaged by meditation and which was never exhausted by fatigue.

For his first two years at Gravesend his only confidante was his sister Augusta. But in 1867 he became acquainted with Mr and Mrs Freese, a couple living in Gravesend who also devoted themselves to social work. Before long Mrs Freese became Gordon's confidante as well as a fellow worker among the poor of Gravesend. Like many shy and lonely people Gordon felt a need for a few sympathetic acquaintances to whom he could pour out his thoughts and feelings in conversation or in correspondence, who did not demand more intimacy than he was prepared to give, and who were willing to confine the extent of their relationship to the somewhat strait limits set by Gordon himself. He was profoundly egocentric, in that he only wanted a sympathetic listener. He was not interested in the other person as a person, although, as he assures us, he regularly remembered many of his acquaintances in his prayers.

He was afterwards to describe his years at Gravesend as the happiest of his life. But he does not seem to have been happy either at Gravesend or at any other period of his life after his return from China. His letters to Augusta are full of anguished self-questioning on the necessity for the subjugation of the flesh. If Gordon had seen the temptations of the flesh merely in the form of the grosser carnal indulgences there would have been no problem, for from these temptations he was singularly free. For him the "flesh" represented worldly ambition. When its satisfaction was within reach, after his return from China, he rejected it; as the possibility of its satisfaction receded during the years at Gravesend, he began increasingly to desire it and increasingly to despise himself for doing so. In his conception of antithesis between spirit and flesh there was no place for compromise, no comfortable intermediate grey between the whiteness of the spirit and the blackness of the flesh. In the light of this creed he judged and condemned himself with a pitiless severity.

In the course of time, since no man, however little hypocritical, can expose himself for too long to the light of truth and live, his personality developed a protective covering. To some extent he succeeded in externalising his inner struggles and began to see himself as a reformer with a mission. The "flesh" in his eyes became identified, not merely with his own unregenerate self but also with that external world of power and influence from which he seemed excluded and for which he longed. His self-criticisms were extended to a fairly sweeping habit of criticising and condemning other people, whom he came to judge with the same severity as he was accustomed to apply to himself. The genuine kindliness and compassion which characterised his social work at Gravesend became transmuted into a more generalised desire to put the world to rights. The unaffected humility which he exhibited towards his ragged "scuttlers"[2] and his destitute old women degenerated into a somewhat ostentatious mock-modesty. All the near-saintliness of his Gravesend days was still there, not far beneath the surface, but, in his own way, as he came back into the world from his exile at Gravesend, he came to terms with the world and padded his bed of nails with a few rags of self-esteem and self-righteousness.

In 1871 Gordon was offered the position of British member of the International Danube Commission which had been set up by the Powers after the Crimean War to control navigation on the Lower Danube, the scene of Gordon's boundary commission duties fifteen years before. The position involved little work and the then high salary of £2,000 a year. It was not one likely to appeal to an ambitious officer. And Gordon was the last man likely to be attracted by the prospect of a well-paid sinecure. But he accepted it, without enthusiasm, as part of that philosophy of fatalism and acceptance of the "unrolling of the scroll", as he called it, which he had developed while at Gravesend.

While at Galatz, the headquarters of the Danube Commission, Gordon heard that his friend and Army contemporary, Wolseley, had been appointed to command the expedition being organised against the Ashantis. This was a command for which, in view of his successful guerrilla experience in China, Gordon might reasonably have considered himself to be well-fitted and, coming on top of his disappointment over Abyssinia four years previously, Wolseley's appointment seems to have convinced him that he could no longer expect any really responsible employment in British service.

In 1872, while on a visit to Constantinople, Gordon met Nubar Pasha, Foreign Minister to the Khedive Ismail, ruler of Egypt. At that time Ismail was pursuing his policy of Egyptian expansion in the Sudan. One of the cardinal points in that policy was to establish Egyptian dominion over the sources of the White Nile in the recently discovered Great Lakes of Central Africa. He had tried to obtain European, and particularly British, support for his ambitions by undertaking to combat the slave trade in that region and had, to that end, engaged the famous British Central African explorer, Sir Samuel Baker, on a four-year contract to lead an expedition up the White Nile to annex the territory and put down the slave trade there. In 1872 Baker's contract had one more year to run; he had succeeded neither in annexing the territory nor in putting down the slave trade, but he had established a number of Egyptian military posts in the direction of Lake Victoria. Ismail was anxious to engage another suitable British officer to carry on where Baker had left off. It is not clear whether Nubar offered the position to Gordon or whether he merely asked Gordon to recommend a suitable officer. At all events, Gordon expressed his willingness to take it on himself, if the British Government agreed. Nothing happened for another year, but, in August 1873, Ismail informed the British Government through Vivian, the acting British Agent in Egypt, that he wished to invite Colonel Gordon to succeed Baker as Governor of the Egyptian territory south of Gondokoro, on the Upper Nile, which he had named the province of Equatoria, and expressed the hope that the British Government would see in the proposed appointment proof of his determination to organise the new province thoroughly and to suppress the slave trade. The British Government replied, with some lack of enthusiasm, that there was no objection to Gordon's taking service with the Khedive, that the War Office were prepared to release him for the purpose, but that the terms of his appointment should be negotiated direct between Gordon and the Egyptian Government and that the British Government could take no responsibility in the matter.

Gordon had sought this appointment in an attempt to escape from the frustration of his career in the British Army, a frustration to which his religious beliefs and his charitable preoccupations had been unable to reconcile him. He professed to regard it as another instalment of the "unrolling of the scroll" and told Augusta that "for some wise design God turns events one way or another, whether man likes it or not, as a man driving a horse turns it to right or left without consideration as to whether the horse likes it that way or not. To be happy a man must be like a well-broken, willing horse, ready for anything."

Gordon, characteristically, refused the salary offered of £10,000 a year and insisted on receiving only £2,000, the amount he was receiving at Galatz. He told his sister: "My object is to show the Khedive and his people that gold and silver idols are not worshipped by all the world."

He went to the Sudan in February 1874 and remained there as Governor of Equatoria until the end of 1876. Virtually all this time was spent on and around the Upper Nile trying to carry out his instructions from the Khedive to develop an organised Egyptian administration in the Upper Nile valley between Gondokoro and the Great Lakes and to suppress the slave trade in that region. In the words of an English writer,[3] "he infused new life into the flagging administration . . . he did what he could to soften the effects of Baker's harshness. . . . Stage by stage he extended the Egyptian sway towards the Great Lakes. He set up a chain of military posts between Rejaf and Dufile where clear water would carry his boats to Lake Albert. He then brought Unyoro and a part of Uganda between Lakes Albert and Kioga within the sphere of Egyptian influence, planting his farthest garrison at Niamyango on the Somerset Nile sixty miles from Lake Victoria."

Gordon's personal efforts were herculean. He was working in a very hot and unhealthy climate with practically nothing in the way of medical or other amenities or comforts. He had a small staff of Europeans who, with the shining exception of Romolo Gessi, an Italian whom he had recruited in Galatz, were of little assistance to him. He had to cope with corrupt and incompetent Egyptian officials and with homesick, discontented and unreliable Egyptian soldiers. His communications with Cairo were tenuous and his instructions from Cairo, when he received them, contradictory and unhelpful. He had no knowledge of Arabic or of the local dialects. He often made things unnecessarily difficult for himself by a bad choice of subordinates, by hasty appointments, by equally hasty dismissals, and by occasional ungovernable outbursts of temper and temperament. He had no previous knowledge of the country, and no previous experience of large-scale administration. The natives, finding it impossible to distinguish between Gordon's "civilising mission" and the raids of the slave traders, were suspicious and hostile. The slave traders were strong and well-organised.

In face of all these difficulties and disabilities the extent of Gordon's achievement was remarkable. He put an end to the use of the Nile as a channel for the slave trade. He established an inter-connected chain of military posts and some sort of coherent administration from Gondokoro to within sixty miles of Lake Victoria. But he came to recognise how ephemeral and how ultimately useless these achievements were. His experiences with Egyptian officials and with Egyptian troops made him lose faith both in the efficacy and the desirability of the Egyptian "civilising mission", although he seems to have retained his faith in Ismail's sincerity. He realised that his policing of the Upper Nile had merely resulted in driving the slave traffic westward to the overland route through Bahr-al-Ghazal, Darfur and Kordofan. He saw that the long and tenuous line of communication via the Nile would have to be supplemented by the shorter route via the east coast at Mombasa if the country round the Great Lakes was to be opened up to trade and civilisation. When an Egyptian expedition sent, on Gordon's suggestion, to achieve this had been ordered to return as the result of the British Government's intervention on behalf of the Sultan of Zanzibar, he abandoned any further attempt to extend Egyptian dominion southward.

He left Equatoria at the end of 1876, mentally and physically exhausted with his labours and determined never to return. He had come to the conclusion that one object of his mission—the extension of Egyptian authority to the Great Lakes—was both militarily impossible and morally undesirable, and that the other object—the suppression of the slave trade—could not be achieved in this way. In Cairo he told the Egyptian Government that he intended to resign his post, giving as his principal reason the lack of enthusiasm for combating the slave trade shown by the Egyptian authorities in Khartum. Ismail tried to dissuade him and the question was still open when Gordon returned to England towards the end of December. He returned, as he had returned from China eleven years before, to find himself comparatively famous.

There was at that time great popular interest in Central Africa as a result of the discoveries of Livingstone, Speke, Grant and others. This interest was stimulated and kept alive by the Royal Geographical Society, the Anti-Slavery Society and by various missionary societies. The region was also beginning to be the scene of political and commercial rivalries and endeavours. The French, the Portuguese and the King of the Belgians were all interested in opening up what had been known as the "Dark Continent" by penetration from the west along the Congo basin. The British and Germans were interested in penetration from the east coast which was under the nominal rule of the Sultan of Zanzibar. And the Khedive Ismail was, as we have seen, interested in penetration from the north by way of the Nile valley.

So much interest was taken in Gordon's achievements in Equatoria. In France it was generally assumed that Gordon was a British agent working in Central Africa under a thin disguise of an Egyptian Government appointment. This was certainly untrue for, although Gordon, during his time in Equatoria, maintained a fairly regular correspondence with Stanton, the British Agent in Cairo, this correspondence was entirely personal (Stanton was a fellow R.E. officer) and he received no instructions, and no requests for information, from the British Government, who seem to have taken little interest in him.

But in the eyes of the Press and public, to whom his exploits in the Sudan had recalled his earlier achievements in China, Gordon was beginning to be regarded as a national hero. In January 1877 there was a suggestion in *The Times* that he should be appointed Governor of Bulgaria with a view to utilising "his genius for government and command" nearer home. But nothing came of it, although, on 11 January, he had an interview with the Foreign Secretary, Lord Derby, in connection with this possibility. Gordon also became interested in the prospect of opening up a route to the Great Lakes from the east coast of Africa and had some negotiation about this with Mr (afterwards Sir William) Mackinnon, who was later the moving spirit in the formation of the British East Africa Company. But nothing came of this either and when, in mid-January, he received a telegram from Ismail, in his best insinuatory vein, asking him to return to the Sudan, he was pleased enough to do so. He wrote to a new friend, the Rev. Horace Waller, whom he had met in the course of his contacts with the Anti-Slavery Society: "The Pillar moves on and goes towards Egypt. After much trouble I find I must go." On the advice of some of his friends Gordon demanded and obtained from Ismail the Governor-Generalship of the entire Sudan as a condition of his returning. He took the view that, without this extension of his authority, he would be able to do nothing effectively to suppress the slave trade, which he regarded as the principal object of his mission to the Sudan. He set off for Khartum at the beginning of March in a mood of euphoria unusual with him. He sent a message to *The Times* in which he wrote: "It will be my fault if slavery does not cease and if those vast countries are not open to the world. So there is an end of slavery if God wills; for the whole secret of the matter is in the government of the Sudan and, if the man who holds that government is against it, it must cease."

But it was not to be quite as easy as that, even though, in August 1877, as the result of an Anti-Slavery Convention between the British and Egyptian Governments, the slave trade was outlawed in the Egyptian dominions. So long as, on the one hand, there was a demand for slaves in the Moslem world and, on the other hand, an apparently unlimited supply of slaves in Central Africa, the slave trade would go on in spite of conventions and other legal bans and in spite of attempts to suppress it by force. The principal, almost the only, economic activity of the Sudan was the slave trade, by which the Arab and Moslem north exploited the human material of the pagan and negro south. And the economy of the south was not less dependent on the trade than that of the north. For, while the north benefited both from domestic slavery and from the profits of the slave trade, the south, for lack of any settled agriculture or legitimate trade, had to dispose of its surplus population by selling it into slavery. All this became gradually apparent to Gordon during his next three years of furious activity, riding the length and breadth of the Sudan on camel-back, alternately fighting, threatening and cajoling the slave traders, promoting and dismissing officials, quarrelling with Cairo, trying in vain to make peace with Abyssinia, and trying, also in vain, to instil some sense of justice, order and humanity into the administration of the Sudan.

He was happier than he had been in the south. The dry air, the wide horizons, the swift movement on camel-back, suited him better than the swamps, the forests and the slow river-borne movement which had characterised his years in Equatoria. Most of all perhaps he enjoyed the despotic authority which he wielded. Within the vast area of the Sudan he had virtually unlimited powers of life and death, reward and punishment, appointment and dismissal. His word was law, his smile fortune and his frown disgrace. He never had to explain or apologise, accommodate his rule to the results of discussion or debate, receive or act upon advice from any but those from whom he chose to ask it. But, as well as the courage, the self-reliance and the decisiveness of the despot, he acquired something of the despot's arrogance and capriciousness, his petulance and vanity, and his habit of confusing the outward forms of obeisance with genuine expressions of gratitude. His long, solitary excursions on camel-back gave him plenty of time for religious meditation and his despotic temper was at all times subject to, and sometimes partly controlled by, the remarkable capacity for self-analysis and self-knowledge which his religious outlook had enabled him to develop. But another part of his religious make-up was responsible for a most serious defect in an administrator and man of affairs. He attributed everything he did either to the direct guidance of God operating on his spiritual self or to the natural impulses of the flesh operating in spite of his spiritual self. The one explained his successes, the other his mistakes. In either case they were outside his control. In this way he justified and rationalised, instead of recognising and trying to correct, an inherent inconsistency, an inability to take a long or objective view, and a tendency to snap judgements and decisions which were frequently reversed almost immediately afterwards. The concept of antithesis between the spirit and the flesh also tended to make him judge men in terms of black and white with no intermediate shades of grey. A man was either a paragon or a villain, and frequently the paragon of one day was the villain of the next and vice versa. Another serious defect was generated by the necessity for omniscience more or less thrust upon him by the necessities of his position. He ceased to be able to distinguish between those things about which he was qualified to express an opinion and those things about which he knew nothing or next to nothing.

In popular British estimation Gordon's administration of the Sudan was a glorious illustration of the superiority of the British character and the Christian religion and a triumphant vindication of the assumed British right to bring the blessings of civilised rule to less well-endowed peoples. An intrepid Englishman, a Christian, an officer and gentleman, the very flower of civilised humanity, was seen to be exhibiting the characteristic British traits of courage and integrity, energy and will-power as a means of bringing order and justice to a people who had so far been deprived of these things. The official view was better informed and became less and less favourable as time went on.

From 1876 onwards the inability of the Egyptian Government to meet the coupons of its accumulated foreign debt led to increasing European interference in the administration of the country. The position taken up by the European bondholders, who were mostly British or French and who were supported by their respective Governments, was that Egypt was a bankrupt estate whose administration had to be supervised by representatives of the creditors in order that these creditors might receive their due. The Khedive Ismail spent three years exercising all his considerable ingenuity in trying to avoid this supervision until, in 1879, Great Britain and France, tired of his manœuvres and acting for once in unison, moved the Sultan of Turkey to depose him.

During the course of these manœuvres, Ismail, in an attempt to avoid the serious investigation into Egyptian finances on which the creditors and the European Governments were trying to insist, announced the appointment of a Commission of Inquiry of his own choosing on which Gordon was to be President, and Lesseps, the founder and head of the Suez Canal Company, Vice-President. The representatives of the Powers, regarding this proposal as an attempt by Ismail to wriggle off the hook of control on which they were trying to impale him, would have nothing to do with it. Ismail, nevertheless, sent for Gordon, who arrived in Cairo from the Sudan in March 1878.

Gordon knew nothing of finance and had only the vaguest understanding of the financial imbroglio in Egypt. But he had an affection for, and a sense of loyalty towards, Ismail and a considerable dislike for the European financiers and other entrepreneurs whom he considered to be battening on Egypt. The short point at issue was this. In 1876, after the Egyptian Government had declared its inability to meet the coupons on the various and onerous foreign loans which it had contracted, an arrangement had been arrived at with MM. Goschen and Joubert, the representatives of the British and French bondholders, for the consolidation of the bonded indebtedness, the capital and interest on which were slightly written down, and for the appointment of an international Debt Commission to collect the sums set aside for the service of the debt from the proceeds of various categories of revenue allocated for the purpose, and to distribute these sums to the bondholders in accordance with arrangements agreed with the Egyptian Government. It soon became clear that the revenue estimates on which the Goschen–Joubert arrangement had been based, and which had been accepted from the Egyptian Government without investigation, were over-optimistic. The foreign creditors, and the British and French Governments, were prepared to consider some new arrangement, but only as the result of the findings of an independent Commission of Inquiry, on which the Debt Commissioners would sit, and which would make a thorough investigation of Egyptian official finances with particular reference to the practice by which the Khedive and his family acquired and maintained large private estates out of public funds. Ismail's invitation to Gordon and Lesseps was an attempt to use the respectability of their names and reputations for the avoidance of such an investigation.

Gordon arrived in Cairo on 7 March 1878, having travelled down from Khartum on camel-back, by river steamer and by train. He went to dinner with Ismail the same evening and immediately accepted his invitation to be President of a Commission of Inquiry on the understanding that Lesseps would be Vice-President and that the Debt Commissioners were not to serve on it. As he explained afterwards: "I was angry with these Commissioners of the Dette because I thought they had been too hard on H.H." Next day, he went to see Vivian, the British Agent, whom he remembered, contemptuously, as "a pretty, black-eyed boy at the R.M.A.", and who reproached him for having agreed to accept the Presidency of the Commission on Ismail's terms. He told Vivian, in effect, to mind his own business. Later in the day, he had another interview with Vivian, together with the French, German and Austrian Consuls-General, who all told him that Ismail would be risking his throne if he went on with his plans and that Gordon was taking a grave responsibility by encouraging him to do so. Gordon, still quite unabashed, offered to convey this to Ismail, "with any remarks I like to make about the futility of your words". He was clearly in a very truculent mood. He conveyed the message to Ismail, who "did not seem to care a bit", and next day he had a talk with Lesseps. Lesseps admired Gordon, but he was a realist and a man of business, which Gordon was not. He had had long business relations with Ismail and had no illusions about him. As President of the Suez Canal Company he had no intention of setting himself in opposition to the British and French Governments in order to oblige a ruler who no longer had the power to be of much use to him. He listened patiently to Gordon's proposals which, characteristically and in advance of any inquiry, he had already worked out, for a settlement of the debt question. These consisted of a suspension of the coupon payment about to fall due, a cancellation of the Sinking Fund provisions in the Goschen–Joubert settlement, and a reduction of the rate of interest from 7 per cent to 4 per cent. After some discussion, Lesseps made it clear that he would only serve on the Commission on terms agreeable to the British and French Governments.

Gordon also met Baring, the British Debt Commissioner, for

the first time. He was not impressed. "Baring was in the nursery when I was in the Crimea. He has a pretentious, grand patronising way about him. We had a few words together. I said I would do what H.H. asked me. He said it was unfair to the creditors and in a few moments all was over. When oil mixes with water we will mix together."

Baffled and bewildered by what he regarded as an atmosphere of conspiracy, with Lesseps, the foreign Consuls, the Debt Commissioners, and even Riaz and Sherif, two of the principal Egyptian Ministers, all banded together against himself and Ismail in a determination to extract their pound of flesh from the Egyptian peasant, Gordon telegraphed to Goschen, the representative of the British bondholders, telling him that he had recommended Ismail to suspend payment of the next coupon and offering to arrange directly with him for an inquiry into the finances. Goschen replied rudely that he would not look at him and that the matter was in the hands of the British Government. Gordon then wrote to Ismail proposing that he should suspend the payment of the next coupon by decree in order to enable arrears of salaries of Government employees to be paid and offering to telegraph Lord Derby, the British Foreign Secretary, that he accepted all responsibility. But Ismail, who preferred more indirect methods, and who had apparently decided that Gordon was too blunt an instrument for his present purpose, made himself inaccessible. Four days later, under strong pressure from Vivian and the French Consul-General, and without telling Gordon, he agreed to appoint a Commission including the Debt Commissioners, with Lesseps as President. Gordon was thrown over, and Mr Rivers Wilson, a Commissioner of the British National Debt, whom the British Government had suggested for the purpose, was appointed Vice-President.

So Gordon, in his own words, "left Cairo, with no honours, paying my passage . . . H.H. was bored with me after my failure and could not bear the sight of me . . . I dare say I may have been imprudent in speech." It was a bitter humiliation, after having arrived in Cairo as the great man from the Sudan, determined to put the financiers in their place, to set the finances to rights and to do justice to Egypt's oppressed peasants. It was Gordon's first serious contact with what is now known as the Establishment; he had been worsted and humiliated and the memory of it rankled until the end of his days. He would have appreciated some lines written by G. K. Chesterton long after his death;

They have given us into the hands of the new unhappy lords,
Lords without anger and honour who dare not carry their swords;
They fight by shuffling papers; they have bright dead alien eyes;
They look at our labour and laughter as a tired man looks at flies.

He, the sword-carrying warrior, coming with anger and honour from the Sudan, had been beaten by paper-shufflers like Vivian, whom he had saved from being bullied at Woolwich, and Baring, the supercilious ex-Gunner who had been in the nursery when he was in the Crimea.

In the eyes of the Establishment, Gordon had made a fool of himself, behaved like a Bull of Bashan in the china shop of Egyptian finance. Rivers Wilson, the man who succeeded Gordon on the Commission of Inquiry, afterwards told Lord Salisbury that "Gordon, for all ordinary Foreign Office work was officially 'impossible', but, if there were anything exceptionally astonishing to do in a wild country, he was the man to do it". When everybody knew, or thought they knew, what was to be done and how to do it, Gordon was of no use, because he thought he knew best and could not be trusted to take the sensible view and obey orders. But when nobody knew what to do, a man like Gordon might somehow work a miracle, and in any case could not make matters worse than they were. In spite of all his absurdities, his ungovernable temper, his distressing naïveté, his curious manners, his religious mania, there was a charisma about Gordon which even his detractors recognised. Perhaps even, in a desire to be something more than fair to a virtuous eccentric whose integrity made them feel uncomfortable, they exaggerated the effect of this charisma and became the unconscious dupes of the crescent Gordon legend.

Gordon returned to Khartum via the Horn of Africa, where

he inspected the Egyptian settlements and dismissed Rauf Pasha, the Governor of Harrar, who eventually succeeded him as Governor-General. He got back to Khartum in June 1878, and, in contrast to his continual movement during 1877, spent the next nine months there, until March 1879, at the unaccustomed business of routine administration. Much of the heart had been taken out of him by his humiliation in Cairo. "Since my visit to Cairo," he wrote, "I feel very different about the Sudan and H.H. It is only a sort of sense of duty that keeps one up to the work." And he soon found that there was a different atmosphere in Cairo. When Ismail had appointed him, it was provided that the Sudan administration should be completely free of the Ministry of Finance in Cairo. But the Commission of Inquiry which Ismail's creditors had forced on him began to start interfering and demanding a contribution from the Sudan revenue. Gordon made a personal appeal to Lord Salisbury, the British Foreign Secretary, and the demand was not persisted in. But when, in the autumn of 1878, a partly European Ministry was installed in Cairo, with Rivers Wilson as Minister of Finance, attempts at interference were resumed. Gordon, who hated finance, and who was once described by Lesseps as keeping the Sudan accounts on odd scraps of paper, with vouchers for expenditure in one pocket and vouchers for receipts in another, set himself to master that country's chaotic finances. He found that there was a small but regular annual deficit. Since it was clear that this deficit would no longer be met by subventions from Cairo, he determined to make the Sudan financially self-supporting. To this end he withdrew the garrisons from the southernmost posts he had opened when in Equatoria and stopped work on a railway from Wadi Halfa in the north.

He also made some attempt to reform the administration. Despairing of the competence and honesty of high Egyptian officials, he adopted a policy of appointing young and mostly untried foreigners to provincial governorships and other important posts. Dr Schnitzler, an Austrian naturalist, was appointed Governor of Equatoria, and Messadiglia, an Italian engineer, as Governor of Darfur, where he was later replaced by Rudolf Slatin, a young Austrian soldier of fortune. Lupton, a young British officer in the Merchant Navy, was made Governor of Bahr-al-Ghazal. Gordon tried, and failed, to secure the services of Sir Samuel Baker and Sir Richard Burton, and those of C. M. Watson, a young R.E. officer who had been with him for a short time in Equatoria. His ablest foreign assistant, and the one closest to him, was Romolo Gessi, who had been with him in Equatoria and who later joined him in Khartum. After making plans, which came to nothing, for sending Gessi on an expedition to try to open up a route to the east coast, Gordon, in 1878, placed him in charge of a military expedition to destroy the slave traders who, after Gordon's attempts to bring them to order the previous year, had risen in rebellion.

Not all of these foreign appointments were suitable and they all created resentment among the Egyptian officials. Gordon's policy, which was the policy later followed by the British administration in the Anglo-Egyptian Sudan, and which was inspired by an exaggerated dislike and mistrust of Egyptian officialdom, was gradually to eliminate the Egyptian element both in the civil administration and in the army and to replace Egyptian officials, officers and soldiers by native Sudanese. In order to facilitate this, and because few Sudanese were as yet deemed capable of filling high positions, Gordon used European officials as a stop-gap. The policy did not work well, partly because it depended on the co-operation of some, at least, of the Egyptian officials, which was not forthcoming, and partly because of the unsuitability of the officials to whom he gave his confidence. Gordon was no judge of men, and his ignorance of Arabic placed him in the hands of those Egyptians and Sudanese whom he chose to trust. And his lifelong habit of instant decision, made on impulse, inspiration and instinct, while appropriate and necessary when fighting a guerrilla war, was the negation of efficient civil administration. He might have made a success of governing a small colony, where his personality and charisma would have carried him through. But the Sudan was too vast to be controlled by force of character alone, particularly when that force of character was exercised by a man of alien race and religion who did not even speak the local language.

In the midst of all his administrative toils and trials Gordon never lost sight of what he regarded as his principal mission in the Sudan—fighting the slave trade. He was by no means a doctrinaire anti-slaver of the Exeter Hall variety and frequently found himself in disagreement with the unrealistic purism of the Anti-Slavery Society. He had no violent objection to domestic slavery and, knowing something about conditions of sweated woman and child labour in some trades in England, to say nothing of underpaid and overworked domestic service, was scornful of English hypocrisy on the subject. But he had seen, and been appalled by, the horrors of slave hunting and slave raiding, the merciless conditions under which slaves were transported, the mutilations, the deaths from wounds, thirst and starvation, the total disregard for human suffering, the utter degradation, characteristic of the slave trade. For Gordon, fighting the slave trade was a moral imperative, transcending any consideration of duty to Egypt or the economics of the Sudan. It was only the question of the slave trade which had induced him to return to the Sudan at all after his years in Equatoria. During his euphoric first year as Governor-General, when he had toured Kordofan and Darfur on camel-back, promoting and dismissing officials, marching and counter-marching, encouraging, threatening and, when necessary, fighting, he began to think he had killed the slave trade by the force of his personality. But he had not. In the spring of 1878 the slave traders, led by Suleiman Zubair, son of the great Zubair Pasha, the "uncrowned king" of the Bahr-al-Ghazal, then in exile in Cairo, rebelled against Egyptian rule in an attempt to re-establish their old autonomy. Gordon suspected, probably correctly, that the moving spirit behind the rebellion was Zubair Pasha, the father.

While Gordon was in Khartum, toiling at finance and administration, Gessi pursued the rebels through the swamps and forests of Bahr-al-Ghazal. In March 1879 he left Khartum to join in the war and, while Gessi was dealing with the *zeribas* in the slave-hunting grounds of Bahr-al-Ghazal, harried the slave caravans and staging-posts in the open country of Darfur. At the end of June Gordon and Gessi met at Tawaisha, in Darfur. By that time the rebellion was on its last legs as a result of their efforts and, after the meeting, Gordon returned to Khartum, leaving Gessi to finish the work. Within a month, Gessi had rounded up the rebel leaders and had had most of them shot, including Suleiman Zubair. This act of Gessi's, which had been authorised by Gordon, was to have important consequences later.

When Gordon returned to Khartum in July he learned of the deposition of Ismail at the instance of the British and French Governments, of the accession of his son Taufiq, and of what he regarded as the subjugation of Egypt to the interests of the European bondholders. This news, and the state of mental and physical exhaustion in which he found himself, determined him to resign his appointment. He had few illusions left about Ismail, but he admired him for the tenacity of his resistance to his creditors and had managed to convince himself that, in fighting his own battles, he had also been fighting the battles of the people of Egypt who were being oppressively taxed in order to meet the coupons on the foreign debt. He disliked the methods and mistrusted the motives of the Europeans who, as he saw it, were battening upon Egypt, and made little distinction between the bankers who advanced the money, the entrepreneurs who benefited from it, the statesmen and diplomats who insisted on its repayment with interest, and the Egyptian Pashas who connived at the whole process.

Gordon's mistrust of the Egyptian Pashas was reciprocated. He had never taken any pains to conciliate them and had, on various occasions, been unnecessarily rude to many of them. He had been a personal favourite of Ismail's, whose likes and dislikes were as capricious as Gordon's own, and, so long as Ismail was ruler, Gordon had enjoyed his protection and done more or less as he liked. But, with Ismail gone, he no longer enjoyed that protection. The new Khedive, Taufiq, was suspicious of all his father's favourites. And Gordon's administration of the Sudan had given rise to a general suspicion among the Pashas that, whether as an individual or as an agent of the British Government, he was adopting a deliberate policy of cutting off the Sudan from Egypt.

With the Europeans in Egypt, who were more powerful than ever since Ismail's departure, Gordon was unpopular both as an "Ismailite" and because of his behaviour over the financial Commission. So, all in all, he neither loved, nor was loved by, influential circles in Cairo and Alexandria.

Gordon, no judge of character and extremely susceptible to flattery, was favourably impressed by Taufiq in spite of his prejudice against him. He allowed himself to be persuaded into undertaking a mission to King John of Abyssinia in an attempt to settle the long-standing frontier dispute between Abyssinia and Egypt. It was a hopeless mission from the first. He achieved nothing with King John, who treated him with the grossest discourtesy. In Cairo, a confidential telegram which he had sent to Taufiq, recommending various territorial concessions to be made by Egypt, was "leaked" to the Press by Egyptian Ministers with the object of demonstrating Gordon's disloyalty to Egypt. On his return to Massawa after a most perilous journey he was greeted by a telegram from the Anglo-French Dual Control, which had just been set up over Egyptian finances, asking for explanations about his financial administration of the Sudan. He had left for Abyssinia in a very depressed state, comparing himself to Job, longing for death and, as he told Augusta, praying to God to visit all the sins of Egypt and the Sudan on his head and make him the scapegoat for the wickedness of their peoples. While in Abyssinia he was elevated as always, in spite of the humiliations he received, by the presence of danger and by a life of action and movement. But, by the time he returned to Cairo at the beginning of January 1880, he was a very angry man indeed, furious with Taufiq, with the Egyptian Ministers, with the Dual Control and with the British Government. His nerves were raw as a result of his exertions and privations and, while in Cairo, he behaved in a very eccentric manner, which heightened the unfavourable impression he had already created. The only person with whom he seems to have got on well was Edward Malet, the new British Agent, and he was alarmed and distressed by Gordon's eccentric behaviour. He was rude to the Khedive when offering his resignation. He quarrelled with Baring, now the British Controller-General, over the slave trade, and challenged Nubar to a duel. He left Egypt disgusted with the extent and manner of European interference and with the Egyptian Pashas for conniving at it. He wrote that "as long as aliens govern Egypt and the voice of the Egyptian people is smothered, so long must Egypt be the basest of kingdoms", and expressed the view that the "announcement of a constituent assembly would stop palatial intrigues and paralyse European ditto and settle the question. . . . The best course is that which is just and right, and that course is the convening of the Notables." That is to say, Gordon was in favour of some popular and indigenous check both on Khedivial absolutism and on alien interference. A few months before, just after Taufiq's accession, Sherif, the Prime Minister, had suggested this and had resigned when Taufiq, with the approval of the British and French Agents, had rejected the suggestion. Sherif had been replaced by Riaz Pasha, a Turk of the old school, who co-operated closely with the Dual Control, and whom Gordon suspected, probably correctly, of being the origin of many of the intrigues against him.

While in Egypt Gordon, unusually for him, consulted a doctor. Although his physique must have been remarkably robust, he was addicted to self-medication and had for some time been erroneously convinced that he suffered from angina pectoris. The doctor told him that there was nothing organically wrong with him, but that he was suffering from nervous exhaustion and recommended several months of complete rest "with no business or political excitement".

Before leaving Egypt, Gordon, in an interview with Moberly Bell, *The Times* correspondent, summed up his work in the Sudan. "I am neither a Napoleon nor a Colbert; I do not profess to have been either a great ruler or a great financier; but I can say this—I have cut off the slave dealers in their strongholds and I made all my people love me." Shortly before he had written that nobody in all the length and breadth of the Sudan could raise his hand without his permission. He had become the dupe of his own charisma. His influence, due to the respect inspired by his personality, was undoubtedly very great in the Sudan, so long as he was there in person. But he had made many enemies, in the Sudan as well as in Egypt, and such benefits as he had been able to bring to the common people of the Sudan were both limited and transient. It was obvious to him, before he left Egypt, that neither Taufiq, nor the European Powers, were prepared to do anything to follow up his reforms in the Sudan. Rauf Pasha, the Egyptian official Gordon had dismissed from the Governorship of Harrar for his harshness, was appointed to succeed him as Governor-General without protest from the British or French Agents. But he seems to have convinced himself, and others, that his influence in the Sudan was such that, if only he could return there with the support of the British and Egyptian Governments, all would be well. This conviction grew upon him, was communicated to and propagated by others, and persisted until, four years later, he was confronted on the spot with the realities of the Mahdist rebellion.

Joseph Reinach, a French fellow traveller, who had been secretary to Gambetta, published an amusing account of conversations with Gordon on the boat between Alexandria and Naples. "Ce diable d'homme, parlant presque à la fois anglais et français, mêlant à des observations d'une expérience profonde, les fantaisies les plus bizarres d'un esprit excité, inventant toutes les heures un nouveau partage du monde et surtout de l'empire ottomane, louant Dieu avec exaltation et accablant de sarcasme le ministère tory—les saltimbanques, les mountebanks." Gordon took his companion to lunch with Ismail, who was living in exile near Naples, and appeared to be completely absorbed by the affairs of Egypt and the Sudan and the Ottoman Empire generally. He passed rapidly through Rome where, he told his sister, he went to see St Peter's and "thought it poor". Then he went to Paris, where he tried to persuade Lord Lyons, the British Ambassador, to intervene with the British and French Governments over the question of a suitable successor to himself as Governor-General of the Sudan in order to provide for its better government and for the effective suppression of the slave trade. Lord Lyons seems to have regarded Gordon as unbalanced and communicated his impression to the Foreign Office.

When he arrived in London at the end of January, Gordon tried to interest the Foreign Office in the Sudan but seems to have found most important doors closed to him. In a letter to Lady Burton, the wife of the explorer, he described himself as "an orb which is setting or rather is set".

Having quarrelled with the Egyptian Government, and having been rebuffed by the British Government, Gordon, absorbed by the slavery question, considered resigning from the British Army and offering his services to King Leopold of the Belgians, to whom he was introduced by Wolseley, for work in the Congo, where Leopold had formed a "Congo Association" with the object of opening up the region for trade under his own auspices. Leopold was actuated by the crudest colonial ambitions for exploitation and gain, but Gordon, who was very naïve about some things, was a great believer in the "civilising mission" of Europeans in Africa and considered that the only ultimate cure for the slave trade was the opening up of Central Africa to European influence by means of "legitimate" trade. This was, to some extent, true, but he overestimated the benefit of substituting one form of exploitation for another and allowed himself to be deceived by the motives of Leopold and other "developers", such as Mackinnon the shipping magnate, who was interested in the formation of a chartered company for opening up the interior of Africa from the east coast. Despairing of any possibility of Egypt, either alone, or in conjunction with Great Britain or France, taking any effective action in the Sudan, Gordon's idea seems to have been to encourage and to participate in the expansion of these European enterprises into the "black" areas of Africa and so cut the Arab slave traders off from the source of their supplies.

Gordon may have felt that the British Government's coldness towards him was to some extent compensated by the interest of the Prince of Wales, who invited him to a luncheon where he met the Duke of Cambridge, cousin of the Queen and Commander-in-Chief of the army. The Duke persuaded him not to send in his resignation and, since Gordon had given his need for rest as the reason for contemplating doing so, invited him to take a year's leave.

At the end of February, Gordon went to Brussels to see Leopold about the Congo. In view of what he had told the Duke of Cambridge, he was no longer free to take service with Leopold immediately and his conversation with the King was inconclusive. But Leopold, who was already employing Stanley, the explorer, in the Congo, was interested and gave Gordon to understand that there was a post open for him.

From Brussels, Gordon went on to Lausanne with a young nephew for a rest. His mind was still on the Sudan and the Near East and, while in Lausanne, he wrote, for private circulation, a memorandum on the treaties of San Stefano and Berlin, in which he criticised Disraeli's intervention in favour of the Ottoman Empire at the Congress of Berlin and advocated a partition of the Ottoman Empire involving an enlargement of Greece, Bulgaria and Montenegro, the establishment of an international régime at Constantinople, the annexation of Egypt by England and Syria by France, and annexations by Italy on the Dalmatian coast and in the Horn of Africa. He proposed that constitutional governments should be set up in Egypt and in what remained of the Ottoman Empire and that Great Britain should retain Cyprus.[4] These proposals, which advocated almost everything in the Near East which the Powers had been trying to avoid for the past fifty years, was greeted contemptuously by the British Government, Disraeli, the Prime Minister, declaring it to be the work of a madman. In retrospect, nevertheless, it seems fairly sensible, although Gordon, characteristically, ignored the almost insuperable difficulties of bringing such a settlement about by international agreement.

In March, while he was still in Lausanne, the Government of Cape Colony asked the Colonial Office for Gordon's services as Commandant of their military forces. The British Government were prepared to release him but Gordon, his mind still on the Near East and the slave trade, and perhaps lacking enthusiasm for the policies of the Cape Government, declined the offer.

Gordon soon got tired of Lausanne, where he was supposed to be resting. He found nothing to occupy him, apart from continual letter and memorandum writing, and the company of his young nephew and the Rev. Mr Barnes, Vicar of Heavitree in Devonshire, with whom Gordon struck up a friendship and who became one of his principal correspondents on religious matters.

He was back in England early in April, attracted thither by the news of the General Election results, which were starting to come through and which showed that the Liberals had ousted Lord Beaconsfield's Conservative administration. Gordon, who had disliked the Conservative Government both because of its Near Eastern policy and because of its attitude towards himself, was delighted. "What a grand victory over those fellows", he wrote to Mr Allen, Secretary of the British and Foreign Anti-Slavery Society, when he heard the news. He had no particular admiration for Mr Gladstone, although he shared his views about Pashas and Bashibazouks, and for turning the Turks "bag and baggage" out of Europe, but he knew and admired Lord Hartington, who had been the Liberal leader at the time of the Election and whom he would liked to have seen as Prime Minister. As soon as he heard of the Liberal victory, and before Gladstone's Cabinet (in which Hartington became Secretary of State for India and, later, Secretary of State for War) had been formed, he wrote to Hartington telling him that he disapproved of the Near Eastern policy of the previous administration. With his letter he enclosed a copy of his memorandum on the treaties of San Stefano and Berlin, advocated the support of Italian claims to Massawa, deplored the Conservative Government's support of Egyptian expansion in the Red Sea, stated that Egyptian revenues were incapable of supporting an expansionist policy and expressed the opinion that "the extension of Egyptian rule is an unmitigated evil".

Gordon seems to have thought that these views were reasonably in accordance with the sort of policy which a Liberal Government might be expected to pursue in the Near East; they were largely in accordance with the views of the Whig section of the Cabinet, of which Hartington was the leader. It seems probable that he had hopes of being restored to official favour and of being offered some important appointment, preferably somewhere in the Ottoman Empire. What he got was a post which he did not very much want, and for which he was almost grotesquely unsuited. Lord Ripon, who had been appointed Viceroy of India by the new Government, offered him a post as his Private Secretary, in spite of being warned by Dilke, Under Secretary at the Foreign Office, "that he would find him too excitable to be possible as a secretary".

It is said that T. E. Lawrence was once offered (and refused) the post of Secretary of the Bank of England by Montagu Norman. Lord Ripon's offer to Gordon is equally incomprehensible. Gordon's acceptance is perhaps less so. He was accustomed to taking decisions on impulse; when they turned out well he gave the credit to Divine guidance; when they turned out badly he blamed the unregenerate promptings of the flesh. But, at the time, he never knew whether the prompting was sacred or profane. In the case of Ripon's offer, he was almost desperately anxious to return from the wilderness into the British "Establishment", and he had welcomed the advent of the Liberal Government as a chance of enabling him to do so. It was not quite what he would have chosen; nevertheless there was the opportunity of being a great power behind the scenes. And, after the slights received in Cairo and the rebuffs experienced in London, it did seem a sort of rehabilitation. His family were anxious for him to accept. Perhaps he saw himself, momentarily, as an *éminence grise* to the most powerful of Eastern potentates. So he accepted, and regretted his acceptance even before he left England, telling Halliday Macartney, his old friend of China days, that he had "decided in haste, to repent at leisure".

He resigned the appointment on 2 June, immediately after landing at Bombay, having accompanied Ripon and the Viceregal party on the voyage out. The immediate cause of his resignation was a disagreement with Ripon over the question of Yaqub Khan, the ex-Amir of Afghanistan, who had been deposed by Lord Lytton, the previous Viceroy. Gordon, who could only have made a cursory study of the affair, considered that he should be reinstated, but British-Indian official opinion was resolutely opposed to this, and Ripon was not prepared to ignore the views of the official hierarchy. But, apart from this, Gordon, on the voyage out, had come to realise that the whole social and official milieu in which he would have to live and work was utterly abhorrent to him. Lord Ripon accepted his resignation with good grace and was no doubt glad to be rid of him, although, like most persons who failed to get on with Gordon officially, he retained a great admiration for him personally. The incident must have confirmed Whitehall officials in their conviction of Gordon's extreme eccentricity.

Meanwhile, a crisis had blown up in China and that country was on the verge of a war with Russia. While Gordon was on his way to India, Sir Robert Hart, Inspector-General of the Chinese Customs, who had known and admired Gordon at the time of the Taiping rebellion, telegraphed to him care of the Chinese Customs agent in London, inviting him to come to Peking with the tantalising, but vague, offer of "really useful work on a large scale". Campbell, the Customs agent, took no action until he read of Gordon's resignation in the London newspapers on 4 June. He then forwarded Hart's telegram to Bombay where Gordon was packing his bags. To him it must have appeared as a providential intervention. He seems to have assumed that the invitation was inspired by his old friend Li Hung Chang, now Governor of Tientsin, with whom Gordon had kept up an intermittent correspondence. He replied to Hart that he was leaving for Shanghai immediately. On the same day he telegraphed the War Office asking for leave of absence until the end of the year: "Am invited to China: will not involve government." Not unreasonably, he was told by return cable that he "must state more specifically purpose and position for and in which you go to China". Gordon, quite truthfully, replied: "Am ignorant; will write from China before expiration of my leave." This elicited the decision: "Reasons insufficient: your going to China is not approved." Gordon, quite determined to go, replied requesting the War Office to "arrange retirement, commutation or resignation of service", and took passage to Shanghai forthwith, giving a newspaper interview on his departure, stating that his fixed purpose in going to China was to "persuade the Chinese not to go to war with Russia". The War Office, having noted this interview and having, at Gordon's suggestion, consulted Campbell, the Customs agent, sent Gordon a telegram, which reached him at Colombo, granting him the leave he had requested on condition of his not taking military service in China. From about this time, and possibly as a result of his luncheon with the Prince of Wales and the Duke of Cambridge a few months before, there is evidence of a guardian angel looking after Gordon at the War Office.

On his arrival in China Gordon found himself in the midst

of a maze of intrigue. The Emperor and Government wanted war with Russia and were confident of their ability to win it. The European Ministers, among whom the German Minister took the lead, wished to avoid war and, as a means of doing so, were encouraging Li Hung Chang, Governor of Tientsin and one of the most influential magnates in China, to rise in revolt and overthrow the Government. The object of Hart's invitation to Gordon appears to have been to induce him to assist Li in this design.

One of the mysteries of Gordon's career lies in the political acumen which he nearly always displayed in China compared with the political obtuseness which he displayed everywhere else. He usually formed a correct appreciation of a situation; it was only in China that he adopted his means to the ends in view. He soon saw the trap which had been laid for him and refused to walk into it. He ignored Hart, who was privy to the plot, and he ignored the British Minister, Sir Thomas Wade, who was not privy to the plot, but who had been warned by the Foreign Office to keep Gordon out of mischief. Having decided to take his own line, Gordon telegraphed once more to the War Office to resign his commission and went straight to Tientsin to see Li Hung Chang. He persuaded him of the folly of the rebellion which was being urged on him by the European Ministers and then went to Peking to deal with the Chinese Government. He managed to argue them out of their determination to go to war by pointing out the certainty of their being defeated. Thus, in the course of a few days, he helped to avert the alternatives of a foreign war on the one hand and a civil war on the other. It was a remarkable exercise in diplomacy, achieved in the face of the hostility both of the foreign Ministers and of the British Government. He improved the occasion by submitting various memoranda to the Chinese Government and to Li Hung Chang about the organisation of the Chinese Army, the administration of China, the folly of the railway construction being pressed on the Chinese Government by the representatives of the Powers, and the means by which China could best preserve her independence of Europe. None of this can have endeared Gordon to the foreign colony in China, about whom he wrote: "Write them down as identical with those in Egypt. . . . Their sole idea is, without any distinction of nationality, an increased power over China for their own trade and for opening up the country, as they call it. . . . No colonial or foreign community in a foreign land can properly, and for the general benefit of the world, consider the questions of that foreign state. The leading idea is how they will benefit themselves."[5] It is strange that Gordon did not apply this judgement to people like King Leopold and Mackinnon, who were "opening up" Central Africa, and seemed to imagine that the annexation of Egypt by England, and the introduction of constitutional government there, would somehow counteract the nefarious activities of Turkish Pashas and European bondholders and merchants.

Gordon did not linger in China. He took ship from Shanghai, having just received a telegram from the War Office declining to accept his resignation, cancelling his leave, and ordering him to return home immediately. He replied reproachfully that he had already booked his passage home before receiving the telegram and asked if they insisted on cancelling his leave. His guardian angel at the War Office intervened and he was granted another six months' leave. But there was no sign of any recognition for his services in China, which may indeed have been regarded as embarrassing by the British Government.

Gordon, his mind still on the slavery question, had been thinking of going to Zanzibar in connection with Mackinnon's colonising plans, but, apparently still anxious to keep on good terms with the British Government, he decided to return to England, where he arrived at the end of October. He was soon bored by inaction and, in November, paid a short visit to the west of Ireland "to have a little shooting and satisfy myself on the state of the lower classes". On his return, after about a month's experience of the country, he wrote a letter to *The Times* advocating the compulsory expropriation of Irish rural landlords by the Crown and the administration of their lands by a Land Commission. As with so many of Gordon's approaches to vexed problems, he was apt to consider that a statement of a desirable end, without any consideration of means, represented a solution. He then wrote to *The Times* advocating the abandonment of Kandahar, in Afghanistan, a country of which his knowledge was even less than his knowledge of Ireland. He also, during the next few weeks, wrote to and for the Press on a number of other subjects, on which he was better informed, such as Abyssinia, the registration of slaves in Egypt and irregular warfare.

By this time he had become a very well-known figure in England. There were frequent references to him in the Press. Early in 1881 an edition of his letters from the Sudan, edited by Dr Birkbeck Hill, was published. On 19 February his cartoon appeared in the famous *Vanity Fair* series after a display of anguished mock-modesty on his part. The caption accompanying the cartoon probably reflected the contemporary popular view of him: "Colonel Gordon is the most conscientious, simple-minded and honest of men. He has a complete contempt for money, and after having again and again rejected opportunities of becoming rich beyond the dreams of avarice, he remains a poor man with nothing in the world but his sword and his honour. The official mind, being incapable of understanding this, regards it as a sign of madness. And as it is found that, besides being utterly without greed he is also entirely without vanity and self-assertion, he is set down by the officials as being 'cracky' and unsafe to employ in comparison with such great men as Lord Chelmsford, Sir Garnet Wolseley and Sir George Colley. He is very modest and very gentle, yet full of enthusiasm for what he knows to be right. This enthusiasm often leads him to interfere in matters which he does not understand and to make in haste statements he has to correct at leisure. But he is a fair, noble, knightly gentleman such as is found but once in many generations."

For the first time, Gordon moved a great deal in Society. He saw a lot of Reginald Brett, afterwards Lord Esher, who was private secretary to Lord Hartington, and whom Gordon had met in connection with the Ripon appointment. He dined with the Duke of Sutherland and met the famous millionairess, Baroness Burdett Coutts, and her young fiancé, Mr Ashmead-Bartlett. He paid several visits to Florence Nightingale.

All this travelling on "the tram of the world" did not interfere with his religious meditations. As a result of his friendship with the Rev. Horace Waller, with whom he stayed at his Northamptonshire rectory in December 1880, Gordon's religious beliefs took a new turn in that, for the first time, he began to attach importance to the Eucharist. He came to regard what he called "worthy reception" of the Eucharist as an essential means of attaining that indwelling of Christ and that subjugation of the flesh which had been the objects of his religious life. He wrote that although "Christ will save a non-communicant . . . that non-communicant will never attain the subjection of the body unless through obedience to his Lord's last wish." In his meditations on the Eucharist, as communicated to his sister Augusta, and to his old Greenwich confidante, Mrs Freese, he came very near to a belief in the Roman doctrine of transubstantiation. But, characteristically, he wore his transubstantiation with a difference.

Neither his religious meditations, nor his social rounds, nor his writings for the Press satisfied his restlessness. As always, he wanted action. But no word came of any appointment from the Government who, like the previous Government, seem to have come to the conclusion that Gordon was "not clothed in the rightest of minds". In April 1881 he telegraphed the Government of Cape Colony, who had asked for his services a year before, offering to assist over the troubles they were having in Basutoland. He received no reply. Despising himself for his worldly ambitions and, perhaps, mortified that nobody seemed willing to gratify them, he played with the idea of devoting himself to social work in the East End of London. He told Florence Nightingale that he could never "bring himself to accept the shibboleth of the Indian or Colonial middle classes" and that he considered his life's work as done. He talked of going to Palestine and working among the sick there.

Suddenly, in his usual impulsive way, he accepted the unimportant post of C.R.E. Mauritius in order to oblige a brother-officer who had been posted there and who was anxious for an exchange. He left England at the beginning of May 1881 and remained in Mauritius for a year. For the first time since Gravesend he was doing a job of straight soldiering in his own Corps. As at Gravesend, he drove his subordinates hard, and kept himself aloof from local society, apart from walking expeditions with some of the young subalterns and naval officers.

He formed a poor opinion of the senior officers at the station, referring in a letter to "a deadly sleep over all my military friends here" who "grudge two hours a week for their duties".

He had plenty of time on his hands. As usual he was torn between religious meditation and a desire for involvement in political affairs. On the one hand he told his sister to stop sending him the English newspapers and concentrated on a study of the Bible and the mysteries of the Eucharist. For the first time he began to regard the Bible as in the nature of an oracle—the direct voice of God—and, in his own words, adopted the belief that "whenever we are in doubt about anything, we should place the matter before God in prayer, then take the Bible wherever we may be reading and, having our attention fixed on the subject of our prayer, seek to get the answer and take it in just the same way as if we heard God's voice". On the other hand, he was still hankering after playing a role in world affairs, preferably in Egypt and the Near East. He wrote two papers for the War Office, denigrating the importance of Malta, the Mediterranean and the Suez Canal, and advocating the continued use of the Cape route and the building-up of coaling stations in the Indian Ocean. A third paper, written in October 1881, dealt with the current situation in Egypt. He criticised the Anglo-French Control and Taufiq for having rejected Sherif Pasha's proposals for a constitution and for having dismissed him as Prime Minister and appointed the autocratic Riaz Pasha in his place. He ridiculed the notion that Egypt had become more prosperous as a result of foreign intervention and wrote: "I do not think that it has altered at all except in improving its finances for the benefit of the bondholders. The army may be paid regularly, but the lot of the fellahin and the inhabitants of the Sudan is the same oppressed lot as before. . . . The only remedy is to form a Council of Notables . . . to amalgamate Controllers with Consul-Generals [*sic*] and to give these latter the position of Residents."

At this time in Egypt matters were moving towards a crisis. In September, before Gordon's memorandum was written, Sherif was back in office as Prime Minister after Riaz Pasha's Government had been overthrown as the result of an army mutiny. The Chamber of Notables was about to be convened and it seemed possible that some genuine control over the Executive might be given to the Chamber. But, in the event, the Controllers, supported by their respective Consuls-General and Governments, refused to allow the Notables any control over the Budget, which was the principal point at issue between the Chamber and the Government. The result was that the Notables made common cause with the mutinous army which, in the spring of 1882, took control of the Government, thus precipitating the British occupation in the late summer.

Gordon's views about the Egyptian situation were not always objective or consistent, and they were usually presented in such a way as to make them even less objective and consistent than they were. He thought that the Ottoman Empire should be broken up, with European Turkey divided into independent Christian states and the Arab lands of Asiatic Turkey partitioned between the Powers. He thought that the Powers should grant a wide autonomy to Egypt and Syria and the more "developed" Arab countries and install benevolent despotisms over the rest with a view to preparing them for self-government. In the rump of Turkey, consisting of Asia Minor, he thought that Midhat's Constitution should be restored. That is to say, he believed that European influence should be forcibly used to promote what was later to be known as "self-determination". As far as Egypt was concerned, this view was obscured and made to seem inconsistent both by his admiration for Ismail and by his own autocratic rule over the Sudan. But his admiration for Ismail was a matter of personal loyalty and the ultimate object of his administration of the Sudan was "self-determination", the liberation of the northern, Arab, Moslem lands from Egyptian, or Turkish, rule, and the liberation of the southern, negro, pagan lands from northern, Arab, Moslem rule. Similarly, in Egypt, he advocated the liberation of the fellahin from that same rule of Turkish Pashas as was weighing on the Sudan. He thought that this liberation could only be achieved with European assistance—through the agency of people like King Leopold and Mackinnon in the southern Sudan and through that of "liberal" European Governments elsewhere in the Ottoman Empire. His main objection to Disraeli's Conservative administration had been what he regarded as their support of despotic and oppressive régimes in Turkey and Egypt in the interests of European bondholders, and he seems genuinely to have believed that the Liberal Government which succeeded it would reverse this policy without leaving Egypt to its own devices.

As usual, Gordon's appreciation of ends was wise and far-seeing. He saw that the development of "self-determination" was the only way to minimise injustice and oppression, and he saw that this development would not come about immediately except as a result of European encouragement in Egypt and Turkey and European intervention in the Sudan. But, also as usual, his appreciation of the means to be employed was absurdly unrealistic. It was absurd to suppose that commercial enterprises like Leopold's Congo Association and Mackinnon's East Africa Company would replace slave-trading with a benevolent despotism. It was unrealistic to suppose that interested European intervention in Egypt and Turkey would be replaced by disinterested intervention. Gordon's support of Hartington and the Whig Imperialists in Gladstone's Government was based on a belief that their Imperialism was somehow more enlightened than Tory Imperialism, whereas it was indistinguishable from it. In effect, there were only two policies which any British Government would have been prepared to pursue towards the peoples and governments of the Near East. One was an interventionist policy designed to achieve or to maintain that "stability" which British strategic and financial interests required, and which normally involved the support of the *status quo*. The other was a policy of withdrawal and evacuation, leaving the governments and peoples concerned to "stew in their own juice". Gordon was perhaps the original protagonist of the policy of the "white man's burden"—the concept of Imperialism as a moral duty laid upon the "haves" to use themselves in the service of the "have nots", the application of Victorian notions of philanthropy to international policy—to which lip service was often given during the nineties and after, but which never, or hardly ever, had any influence on British policy, or on that of any other Colonial Power.

Gordon was even more unrealistic about the French than he was about the British Government. He apparently believed that the bondholders and financial interests generally had been able to exploit Anglo-French differences over Egypt for their own ends and that an Anglo-French agreement over Egypt and the Ottoman Empire generally would enable an altruistic policy to be pursued without reference to the interests of the bondholders. The truth was almost exactly the opposite. Concerted Anglo-French action, when it was achieved, was, after Ismail's deposition, invariably in support of the *status quo*; Anglo-French discord gave indigenous movements of liberation the possibility of playing off one against the other. And the French Government, far more than the British Government, was committed to the interests of the bondholders.

Gordon's denigration of the fashionable Mediterranean in favour of an Indian Ocean strategy was probably due to the fact that he was stationed in Mauritius and not in Malta. Later, after the British occupation of Egypt, and after he had become convinced that this occupation, so far from leading to reforms in Egypt, involved "neither governing nor taking responsibility" but "supporting an unpopular sovereign . . . [and] the Turco-Circassian Pashas", he realised that the importance of the Suez Canal conferred by a Mediterranean strategy meant a continuation of this policy. But, characteristically, since by that time he was in Palestine and not in Mauritius, he advocated, not a reversion to the Cape route and an Indian Ocean strategy but the digging of a canal through Palestine to displace the Suez Canal and so deprive Egypt of strategic importance.

But Imperial questions were part of Gordon's Agag—that aspect of himself which he was trying to suppress—part of the equipment of the "tram of the world" which he was trying to ignore. More appropriate to the "casting off of anchors"—as he called his attempts to separate himself from the world—were the researches into which he plunged about the location of the Garden of Eden, which he satisfied himself, by means of intricate surveying calculations, lay at the bottom of the Indian Ocean in the vicinity of Mauritius, and the nature of the forbidden fruit, which, after a visit to the Seychelles, he identified with the coco de mer, a giant nut found only in that island.

In spite of all these speculations, Gordon was restless in Mauritius. He realised, as he had at Gravesend, that the military work he was expected to perform was a waste of time. What he concluded was needed adequately to defend the island was greatly improved fortifications manned by a garrison half the size. On any subject connected with irregular warfare or military engineering Gordon's opinion was probably the best in the British Army and quite unaffected by the vagaries which affected his judgement in other matters. But the War Office took no more notice of him over Mauritius than they had when he criticised the Gravesend forts.

At the beginning of 1882 Gordon was promoted Major-General and had thus outgrown his post as C.R.E. He might have been appointed G.O.C. the station and did act in this capacity for the next few months. But he was not confirmed in the appointment. As soon as it was known that he was once more "*en disponibilité*" the Cape Government which, two years before, had asked for his services, asked the Colonial Secretary whether he could be made available and was willing to "come to this Colony for the purpose of consultation as to the best measures to be adopted with reference to Basutoland . . . to assist in terminating the war and administering Basutoland". The British Government had no objection and an invitation was sent to Gordon, who immediately accepted it and left Mauritius for Cape Town in a sailing ship at the beginning of April 1882.

He had been thinking of going either to Palestine or Zanzibar after laying down his command. He realised that part of the reason for his thinking of Palestine was the unregenerate desire, which he was trying to suppress, to intervene in Egyptian affairs. The other alternative, Zanzibar, seemed purer to him, since he hoped to work, with Mackinnon, on his old dream of opening up Central Africa from the east coast for the purpose of legitimate trade as a means of putting an end to the slave trade. He was undecided about what to do when the offer came from the Cape Government. He accepted it without hesitation, but without much enthusiasm, as he had accepted so many unsuitable offers. Presumably this was the immediate work which God intended him to do.

The Cape Government had for some time been troubled with insurrection in the native territory of Basutoland and, on the strength of Gordon's Sudan reputation, were anxious to have his services for the purpose of "restoring order" there, a process which they regarded principally, if not entirely, in terms of a military operation. Gordon arrived at Cape Town at the beginning of May in a depressed state after an uncomfortable sea voyage. He soon found himself at odds with the Cape Government. He made it clear that he thought Basutoland should be given a large measure of autonomy under its own chiefs. The Cape Government wanted to "restore order" under the authority of the white magistrates. The principal instrument of pacification was to be the white-officered volunteer Cape Army which they wanted Gordon to command, a position which he had been offered, and had refused, two years before. Gordon now accepted the appointment, but insisted that his principal task was to make political recommendations about the future of Basutoland. Within a month of his arrival, after some conversations with the Chief Magistrate of Basutoland at Grahamstown, but before making a visit to the Basuto territory, he submitted a report to the Cape Government advocating a drastic change of policy in the direction of representative institutions for the Basutos. The Cape Government gave no immediate reply to this and Gordon in the meantime devoted himself to making a long report on the re-organisation of the Cape armed forces, which he submitted on 6 June. (One of the reasons why Gordon's recommendations, on this and on other occasions, did not receive the attention they deserved, was the speed at which they were produced, which precluded any detailed examination of the matter in hand. He was very often right in his conclusions, but he never condescended to argue a case or to forestall any of the more obvious objections to the course which he was advocating.) The Cape Government, which was beginning to find Gordon an embarrassment, then sent him off to make a report about the administration of the Transkei which he produced in the middle of July and which was critical about the work of the white magistrates in that area. In August, after the Cape Government had replied to his recommendations about Basutoland, dissenting from most of his conclusions, he visited Basutoland in company with the Cape Secretary for Native Affairs. Recognising the extent of his differences with the Cape Government over Basutoland, he went most unwillingly. The visit was a complete disaster. He was put into a false position by being induced to discuss a project for a Convention with one of the Basuto chiefs at a time when the Cape Government was inciting another chief to attack him. When he heard about this he offered his resignation in a telegram sent from Williamstown in which he told the Prime Minister of the Cape that bad magistrates cause wars, which he as Commandant-General would be expected to put down, that he was not a colonist and not therefore bound to wage unjust wars, and that though the Government recognised the existing administration as bad they refused to make any changes. It was not a tactful telegram. The Prime Minister replied accepting his resignation and agreeing that it should take immediate effect since, "after the intimation that you would not fight the Basutos . . . the continuance in the position you occupy would not be conducive to the public interest". So, after a long telegram dated 6 October in which he defended the line he had taken, Gordon returned to Cape Town, took his leave of Sir Hercules Robinson, the Governor, and set sail for England on 14 October, arriving home on 8 November.

His mission to the Cape had been a complete fiasco. What the Cape Government had wanted was a military commander who would subdue the Basutos by force of arms. What they got was a political reformer who made political recommendations which they regarded as subversive and who refused to undertake military operations in support of a policy with which he was in disagreement. None of his recommendations which were, for the most part, sound both from the political and military points of view, were accepted (although many of his political recommendations about Basutoland were in line with the policy adopted there later). He left Cape Town irritated and almost penniless after five and a half months of frustration. As he wrote to his sister: "What a queer life mine has been, with these fearful rows continually occurring."

While he was in South Africa, Gordon had had several

letters from Mackinnon, whose plans for East Africa were hanging fire owing to the hesitations of the British Government and the activities of the Germans, urging him to follow up his interview with Leopold two years before and take service with the Congo Association. He had been in occasional correspondence with Leopold since his interview with him and, immediately on his arrival at Southampton, wrote offering his services on condition that some kind of international status was conferred on the Congo Association. (This came to pass when the Congo Free State was accorded international recognition in 1885, after Gordon's death.) Leopold replied telling him that this matter would soon be solved and offering him an immediate appointment. "For the moment I have no mission to give you, but I wish much to have you at my disposal and to take you from this moment as my counsellor. You can name your own terms." (He intended to appoint Gordon as his Representative in the Congo in succession to Stanley, but could not do so until Stanley's contract had expired.) Gordon replied that he was ready to enter H.M.'s service at any time on the understanding that he would be employed in the Congo and provided that the question of international status was in a fair way to being settled. Meanwhile, he would be visiting Palestine, whence he would be ready to return as soon as the King should be able to employ him in the Congo. He had no wish to hang about Brussels in an advisory capacity.

On 17 November, soon after his arrival in England, Gordon was sent for by Lord Granville, the Foreign Secretary, to talk about the Sudan, where the Mahdist rebellion had broken out. This was the first occasion on which the British Government had asked Gordon's advice about any major matter of policy. Since his departure from Egypt at the beginning of 1880, Egypt and the Sudan had never been far from Gordon's thoughts, in spite of occasional protestations to his sister that "events in Egypt do not move me". In his conversation with Granville Gordon deprecated the seriousness of the rebellion and put it down to discontent with Egyptian rule and to the unpopularity of his own anti-slavery measures. He suggested that Sir Charles Wilson, the Military Adviser to the British Agent in Egypt, should be appointed Governor-General of the Sudan, with the moral authority of the British Government behind him, and expressed the view that he would have no more difficulty in maintaining order there than Gordon had experienced himself. He also advised that the Egyptian Government should "go easy" on anti-slavery proclamations and measures in the Sudan, as these would be ineffective and extremely unpopular.

It is evident from this advice that Gordon underrated the seriousness and completely ignored the religious significance of the Mahdist rebellion. His advice about Sir Charles Wilson was not taken. The Egyptian Government had as yet no desire to repeat the experiment of a British Governor-General. And the British Government, still thinking in terms of a military withdrawal from Egypt in a matter of months, were not anxious to involve themselves in the Sudan. But Granville was no doubt encouraged by Gordon's opinion to believe what he wished to believe—that the Sudan problem would solve itself if it were left alone—and this opinion may have been one of the reasons why the British Government refused to consider the proposals which Sir Charles Wilson was making for British involvement.

One of Wilson's proposals was for the appointment of Gordon as Governor-General. It is not clear from Granville's account of the interview,[6] the only one in existence, whether or not this proposal was mentioned to Gordon. But Gordon, who had friends in the War Office, probably learnt about it. And when he departed for Palestine at the beginning of January 1883, he appears to have been aware of the possibility that his services might be called upon in connection with the Sudan, and he lived in hope, tempered with the chastening thought that Agag was still very much alive.

Gordon, at this time, made no secret of his feelings about the Egyptian policy being pursued by the British Government. On his way home from Cape Town he wrote to W. S. Blunt, the foremost English champion of Egyptian nationalism, deploring the reinstatement in Egypt of the "parasite ring of Pashas" and expressing the opinion that Dilke, the Under Secretary of State for Foreign Affairs in the British Government and a leading advocate of the occupation policy, was an "imposter". While in England he wrote a letter to *The Times* criticising Khedive Taufiq. On 8 December, about three weeks after his interview with Granville, he saw Blunt and had a talk with him about Egypt and the Sudan. He expressed his sympathy and support for Ahmed Arabi and the other leaders of the military coup which had precipitated the British occupation, and whose trial, resulting in sentences of perpetual exile, had just taken place. According to Blunt[7] he expressed his confidence that the British Government intended to "restore Arabi as soon as public opinion should have cooled down".[8] As regards the Sudan, Blunt's recollection was that Gordon "expressed himself . . . in entire sympathy with the Mahdi as the popular leader of a revolt against an iniquitous Government . . . [but] . . . insisted on the retention of Khartum as a necessity for Egypt in connection with the Nile water supply and as an outpost to be held politically."

On 2 January, on the eve of his departure to Palestine, Gordon wrote to Blunt expressing his confidence that "Arabi would be back in a couple of years", and telling him that he had seen his friend Brett at the War Office, where he was private secretary to Hartington, the Secretary of State, and begged him to "urge the Government to assemble the Notables at once". He also told him of the imminent recall of Sir Auckland Colvin, previously the English Controller-General, who had been appointed Financial Adviser after the occupation and the abolition of the Anglo-French Control. Colvin was regarded by Blunt, and to some extent by Gordon, as the evil genius of Sir Edward Malet, the rather pedestrian British Agent in Cairo, the champion of the foreign bondholders, and the principal architect of the British occupation policy. They apparently hoped that his recall (Gordon's information about this was correct) presaged a change of policy in the direction of constitutionalism. By this time Lord Dufferin, the British Ambassador in Constantinople, was in Cairo preparing recommendations for the future of Egypt, and both Gordon and Blunt, whose views on Egypt were at that time similar, no doubt hoped for that change of policy which Gordon, through his contacts in the War Office, was urging on the Government.

Gordon spent almost the whole of the year 1883 in Palestine. For the first six months he lived at Ain Karim, a village just outside Jerusalem, immersed, or almost immersed, in investigations about the architecture of the Temple, the site of the Crucifixion, the line of demarcation between the tribes of Benjamin and Judah, the sites of the Gibeons of Scripture, and the location of Emmaus. He also continued his speculations, begun in Mauritius, about the location of the Garden of Eden, and satisfied himself that Noah's Ark came to rest, not on Mount Ararat, but in the vicinity of Jerusalem. In the intervals of these researches he maintained a voluminous correspondence on religious matters with his sister Augusta and with the Rev. Mr Barnes, the clerical friend he had met in Lausanne. In these letters the tone is less agonised, and certainly much more orthodox, than before, but he was still as remote as ever from serenity and still acutely conscious of the war within himself between worldly ambition and the spiritual life. He told his sister that he was "trying the experiment of giving up all hindrances to a holy life . . . [but] . . . I am yet empty of any increase in spiritual joy". His mind still constantly reverted to the affairs of Egypt and the Sudan. In writing to his sister about hindrances to a holy life he referred, in what nowadays would be described as a Freudian allusion, to the necessity of "avoiding going down into Egypt, i.e. the world". In another letter, written at the end of February, he praised God for the Mahdist rebellion. "Look at His work. He has upset the Egyptian people thoroughly and they will get their liberty from the oppressing Pashas. He has permitted this revolt which will end I believe in the suppression of the slave trade and slave holding . . . I foresaw the Egyptian and Sudan affair and was not listened to . . . I am sorely tempted to write Lord Dufferin my ideas; but I will not, for Jesus is Lord and He knows what to do." A few days later he reflected that "God governs the Sudan as much as He did when I was there . . . this comforts me for I feel that their welfare and the course of events that takes place are being conducted by the same Hand, whether I am there or not." In mid-April, after he had read Dufferin's recommendations for the future of Egypt (published in a Blue Book), he told his sister that he cared no more about Egypt and added, in the light of Dufferin's report, "even had I gone it would have been another fiasco". (Dufferin, in his report, had said that the Sudan was a drain upon Egypt, but that the Egyptian Government could not be made to realise this, and he suggested that "someone like Gordon" might be able to maintain a "fairly good government" in the Sudan without calling upon Egypt for men or money.) In April he wrote to Blunt praising Nubar, whom previously he had detested, as "the only man who would work with Arabi, give quiet to Egypt and some hope of benefiting the people". In May he referred to a letter he had received from Egypt "which is not very sanguine about the state of affairs, all because our Government will not say they will stay; yet stay they must whether they like it or not". (Gordon had several friends in Egypt, either in the British Army or seconded to the Egyptian Army, and he was kept well posted about events there while he was in Palestine.)

In July, Gordon, restless as ever, moved from Ain Karim down to Jaffa, on the coast. In August he wrote to Blunt, again praising Nubar as "the only man who can rule that country" and advocating that Hicks, who was about to start on his ill-fated expedition, "must be made Governor-General, otherwise he will never end things satisfactorily". At about this time Gordon, in correspondence with Laurence Oliphant, ex-diplomatist, writer and Orientalist, who was living on Mount Carmel, developed the idea of making a canal between the Mediterranean and Red Sea via Esdraelon, the Jordan valley, the Dead Sea and Wadi Araba. He regarded such a canal as the fulfilment of a Scriptural prophecy, but his advocacy of it was mainly due to the belief that it would replace the Suez Canal, thus depriving Egypt of its strategic importance and enabling the British to leave. For he had come to despair of the British occupation bringing any benefits to the people of Egypt and the Sudan. Writing to Oliphant, he complained that "The British Government will not take a decided line in re Egypt and the Sudan; they drift but at the same time they cannot avoid the onus of being the real power in Egypt. . . . They maintain Taufiq and the Pashas in power against the will of the people; this alone is insufferable. . . . Also they cannot possibly avoid the responsibility for the state of affairs in the Sudan where a wretched war drags on in a ruined country. . . . To avoid all this, if the British Government will not act firmly and strongly and take the country . . . let them attempt to get the Palestine canal made and quit Egypt to work out its own salvation. . . . Anything is better than the wretched want of sympathy between us and the Egyptians which is now increasing into a deadly hate. We must have a Nemesis unless we show more sympathy. What single good thing have we done for the people?"

In October he received a telegram from Mackinnon, sent on behalf of Leopold, reminding him of his promise to go to the Congo as soon as the question of international recognition was on the way to being settled (which it was by this time) and claiming his services. Gordon telegraphed to the War Office for permission to accept H.M.'s offer, and Mackinnon, in reply to a War Office request for information as to the capacity in which Leopold proposed to employ Gordon, told them that it was intended he should succeed Stanley as Leopold's principal Representative in the Congo. Hartington, Secretary of State for War, referred the request to Viscount Wolseley, Adjutant-General, who replied: "Looking at the fanatical character of the man and the chances of a collision with the French authorities I think it very doubtful whether permission should be given." Lord Granville, being informed by the Foreign Office that Gordon's appointment might involve Great Britain in international complications, and after consulting Gladstone, told Hartington that he disapproved of a British officer on full pay "being connected with this non-descript Association". The War Office replied accordingly to Gordon, turning down his request. There was some misunderstanding arising from the fact that the War Office telegram was wrongly transcribed by the telegraph clerk at Jaffa, who changed the word "declines" to "decides", but this was soon cleared up and, before Gordon left Palestine for England at the beginning of December, it was clear to him that he would only be able to enter Leopold's service by resigning his commission in the British Army.

There is no reason to suppose that the British Government's refusal of Gordon's request was connected with any intention to employ him themselves in the Sudan or elsewhere. The whole question of Leopold's enterprise in the Congo had important international implications, particularly in connection with the disputed boundary between the territory claimed by the Congo Association and the hinterland of French Equatorial Africa, and

Wolseley's apprehensions about possible difficulties arising with the French as the result of the employment of a British officer of Gordon's character and reputation were perfectly comprehensible.

Gordon, while still under the impression that permission had been given, was resigned rather than enthusiastic. Writing to his sister on 5 November he told her: "Should my going to the Congo be settled I hope you will not mind; you know what little rows I get into while in England and I am far better away." And to his brother on the following day he wrote: "There is no help for it; I must go to the Congo unless anything that I do not see turns up." Can he still have been thinking of a possible appointment in Egypt or the Sudan? On 17 November he learned that the British Government would not after all give him permission to serve in the Congo. But his mind was made up; he wrote to his sister: "I was not moved at the information which told me the true version." A few days later he wrote again: "As for the Sudan, I am much interested, but should feel great repugnance to going back there; and that is a great gain for I had a sneaking desire to return there when I first came out here. As for the Congo, I have not much choice left me." And to Horace Waller, in his Northamptonshire rectory, he wrote: "If by the keeping of my promise [to Leopold] I would get a free and speedy passage to it [i.e. death] . . . I would be very glad, and it seems that the Congo is the route which is quickest to it if, as I think, I am called there."

In this mood he left Jaffa for England at the beginning of December. The ship was delayed by a storm and put into Haifa where he stayed for a few days with Laurence Oliphant. The two men talked much of the Sudan. Gordon told Oliphant that he thought that the Sudan should be granted independence under its own rulers and that a Commissioner should be sent out from England to arrange matters accordingly with the Mahdi. If the Mahdi objected various Sudanese chiefs might be encouraged to combine against him. Oliphant tried to persuade Gordon to give up the idea of the Congo and volunteer his services for the Sudan. But Gordon told him that he was in honour bound to Leopold and that, in any case, "he had already had too many differences with the heads of departments under which he had served, and was regarded with too little favour, on account of his refusal to look at every question through official spectacles, to be a *persona grata* to the English government".[9] As we shall see, at the same time as Oliphant was urging him to volunteer for the Sudan, other suggestions and proposals were being made to the same end.

On 18 December Gordon, having walked the twelve miles from Haifa to Acre, embarked on a French steamer bound for Marseille. He was about to start on his strange and splendid Via Dolorosa, towards a fame which he both sought and despised himself for seeking, and towards a Calvary for which he had, long since, prepared himself.

CHAPTER TWO

THE BACKGROUND TO THE MISSION

NAPOLEON IS SAID to have expressed to the Governor of St Helena his opinion that Egypt was the most important country in the world. During the course of the next 150 years both British and French statesmen often behaved as though they believed this statement to be true. British official interest in Egypt dated from the time of Bonaparte's invasion of that country in 1798. From then on, until the end of the nineteenth century, successive British Governments were hag-ridden by the fear lest British communications with India, and even British possession of India, should be threatened either by a Russian occupation of Constantinople or by a French occupation of Egypt, or both, leading to a partition of the Ottoman Empire between France and Russia. British Near Eastern policy concentrated on "the preservation and territorial integrity of the Ottoman Empire", of which Egypt was a part, as a means of countering this threat. This was the thinking behind Palmerston's successful opposition to Mohamed Ali's expansionist schemes in 1839–41 which he feared might result in installing the Russians on the Bosphorus and the French on the Nile. And it was the thinking behind his unsuccessful opposition, between 1856 and 1865, to the French-sponsored Suez Canal, which he saw primarily as a French plot to install a permanent French military presence in Egypt.

The threat seen to be posed by Mohamed Ali was eliminated by diplomatic action isolating France from the rest of the Concert of Europe and by forcible action which restored a measure of effective Ottoman control over Egypt. The threat seen to be posed by the Suez Canal, which was a commercial enterprise-cum-financial racket and not a French Imperialist plot, was seen by Palmerston's successors to be illusory.

But, hardly had the alarm over the Suez Canal subsided, than another threat was seen to be developing. From about 1856 onwards Egypt had become a happy hunting-ground for European speculators and developers eager for profitable investment, lucrative concessions and favourable markets. Their activities were encouraged by two successive ambitious, modernising, but undiscriminating rulers, Said and Ismail, who enjoyed more or less absolute power over the disposal of Egypt's domestic resources, and were assisted by the foreign privileges and immunities which had grown up under the cloak of the Ottoman Capitulations. Mainly as a result of these activities Egypt had, by 1876, incurred a foreign debt of about £90 million, with very little to show for it. In spite of oppressive taxation the Egyptian Government was unable to maintain the service of this debt and was compelled to seek an arrangement with its European creditors, mainly in France and England, who, to a large extent in the case of the French and to a lesser extent in the case of the British, creditors, had the backing of their respective Governments. Some three years of complicated haggling followed which resulted (*a*) in the deposition of Ismail, who had been responsible for most of the indebtedness, and his replacement as Khedive, or Ruler, by his son Taufiq; (*b*) in the setting up of an Anglo-French Control over Egyptian finances and Egyptian administration generally; and (*c*) in an international agreement regulating and policing the service of the foreign debt, which was made a first charge on Egypt's revenue.

The collapse of indigenous authority resulting from Ismail's departure, the oppressive weight of taxation and the economies in the public services, particularly the Army, necessitated by the service of the debt, and the resentment caused by the pervasiveness of the Anglo-French Control, combined to give rise to a movement of popular discontent, which soon coalesced into a recognisable national protest directed both against Egypt's rulers, who were for the most part not native Egyptians but Turks and Circassians, and against the European Controllers. This national movement was made up of three elements: (i) a section of the Ulema, or Moslem religious leaders, which saw an acceptable and desirable national future in terms, not of a progressive assimilation to the West, but of a liberalised and modernised Islamic theocracy; (ii) educated, able and ambitious Egyptians who were frustrated by the inefficient and foreign-controlled despotism under which they lived and who had been influenced by the constitutional ideas seeping from Europe into Constantinople and the Near East; (iii) Egyptian Army officers who were influenced by both these currents of opinion and whose careers were being particularly affected both by the favouritism shown to Turks and Circassians and by the retrenchment in Army establishments insisted upon by the Anglo-French Controllers.

The coalescence of these three currents of opinion ensured popular support for a series of Army mutinies. By the middle of 1882 the government of the country had passed into the hands of an army clique headed by Colonel Ahmed Arabi, the principal mutineer. The authority of the Khedive and that of the Anglo-French Control had been reduced to a nullity. In France, and in most other European countries, the situation was seen mainly in terms of the impaired security of the debt and a possible threat to the lives and property of European nationals resident in Egypt. But the British Government saw the situation primarily in terms of its effect on communications with India. The real danger, in their eyes, was lest some European Power, or combination of Powers, should take advantage of the situation to occupy Egypt and so realise the threat which had haunted British statesmen for the past eighty years. In the circumstances of the time this threat could have been eliminated by diplomatic means. But increasing British involvement in Egypt, and ambition for Imperial expansion which was becoming fashionable in some circles both for sentimental and for material reasons, contrived to obscure the nature and the intensity of the real danger and to divert popular and political attention to various side-issues. It was urged that the British Government had a duty to restore the authority and to protect the life of the Khedive Taufiq, who had been called to the throne under European auspices and who had co-operated loyally with the Anglo-French Control. It was claimed that the fanaticism and anarchical character of the rebel régime endangered both the lives of European residents and the freedom of passage through the Suez Canal. It was alleged that the rebel régime had set aside international agreements covering the operation of the Anglo-French Control and the service of the foreign debt.

Mr Gladstone's Liberal Government, which had succeeded Lord Beaconsfield's Conservative Government in 1880, was ideologically opposed to the interventionist and imperialist policies of its predecessor, and many of its Parliamentary supporters viewed the Egyptian national movement sympathetically. The Cabinet, apart from the ideological outlook of many of its members, was opposed to military intervention in Egypt both on diplomatic and on domestic grounds. Diplomatically, a British occupation of Egypt would cause endless complications both with Turkey and with the other Great Powers and would jeopardise the grand design of preserving the independence and territorial integrity of the Ottoman Empire which had been one of the bases of British foreign policy for so long. Domestically, it would cause dissension in the Liberal Party, provoke criticism from the Opposition and be a certain source of financial expense. Nevertheless, Lord Granville, the Foreign Secretary, having first allowed himself to be manœuvred by Gambetta's French Government (which was mainly concerned with the security of the Egyptian debt) into accepting the principle of Anglo-French or, if possible, Turkish, intervention, eventually found himself committed by Turkish procrastination and by the defection of Freycinet's French Government which succeeded that of Gambetta, first to the bombardment of Alexandria by a British naval squadron and then to a British military invasion and occupation of Egypt, which took place in the autumn of 1882.

The first few years of the occupation were a nightmare for the British Government. Internationally, they incurred the enmity of Turkey, who considered that her suzerainty over Egypt had been infringed, and of France, who was deprived by the occupation of the French half-share in what had virtually been an Anglo-French Condominium over Egypt. Domestically, they were harried, on the one hand by a heterogeneous but powerful lobby of those who for business, altruistic or jingoistic reasons, wanted to absorb Egypt into the British Empire, and on the other hand by those, mostly but not entirely within the Liberal Party and tradition, who deplored the fact and circumstances of the occupation and clamoured for a speedy withdrawal. In Egypt itself difficulties abounded and multiplied.

The machinery of government and the tradition of authority had broken down, but the British Government were committed, both by their undertakings to the Powers and by their own frequently and publicly expressed views, to a speedy withdrawal, and thus to an attempt to restore discredited Egyptian authority rather than to replace it by direct British rule. In spite of the impoverished condition of the country, due to the dislocations caused by the rebellion, a continuation of oppressive tax-collecting and a parsimonious policy of administrative economy were necessary in order to pay the coupons on the foreign debt. Attempts at reform which might have mitigated the oppression and humanised the economies were vitiated by a determination to restore rather than replace the *status quo ante* the occupation. The possibility of a reduction in the burden of the foreign debt was nullified by the British Government's determination not to make themselves responsible for it. The resultant state of affairs in Egypt exposed British policy to criticism from almost every shade of opinion, both at home and abroad.

In addition to all the troubles in Egypt proper a rebellion was raging in the Sudan. For some time, the British Government, plagued by all the other intractable problems—financial, administrative, political and diplomatic—which the occupation had thrust upon them, tried to ignore the implications of the rebellion, maintaining the fiction that it was the responsibility of the Egyptian Government. But, by the end of 1883, the manifest inability of the Egyptian Government, unaided, to check the progress of the rebellion made it necessary for the British Government to extend to the Sudan the same responsibility which they had, reluctantly and indirectly, assumed for most other aspects of Egyptian affairs. For the next eighteen months the Sudan, in British popular estimation and to some extent in fact, became the most important, the most controversial and most troublesome aspect of the whole complicated Egyptian problem.

The Sudan—meaning literally "the country of the black people"—was a large, ill-defined region forming the African hinterland of Egypt and consisting essentially of the valley of the Upper Nile, from the 1st Cataract at Aswan, the traditional southern boundary of Egypt proper, to the sources of the White Nile in Central Africa. At the beginning of the nineteenth century it was a region almost entirely unknown to the outside world. It was vaguely believed to contain rich resources and was a natural area for penetration and colonisation by an expansionist Egypt. It was invaded in 1820 by Mohamed Ali who succeeded in establishing some sort of permanent Egyptian administration along the White and Blue Nile Valleys, among the Arabised Moslems of the north, to about as far south as lat. 14 N. Subsequent attempts to extend eastwards brought the Egyptians into contact and conflict with the Abyssinians, with whom an endemic state of warfare came to exist along the foothills between the Nile Valley and the Red Sea. Westwards there was some expansion away from the White Nile Valley into the rolling, semi-desert country of Kordofan, also inhabited by Arabised Moslem tribes.

The fabled riches of the Sudan were illusory. The gold which Mohamed Ali sought proved to be almost non-existent. But there was one valuable article of commerce—black slaves—on which the economy of the Sudan largely depended. Arab Moslem settlement in the Sudan extended south to about lat. 10 N. The country south of this line, where the rainfall was greater and where the arid deserts of the north began to change into the rainland forests of Central Africa, was inhabited by pagan tribes whose poverty, lack of organised government and primitive way of life made them an easy prey for Arab slave hunters from the east and north.

In Islam, domestic and, to some extent, economic life was based on the institution of slavery. Deep in the Moslem consciousness was the conception of themselves as a master-race, who used the people they conquered as hewers of wood and drawers of water. In the eras of Arab and Turkish conquest there was a plentiful supply of white slaves from the conquered peoples of Asia Minor, the Caucasus and the Balkans. When this supply began to dry up the apparently limitless human resources of Central Africa were exploited to supply the slave markets of Islam. The Moslem Arabs of the northern Sudan had a twofold interest in slavery. On the one hand every family of any substance relied on slave labour in their households and in their gainful occupations. On the other hand a large number of them had a direct or indirect interest in the lucrative business of exporting slaves to the rest of Islam. The market for slaves, both for the domestic and the export markets, was supplied mostly by Khartum merchants who developed a highly organised system of slave procurement in the pagan south. This demanded big resources. Private armies had to be raised and arms and ammunition procured for the slave-hunting expeditions. Depots had to be established in the south for the collection of slaves, boats and guards provided for their transport from the south. Other, more complicated, arrangements had to be devised for transporting slaves for export, either down the Nile to Egypt or across the desert to the Red Sea ports for shipment to Arabia. Middlemen had to be employed for dealing with the domestic market. The slave traders were the richest and most powerful men in the country. The Egyptian administrators connived at the trade and some even engaged in it. Egyptian rule was inefficient, oppressive and unpopular and the rulers could not afford to alienate such an important vested interest.

In spite of the recognition given to the slave traders, and in spite of the semi-official concessions, sometimes disguised as ivory concessions, which enabled taxes to be collected from them, very little of the considerable profits of the slave trade ever reached the Egyptian Treasury. The Sudan, although on the whole self-supporting from the revenue point of view, was never a source of profit to Egypt.

The prevalence of the African slave trade was a subject of concern in Europe, and particularly in England where there was a strong and well-established movement dedicated to putting an end to the slave trade and the institution of slavery. For years the British had been active in trying to put down the slave trade between Zanzibar and Arabia. In 1857, as a result of British initiative, the Sultan of Turkey was persuaded to decree the abolition of slavery in the Ottoman dominions. Like so many Ottoman decrees, this remained largely a dead letter. But it enabled British and other European Consuls to apply pressure to the Ruler of Egypt, which was part of the Ottoman dominions, to take steps about slave trading in the Sudan.

Said, who ruled Egypt from 1854 to 1863, who was unenthusiastic about the Sudan and who, at one time, considered an Egyptian withdrawal from it, established, at the instance of the European Powers, a control post at Fashoda, at about lat. 10 N. on the White Nile, in a rather ineffectual attempt to block the principal slave route from the south.

Said's successor, Ismail, had large ideas about the Sudan. He was determined to establish an Egyptian Empire, including the whole of the Nile Valley to its headwaters in the Great Lakes which had recently been discovered, and extending eastwards to the Red Sea and the Horn of Africa and westwards to include the desert kingdom of Darfur. His first step was to obtain from his suzerain, the Sultan of Turkey, the Governorships of Suakin and Massawa. This, for the first time, extended the frontiers of the Sudan to the Red Sea. His next step was to try to extend the Egyptian dominion southwards up the White Nile towards the Great Lakes. In order to secure British benevolence towards this design he associated it with an expressed determination to strike a blow at the slave trade by policing the principal transport route along the Upper Nile and by opening the country to legitimate trade. With these ends in view, he engaged Sir Samuel Baker, the noted English Central African explorer, as Governor of the *soi-disant* province which he called Equatoria, to lead an Egyptian expedition southwards from Gondokoro, on about lat. 5 N., at that time the southernmost Egyptian post on the White Nile, to Lake Victoria with a view to annexing the whole area to Egypt and establishing a chain of military posts so as to police the slave trade, keep the peace and open up the country generally. Baker's mission, which lasted from 1869 to 1873, was not very successful. He established a few isolated posts, but failed to reach Lake Victoria. More importantly, he failed to conciliate the local inhabitants, who were unable to distinguish between Baker's civilising mission and the activities of the slave raiders. In 1874, Baker was succeeded as Governor of Equatoria by Colonel (as he then was) Gordon, whose first experience of Africa this was. Gordon, during his three years in Equatoria, succeeded very little better than Baker. A few more posts were established and a rudimentary form of administration introduced. But the only effect on the slave trade was to divert the main transport route away from the Nile to the inland route westwards through Bahr-al-Ghazal, Kordofan and Darfur. Within a year or two the idea of pushing Egyptian territory to Lake Victoria had been tacitly abandoned and the southernmost posts were evacuated.

Meanwhile Ismail had been extending his dominions westward and eastward. In the district of Bahr-al-Ghazal, one of the main haunts of the slave traders, the Egyptian Government, after a vain attempt to break the power of the principal slave trader, Zubair Rahmat al-Mansur, with a military expedition from Khartum, which Zubair defeated with his private army, was compelled to recognise the *fait accompli* and appointed Zubair Governor of the province of Bahr-al-Ghazal (1870). Three years later Zubair, ostensibly in the name of the Egyptian Government, and with a little assistance from the Egyptian Governor-General, who sent an expedition from Khartum, invaded the Sultanate of Darfur, captured al-Fasher, the capital, killed the reigning Sultan, and annexed his Sultanate (1874). This brought the whole of the Western Sudan virtually under the control of the slave traders. Zubair then went to Cairo to assert his claim to the Governorate of Darfur, as well as that of Bahr-al-Ghazal, leaving his son Suleiman as his deputy.

In the east, Egyptian rule had been extended without much opposition along the African coasts of the Red Sea and the Gulf of Aden to Cape Guardafui and inland to the provinces of Harrar and Bogos on the borders of Abyssinia. Attempted expansion inland from Massawa brought Egypt into renewed conflict with Abyssinia, as a result of which the Egyptians suffered two heavy defeats in 1875 and 1876.

In 1877 Ismail, in a series of attempts to purchase British benevolence in his efforts to avoid reforms and financial controls sought to be imposed by the Powers, signed with the British Government an anti-slavery convention which, *inter alia*, formally prohibited slave trading in the Egyptian dominions, gave wide powers of search and control to British naval vessels in the Red Sea, and decreed that slavery should be abolished in Egypt in 1884 and in the Sudan in 1889.

Gordon, after three years in Equatoria, relinquished his appointment at the end of 1876, conscious of his failure to achieve any permanent good there, disillusioned with Egyptian rule in the Sudan, and suspicious of Ismail's sincerity in wanting to put down the slave trade. But, seduced by Ismail's charm and beguiled by his own belief in predestination, he allowed himself to be persuaded by Ismail to return in 1877 as Governor-General of the whole Sudan. He ruled the Sudan for three years in this capacity. Apart from some unsuccessful attempts to make peace with Abyssinia, he devoted most of his time and energy to waging war against the slave traders in Bahr-al-Ghazal and Darfur. He was successful in his immediate aims. The large-scale slave trading organisations were broken up, the private armies dispersed and the slave depots destroyed. Suleiman, Zubair's son, was caught and shot by Romolo Gessi, who was one of the many Europeans introduced by Gordon into the Sudan administration and who bore the brunt of the campaign against the slave traders.

But the success of this concentrated effort, together with Gordon's neglect of other aspects of the administration, and his capricious and arbitrary methods generally, had a seriously weakening effect on the Egyptian administration of the Sudan. The violent methods he employed against the slave traders disrupted the economy of the country and antagonised many important elements who, directly or indirectly, had an interest in the slave trade. His employment of sometimes not very well qualified Europeans in high positions, his capricious dismissals, promotions and transfers of Egyptian officials, impaired the prestige, efficiency and *esprit de corps* of the administration. He was generally suspected of being an agent of the British Government, and his ill-concealed contempt for Egyptian methods, and for most of his Egyptian civil and military staff, did much to undermine the rickety foundations of Egyptian rule.

As Gordon himself came to recognise (but not to regret), this was a contributory factor to the rebellion which broke out in 1881, less than two years after his departure at the end of 1879. It was not the only, nor the most important, factor. The other two factors were religious fanaticism and the army mutinies in Egypt, in that order of importance.

The rebellion in the Sudan can be taken to have started in May 1881, in which month, Mohamed Ahmed, who had gained some local reputation as a *faqir*, or holy man, leading a life of prayer, meditation and fasting on the island of Aba, on the White Nile about 200 miles south of Khartum, sent emissaries to all provincial Governors and heads of tribes throughout the Moslem Sudan with a written proclamation announcing that he was the Mahdi and that "whosoever doubts my mission does not believe in God or in his prophets and whosoever is at enmity with me is an unbeliever and whosoever fights against me will be forsaken and unconsoled in both worlds".

In the strict theological sense, Mahdism has no place at all in the orthodox beliefs of Sunni Islam. It derives from the messianic doctrine of the heretic Shiis who believe that the divine attributes have descended from the Prophet Mohamed by a sort of apostolic succession through a line of Imams, and that either the twelfth of this line (according to the majority of Shiis) or the seventh (according to some Shii sects) has been taken up into Heaven and become the "hidden Imam" who will one day become manifest on earth as the Mahdi, meaning literally "one who guides people in the right path". This Shii belief had been popularly adopted in many unsophisticated Sunni Moslem communities and, from time to time in such communities, some local holy man had proclaimed himself as the Mahdi, usually as a preliminary to leading a rising against authority. The Sudanese Moslems were an unsophisticated community, remote from Moslem theological centres and relying for religious instruction mainly on the ministrations of *fikis*, uneducated and self-appointed holy men who, in the great majority, accepted and propagated Mohamed Ahmed's sensational claim.

Rauf Pasha, the Governor-General who had succeeded Gordon, did not at first treat the matter very seriously. Having been assured by the Ulema of Khartum, on various cogent theological grounds, that Mohamed Ahmed was an imposter, he summoned him to Khartum and, after he had refused to come, sent an armed force to fetch him. A fight ensued in which most of the force sent by Rauf Pasha was killed by the Mahdi's followers (11 August 1881). The survivors returned to Khartum by the steamer in which they had come and Mohamed Ahmed and his followers retired to the Nuba Mountains in the south of Kordofan, there to raise the standard of rebellion against the Egyptian Government.

The Mahdi, as we shall now call him, proceeded to recruit an army by appeals to religious fanaticism and to maintain it in a state of fighting fitness by the application of a strict code of religious discipline. His troops became known as Dervishes, which implied that they were regarded, and regarded themselves, as a religious order; they wore as a uniform a patched *jibba*, or cloak, characteristic of such an order. In organising his army, the Mahdi appointed four Khalifas, or deputies, one of whom, Abdullahi, was nominated as his successor. (In fact only three of the four Khalifas were actually appointed; the fourth nomination, the leader of the Senussi sect in Libya, refused to join the rebellion.) Below the Khalifas were a number of Emirs, commanding the various units of the growing rebel army.

Southern Kordofan, which the Mahdi had chosen as his headquarters, was in the country of the Baqqara Arabs, a conglomeration of warlike, semi-nomad, cattle-raising tribes who had been interested in slave-raiding and slave-trading and who had in consequence been hard-hit by Gordon's anti-slavery campaigns. Abdullahi, the Mahdi's chosen successor, and his right-hand man generally, was a Baqqara.

For the next two years the Mahdi was to remain in Kordofan, consolidating his hold on that province and extending it westward into Darfur. At the same time he sent his emissaries throughout the Moslem Sudan calling upon the people, not merely to rise against the Egyptian oppressor but to enforce throughout the Moslem world the New Order proclaimed by him.

By the time of the British occupation of Egypt in September 1882 the Mahdi's increasing army based on the Nuba Mountains had defeated two Egyptian forces sent against him, were besieging the Egyptian garrison in el-Obeid, capital of Kordofan, and were in effective occupation of most of Kordofan and the country eastwards between the White and Blue Niles. Sennaar, on the Blue Nile, some 200 miles south of Khartum, was besieged, and the provinces of Darfur, Bahr-al-Ghazal and Equatoria, each with a European Governor and an Egyptian garrison, cut off by the rebels from Khartum. East and north of

Khartum the country was still under effective Egyptian control, but the Mahdi's emissaries were active and the tribal leaders, affected more perhaps by prudential than by messianic considerations, were anxiously watching the course of events in Cairo, in Khartum and in Kordofan. It was important to try to remain uncommitted until the winning side could be discerned.

For some months nothing in the way of effective advice or assistance had reached Abdul Qadir Pasha, the capable Governor-General who succeeded Rauf Pasha in May 1882. The army mutinies, the constitutional crises, the British invasion, the defeat of the Egyptian Army at Tel-al-Kebir and its subsequent disbandment, meant that the Sudan was left to its own devices. News of events in Egypt filtering through to the Sudan had no doubt assisted recruitment to the Mahdi's standard and affected the minds of many of the wavering tribal leaders.

In the very early days of the British occupation, Sir Charles Wilson, who had been Chief Intelligence Officer to the British expedition and who was afterwards attached to the British Agency as Military Adviser, turned his attention to the position in the Sudan. At the end of September, less than a fortnight after the battle of Tel-al-Kebir, he recommended to Sir Edward Malet, the British Agent, that Darfur and Kordofan should be abandoned, that Bogos and Qallabat in the eastern Sudan be ceded to Abyssinia, that Massawa be made a free port, with the import of arms prohibited, and that British officials be appointed to most of the senior posts, including that of Governor-General, in what would remain of the Sudan. He also recommended that two British officers should be sent to the Sudan immediately to report on the situation with a view to possible operations to be conducted during the coming winter.[1] The only part of this report endorsed by Malet when forwarding it to London was the sending of two British officers to report. During October, Omar Lutfi, the newly appointed Egyptian Minister of War, told Malet that the Egyptian Government, in response to requests from Abdul Qadir Pasha, were raising a force of 10,000 men from the *débris* of the now disbanded Egyptian Army to assist in the defence of Khartum.

Malet passed this information on to London without comment, as he did another report submitted by Sir Charles Wilson at the end of October. This report stated that the situation in the Sudan was deteriorating, that Khartum was in danger, and that the fall of Khartum would have a bad effect on political stability in Egypt and might even lead to an attempted invasion of the country. He recommended that British officers should be sent to Khartum to organise the defence of the town and that the Indian contingent of the British expeditionary force, then on its way back to India, should be landed at Suakin. He also repeated his previous recommendations about ceding territory to Abyssinia and the appointment of Englishmen to the posts of Governor-General and Commander-in-Chief in the Sudan and urged that all military operations in the Sudan should be placed under the control of the officer commanding British troops in Egypt. He expressed the opinion that Gordon would be the best choice as Governor-General if he could be persuaded to accept the appointment, and drew attention to the fact that Gordon was then out of employment.[2]

The British Government telegraphed their reply to Wilson's recommendations on 30 October. They turned down the suggestion to land Indian troops at Suakin and rejected any idea of employing British officers in the Sudan. They did, however, agree with Wilson's (and Malet's) recommendation that two British officers should be sent to the Sudan to report and, in the middle of November, after consultations between Malet and Alison, the British C.-in-C., Lieut.-Colonel D. H. Stewart, accompanied by M. Messadiglia, an Italian who had been employed by Gordon as Governor of Darfur, went to the Sudan to report to Malet on "the amount of danger from the insurrection to the Egyptian people and nation and the nature and extent of the measures which should be taken against such danger", and with the understanding that they should "under no circumstances act in any military capacity".[3] The British Government also asked for details of the Egyptian force which it was proposed to send to the Sudan and asked "whom it was proposed to place in command and whether the reconquest of the Sudan is contemplated in case the False Prophet has obtained possession of that district?" With regard to the suggestion about Gordon, they inquired as to the capacity in which it was proposed that he should be employed (although this was clear from Wilson's report) and what Sir Archibald Alison, the C.-in-C., thought about it.[4] Malet replied that the Egyptian Government proposed to appoint Ala-ed-Din Pasha as C.-in-C. of the Egyptian forces in the Sudan (thus superseding Abdul Qadir Pasha in his military capacity), and that the intention was to reconquer the Sudan. With regard to Gordon, Malet replied that Wilson's proposal was that he should go as Governor-General, but stressed that this proposal did not come from the Egyptian Government, who would not appoint Gordon unless the British Government insisted.[5] The British Government replied that "in default of fuller information the responsibility must rest with the Egyptian Government".[6]

Meanwhile, the British C.-in-C. was considering the matter, in the light of the defence of Egypt, with Valentine Baker Pasha, an ex-British Army officer who, at that time, was engaged in raising a new Egyptian Army under British auspices. Alison and Baker thought that the proposed reinforcement of 10,000 Egyptian troops under Ala-ed-Din Pasha might hold the Mahdi at bay but that, if it failed to do so, a British force, or Baker's new Egyptian Army if it were ready in time, should be made available in the region of Aswan to check a possible advance into Egypt by the Mahdi. Alison disagreed with Wilson's suggestion for using Indian troops at Suakin, but recommended that two British officers be sent there "to report on the route between Suakin and Berber, and thence to Khartum to ascertain exactly the general situation and examine the defensive capabilities of Khartum".[7] When forwarding this report Malet expressed the opinion that the Egyptian Government should be allowed to take their own measures in suppressing the revolt "without aid or advice from H.M.G. . . . lest at some future period, should measures be taken at our suggestion or in accordance with our advice have proved inefficacious, England would inevitably be drawn into military operations in the Sudan." If the worst came to the worst, Egypt could be defended by the British troops stationed there.[8]

On 17 November Lord Granville, the Foreign Secretary, interviewed Gordon, who had just returned from Cape Town.

Gordon told him that the perils of the Mahdist rebellion had been greatly exaggerated, and suggested that if Sir Charles Wilson were appointed Governor-General he would have no difficulty in restoring order. He also warned Granville against trying to get the Egyptian Government to enforce anti-slavery edicts in the Sudan, having taken the (partially correct) view that the Mahdist rebellion was the result of his own anti-slavery campaigns.[9]

During November Lord Dufferin, the Ambassador in Constantinople, was sent to Egypt to advise the British Government on the future administration of Egypt on the understanding that the British occupation should "last for as short a time as possible" and that the Egyptian administration should be reconstituted "on a basis which will afford satisfactory guarantees for the maintenance of peace, order and prosperity, for the stability of the Khedive's authority, for the judicious development of self-government and for the fulfilment of obligations towards the Powers".[10] The Sudan was not among the matters which Granville especially commended to his attention, except in so far as it was included in an instruction concerning the prevention of the slave trade. During his time in Egypt Dufferin in effect superseded Malet as the principal British Representative in Egypt.

At about the same time as Dufferin arrived in Egypt, it was decided at the War Office that Baker Pasha could not retain his command of the Egyptian Army, as the circumstances of his leaving the British Army made it inappropriate that seconded British officers should be required to serve under him. (He had been convicted of indecent assault by the civil power.) General Sir Evelyn Wood was therefore appointed in his stead. Dufferin, partly to solace Baker, suggested privately to Granville that he might be appointed as C.-in-C. the Egyptian Army in the Sudan. But the Khedive objected and the matter was not pressed.[11] The Egyptian Government did, however, want some British officers in the Sudan, and Dufferin, after consulting Granville, told Sherif Pasha, the Prime Minister, that there would be no objection to the employment of British officers on the retired list for this service.

As a result of this permission, Colonel Hicks, an ex-officer of the Indian Army who had been with Napier's expedition to Abyssinia in 1867, and a number of other British and European retired officers, were engaged by the Egyptian Government and left for the Sudan in February 1883. At about the same time, Ala-ed-Din Pasha, who had originally been intended as C.-in-C. in the Sudan, was sent to Khartum to take over as Governor-General from Abdul Qadir Pasha; Suleiman Niazi, described by Stewart as "a miserable-looking old man of 74 or 75" was sent as C.-in-C. Hicks was appointed C.O.S. to the C.-in-C., who was instructed to take Hicks' advice on all military matters.

By this time the situation in the Sudan had still further deteriorated in that, in January 1883, el-Obeid, the capital of Kordofan, had fallen after a desperate resistance which had cost the lives of some 10,000 of the Mahdi's followers. This made the Mahdi the master of the whole of Kordofan and cut Darfur off completely from Khartum.

In March 1883, Lieut.-Colonel Stewart, who had been in the Sudan with Messadiglia since November, submitted a detailed report to Dufferin[12] in which he recommended that Egypt should withdraw from Darfur, Kordofan, Bahr-al-Ghazal and Equatoria, as well as from Massawa and the Horn of Africa, and concentrate on retaining and improving their administration in the rest of the country. Dufferin expressed his agreement with Stewart's recommendations, but did not urge them strongly on either the British or Egyptian Governments. The British Government, as we have seen, were reluctant to extend their Egyptian responsibilities to the Sudan, and the Egyptian Government, intent on retaining such remnants of prestige as were left to them after the British occupation, ignored Stewart's advice and remained intent on using their reinforced army in Khartum to advance into Kordofan and annihilate the Mahdi's main force, in spite of Stewart's warning that another defeat in Kordofan would probably involve the loss of the whole of the Sudan.

In Khartum, Hicks found himself in an unenviable position. Abdul Qadir Pasha, Governor-General and C.-in-C., was on the verge of being superseded. His successor as Governor-General, Ala-ed-Din Pasha, was intriguing against Suleiman

Niazi, the new C.-in-C., to whom Hicks was C.O.S. The reinforced Egyptian Army was under-trained, under-equipped and of low morale. His relationships with the British and Egyptian Governments were obscure and anomalous. While in Cairo, and before leaving for the Sudan, he had been in close touch with Baker Pasha, who had just been appointed head of the Egyptian Gendarmerie, and who appears to have persuaded Hicks that he was acting for the Egyptian Government in respect of military operations in the Sudan. Although Dufferin impressed on him that the British Government had no responsibility for his activities in the Sudan, arrangements were made for him to communicate with the British Agent by means of the F.O. cipher which Stewart was instructed to hand over to him before he left Khartum. In view of this, and in view of his apparently thinking that Baker had connections with, or instructions from, the British Government, he seems to have assumed that the British Government were more involved in the affairs of the Sudan than they were. He used the F.O. cipher to route most of his communications with the Egyptian Government through Malet who, on Dufferin's return to Constantinople in May, once more became the principal British Representative in Egypt. In this way Malet, and through him, the British Government, were kept informed about everything which passed between Hicks and the Egyptian Government.

During the summer Hicks induced the Egyptian Government to appoint him C.-in-C. in place of the incompetent Niazi Pasha, who was sent to the Eastern Sudan as Governor. He also extracted from them some reinforcements in men and money and won some victories against the Mahdist forces in the Gezira area between the Blue and White Niles south of Khartum. Thus encouraged, he proceeded with plans for leading an expedition into Kordofan in the autumn against the main Mahdist forces.

Malet, in spite of Granville's oft-repeated instructions to avoid any responsibility for military operations in the Sudan, became alarmed at the financial implications and military risks of an advance into Kordofan. In June he suggested to Granville that Hicks "should be instructed to confine himself to maintaining the present supremacy of the Khedive in the regions between the White and Blue Niles".[13] In reply he was told to keep the British Government informed of what was happening, "taking care to offer no advice, but pointing out that . . . the Egyptian Government should make up their minds what their policy is to be and should consider carefully the financial side of the question".[14] Malet was not the man to persist in making unwelcome suggestions to his Government; nor was he the man to exceed his instructions by giving what he considered appropriate advice to the Egyptian Government. So, in congratulating Hicks on his appointment as C.-in-C., he was careful to point out that the appointment was "spontaneous on the part of the Egyptian Government" and that, although he was willing to continue to transmit the contents of Hicks' cipher telegrams to the Egyptian Government, his instructions debarred him from making any recommendations or suggestions either to Hicks or to the Egyptian Government, since it was the British Government's policy to abstain from interference in the Sudan.

As Lord Cromer stated later, "What was most of all required was that an alarm bell should be rung to rouse the British Government from its lethargy and show that the consequences of inaction might be more serious than those of action."[15] But no alarm bell was rung, and Hicks, encouraged by his successful skirmishes in the vicinity of Khartum, bound by his instructions from the Egyptian Government, and, apparently, not unduly pessimistic of his prospects of success, set out from Khartum on 8 September with a force of some 10,000 men to seek out and destroy the Mahdi's main force in Kordofan. Power, the young *Times* correspondent in Khartum who accompanied the expedition for a few days until, fortunately for himself, he fell sick and had to return to Khartum, described Hicks' force as "9,000 infantry that 50 good men would rout in 10 minutes and 1,000 cavalry Bashibazouks (irregular troops) that never even learnt to ride. These, with a few Nordenfeld guns, are sent to beat the 69,000 men the Mahdi has got together."

The result was foreseeable. On 5 November Hicks' force, having penetrated deep into Kordofan, being short of water and having apparently lost its way, was attacked by the Mahdi's forces at Kasghil, some fifty miles south of el-Obeid, and almost completely annihilated. Hicks and all his European staff were killed, as well as the Governor-General, Ala-ed-Din Pasha, who had insisted on accompanying the expedition.

Meanwhile, in August, before Hicks' force had left Khartum, the rebellion had spread to the Eastern Sudan. On 5 August, Osman Digna, a former slave dealer of Suakin, whom the Mahdi had appointed as his Emir, or Lieutenant, in the Eastern Sudan, having gathered together a force in response to the Mahdi's proclamation urging the inhabitants of the Eastern Sudan to "advance against the Turks and drive them out of the country", laid siege to the small Egyptian garrison at Sinkat, in the Red Sea hills on the route between Suakin and Berber and covering the port of Suakin. Within the next few weeks the garrison of Tokar, about twenty miles from the sea and forty-five miles south-west of Suakin, was also besieged. Attempts to relieve Sinkat and Tokar were successively mounted from Suakin and successively defeated by Osman Digna. In the attempt to relieve Tokar on 3 November, a British officer, Captain Moncrieff, R.N., the British Consul at Jidda, who had accompanied the expedition, was killed. A particularly disturbing feature of these defeats was that in each case the Egyptian force was ignominiously routed by an enemy inferior both in numbers and in armament.

Definite news of the Hicks disaster reached Cairo on 22 November, although rumours of it had been rife for some days. It was now clear, not only that Khartum was threatened, but that Osman Digna's victories in the Eastern Sudan had closed the normal route via Suakin and Berber for reinforcing Khartum. Whereas before there had been a tendency to underrate the power of the Mahdi there was now a tendency in Cairo to overrate it and a fear lest the loss of Khartum might lead to a Mahdist invasion of Egypt. The British Government's policy of dissociating themselves from responsibility for the Sudan had become impracticable, although it was persisted in for several more critical weeks.

In September Sir Edward Malet had been replaced as British Agent in Egypt by Sir Evelyn Baring, who had had previous experience in Egypt both as British Debt Commissioner and as British Representative on the Anglo-French

Control. He was to remain as British Agent in Egypt for twenty-four years and was destined to be instrumental in converting the British occupation from the humiliating disasters which appeared to threaten it in 1883 to the triumphant success with which it was generally regarded twenty years later. For the time being, however, he was beset with a number of apparently insoluble difficulties and complications, of which the most immediate and most serious was the crisis over the Sudan.

Soon after Baring arrived in Cairo he had a discussion with Sherif, the Prime Minister, about the future of the Sudan. On the assumption of the success of Hicks' expedition Sherif told him that the Egyptian Government proposed to abandon the direct administration of Darfur, making it into a tributary state, to appoint a commission of three, including possibly one European, to reorganise the administration of the Sudan, and to construct a railway between Suakin and Berber. Baring told the British Government that, in accordance with his instructions, he had "abstained from giving any advice".[16] Granville approved his attitude and supported the idea of a railway, in which various British capitalist groups were interested.[17] But, as the weeks went by, apprehensions began to be expressed about the fate of the Hicks expedition. Baring had an interview with Giegler Pasha, who had been in the Sudan service and who had at one time acted as Governor-General. He expressed the opinion that Khartum could not be held if Hicks were defeated. After this interview Baring telegraphed Granville expressing his anxieties about Hicks and his fears about the safety of Khartum in the event of Hicks having been defeated. He stressed the inability of the Egyptian Government to send either money or military reinforcements to the Sudan and warned that they would be likely to call for the assistance of British or Indian troops. He asked Granville to confirm his expectation that British or Indian troops could not be made available and suggested, while deprecating, the possibility of calling for Turkish aid. He stated his own opinion that the wisest course would be for the Egyptians to "fall back on whatever point on the Nile they can hold with confidence", and concluded that it was no longer possible for the British Government to "maintain a purely passive attitude and to give no advice whatever".[18] Granville replied confirming that British or Indian troops would not be made available, expressed the view that Turkish intervention "would not be for the advantage of Egypt", and recommended "the abandonment of the Sudan within certain limits".[19]

The Egyptian Government, after having received definite news of the Hicks disaster, started making arrangements for sending a force to Suakin with the objects of defending that port, of relieving Tokar and Sinkat, and, if possible, of reopening the Suakin–Berber desert route as the quickest method of reinforcing the Khartum garrison. The force which they proposed to dispatch consisted of 2,000 Gendarmerie, a para-military force which had recently been raised for internal security duties under the command of Baker Pasha, and 6,000 Sudanese troops which had been raised by, and which it was proposed to put under the command of, Zubair Pasha, the ex-slave trader who had been compulsorily detained in Cairo by the Egyptian Government since his visit there in 1875 in connection with the Governorship of Darfur. Baker, with his 2,000 Gendarmes, left Suez for Suakin in the middle of December, just after news had been received that another attempt to relieve Tokar by an Egyptian force from Suakin had been ignominiously defeated.

Baker's instructions were to defend Suakin, to relieve Tokar and Sinkat, and to open up the Suakin–Berber road if possible. Before he left, Baring impressed upon him that "the necessity for avoiding any disaster must come before any other consideration" and advised him that "it would be hazardous to commence any military operations before receiving the reinforcements which shall be sent to you with Zubair Pasha".[20] It had been intended that Zubair should follow with his Sudanese before the end of the month. But unexpected difficulties arose. At the beginning of December news of Zubair's appointment, with disapproving comments from *The Times* correspondents in Cairo and Khartum, appeared in the English Press. The Anti-Slavery Society, which had a powerful lobby in England, began to make disapproving noises. Baring telegraphed Granville on 9 December pointing out that though "under ordinary circumstances his employment would have been open to considerable objections", both the Egyptian Government and Baker himself were anxious to have Zubair's services. He reminded Granville that "the whole responsibility for the conduct of affairs in the Sudan has been left to the Egyptian Government" and expressed the view that "it would not have been just . . . to have objected to that Government using their own discretion on such a point as the employment of Zubair Pasha".[21] In reply, Granville, who had refused to interfere with the dispatch of the Hicks expedition to Kordofan, and who had reiterated *ad nauseam* the British Government's refusal to accept any responsibility for the Sudan, told Baring that he regarded the proposed employment of Zubair as "inexpedient both politically and as regards the slave trade". As a result, Zubair's appointment was cancelled. On his Sudanese troops refusing to leave without him, they were rounded up and embarked for Suakin literally at sabre-point by Egyptian troops under the orders of British officers. This grotesque expedient, adopted in deference to the views of the Anti-Slavery Society, in the opinion of one of the British officers serving with Baker, "rendered the Suakin expedition almost hopeless from the first".[22]

Meanwhile, Colonel Coetlogon, a British officer whom Hicks had appointed to command the Kordofan garrison after his departure for Kordofan, had been sending alarming messages to Sir Evelyn Wood, the British C.-in-C. of the Egyptian Army. He told him that Khartum and Sennaar could not be held, that they had only two months' supply of food in Khartum, and recommended an immediate retreat on Berber and the opening of the Suakin–Berber route by an expedition from the Suakin end. Power, *The Times* correspondent in Khartum, was telegraphing in similar vein: "The Mahdi has 300,000 men with rifles and artillery and we have barely 2,000 soldiers."

There seems no doubt that Coetlogon's panicky messages (panicky in the light of the fact that Khartum was to hold out for another fourteen months without receiving any reinforcements) affected the views of the British military authorities in Cairo—General Stephenson, who had replaced General Alison as C.-in-C. British troops in Egypt, and General Sir Evelyn

Wood. They told Baring that, in the event of the Mahdi's advancing, it would be impossible to hold Khartum with the means at the Egyptian Government's disposal, in view of the demoralisation of the garrison, the non-availability of reinforcements, and the difficulty of maintaining communications. They also doubted whether Baker would be able to open the Suakin–Berber route. They recommended that such an attempt should be made, not in order to try to hold Khartum but to facilitate the evacuation of the garrison from Khartum. They thought that, once Khartum had been evacuated, it would be necessary to abandon the whole of the Nile valley down to Wadi Halfa. These views were communicated by Baring both to the British and the Egyptian Governments. The Egyptian Government's reaction was to ask the British Government either to invite the aid of Turkey or to provide British or Indian troops themselves. Granville, replying on 13 December, reiterated for the *n*th time that the British Government had no intention of providing British or Indian troops, but that they had no objection to the use of Turkish troops provided that they were paid for by the Ottoman Government and provided that they were based on Suakin and did not enter Egypt proper. He recommended the Egyptian Government to "take an early decision to abandon all territory south of Aswan or at least of Wadi Halfa", and intimated that the British Government would be "prepared to assist in maintaining order in Egypt proper and in defending it as well as the ports of the Red Sea". The pressure of events was steadily pushing a reluctant British Government into assuming responsibility for Egyptian policy in the Sudan.

In reply to Granville's recommendation Sherif Pasha informed Baring, on 22 December, in a written note, that his Government could not agree to "the abandonment of territories which they consider absolutely necessary for the security and even for the existence of Egypt". He also pointed out that, under the Sultan's Firman of 1879 appointing Taufiq as Khedive, Egypt was forbidden to cede any territory forming part of the Khedive's dominions.

It is to be noted at this point that the recommendation for the abandonment of the Nile valley down to Wadi Halfa, made by Generals Stephenson and Wood, transmitted to London by Baring, approved by the British Government, and subsequently enforced on the Egyptian Government, had been made on the basis of a number of telegrams sent by a not very distinguished and apparently badly rattled retired officer in Khartum. It is further to be noted that the evacuation of the Khartum garrison implied by this abandonment was recognised to be dependent on the opening of the Suakin–Berber road, although doubt was expressed whether Baker would be able to accomplish this. It seems surprising that no attempt was made at this time (*a*) to send a qualified British officer, like Stewart, to Khartum to report on whether the place could be held in the event of the Suakin–Berber road being opened and (*b*) to send a qualified British officer to Suakin to report on the force necessary to open and keep open the Suakin–Berber road. And since, if the Khartum and Sennaar garrisons were to be extricated, it was probably necessary to reopen the Suakin–Berber road anyway, it is surprising that nobody seems to have asked whether the defence of "Egypt proper" and of the Red Sea ports, for both of which the British Government had assumed responsibility, would be rendered easier or more difficult as a result of a withdrawal to Wadi Halfa.

Baring had already, on 10 December, warned Granville that the Egyptian Government were "drifting on without any definite or practical plan of action", and that "more definite instructions must shortly be sent as to the attitude of the British Government and as to the advice to be given to the Egyptian Government". This had produced Granville's telegram of 13 December. On 22 December, after receiving Sherif's note, Baring telegraphed Granville recommending that he be authorised to inform the Khedive that the British Government insisted on their recommendation for the abandonment of the Sudan being adopted and that "if the present Ministers will not carry it out he must find others who will do so". He also recommended that, in view of the importance of the decision to be taken, the Cabinet should consult Mr Cross, Under-Secretary at the India Office, who had spent two months in Egypt and who was due back in England on Christmas Eve. This gave the members of the Cabinet, to whom Baring's telegram was circulated, plenty of time for consultation and consideration. Gladstone was not averse to the employment of Turkish troops if they could be obtained and was not convinced that the Egyptian Government should be induced to abandon the Sudan.[23] Northbrook, First Lord of the Admiralty, was in favour of abandoning the Sudan, of defending Egypt, and of doing what was possible, by policing the Red Sea and the Nile and the caravan routes at the Egyptian frontier, to check the export of slaves from the Sudan.[24] Granville was in favour of abandonment because he did not think that Turkish troops could be made available.[25] Cross told Granville that, although the Pashas in Egypt objected to the abandonment of the Sudan, there was no popular feeling on the subject. Neither Stephenson nor Wood thought the retention of Khartum necessary for the defence of Egypt, although Valentine Baker, supported by his brother, Sir Samuel Baker, the explorer, disagreed with them. Cross also told Granville that the Egyptian ruling class was terrified at the prospect of a British withdrawal and that, if it came to the point, the Khedive would accede to British advice to abandon the Sudan and be able to find Ministers to implement that advice.[26]

On 3 January a meeting of the Cabinet was held at which the reply to Baring's recommendation was agreed upon. It was contained in two telegrams sent on the following day. The first of these reiterated the British Government's refusal to employ British or Indian troops and raised no objection either to the use of Turkish troops at Suakin, provided that it would not increase "the expenditure falling on the Egyptian Treasury or cause the Egyptian Government to delay coming to a decision as to the movements of their troops from the interior of the Sudan", or to the handing over of the Red Sea ports and the Eastern Sudan to Turkey. It stated that the British Government "do not believe it to be possible for Egypt to defend Khartum and, while recommending the concentration of Egyptian troops, they desire that they shall be withdrawn from Khartum itself as well as from the interior of the Sudan". It urged that "all military operations excepting those for the rescue of outlying garrisons should cease", and promised British assistance for the protection of the Red Sea ports and the defence of "Egypt proper" north of Wadi Halfa or Aswan. The second telegram laid down the principle that "in important questions affecting the administration and safety of Egypt, the advice of Her Majesty's Government should be followed as long as the provisional occupation lasts. Ministers and Governors must carry out this advice or forfeit their offices."[27]

Informed of the contents of these two telegrams, Sherif Pasha and his Government resigned and Nubar Pasha agreed to the Khedive's request to form a Government. Nubar had been in and out of Egyptian Governments for the previous twenty years. He was a cosmopolitan and highly intelligent Armenian who was well versed in the administrative and international complications which beset Egypt. He considered himself as particularly adept at getting on with, and getting his own way with, Europeans, with whom he had had long experience over the Suez Canal, the Mixed Courts, Egypt's finances and many other matters. He was perfectly prepared to do what the British Government wanted over the Sudan and he counted on extracting from Baring a *quid pro quo* in other matters. So in effect he handed over the Sudan problem to the British Government to make the best they could of it, telling Baring that he "entirely concurred with the wisdom of abandoning the Sudan, retaining possession of Suakin".

A curious feature of all the correspondence which passed between Cairo and London, and of all the consultations which took place between British Cabinet Ministers, on the subject of the evacuation, was that no serious thought appears to have been given to the way in which this evacuation was to be carried out, or indeed whether it was a practicable operation. The only apparent reference to this aspect of the matter was a statement by Baring, in his telegram of 22 December, that "it would be necessary to send an English officer of high authority to Khartum with full powers to withdraw all the garrisons in the Sudan and to make the best arrangements possible for the future government of the country". It was only after the policy of abandonment had been agreed to by the British Government and enforced on the Khedive that the mechanics of the operation began seriously to be considered. In

Cairo Nubar and Baring agreed that Abdul Qadir Pasha, the ex-Governor-General of the Sudan, who had been dismissed by the previous Government and who had just been appointed Minister of War by Nubar, should be sent to Khartum to conduct the evacuation. "That officer made a sensible survey of the practical difficulties involved in the operation and reported that in view of the many thousands of soldiers and civilians resident in Khartum he would require thousands of camels for transport across the desert and that it would take from seven months to a year to carry out the task. When he heard that it was intended to proclaim publicly the intention to abandon Khartum he said that such an announcement would render him powerless and he refused to undertake the mission. A similar warning of the physical difficulties of evacuation was also given by Husain Pasha Khalifa, Governor of Berber."[28]

Meanwhile, the situation around Khartum appeared to be deteriorating. On 30 December Power, *The Times* correspondent, whom Baring had appointed as British Consular Agent in Khartum, reported that "the state of affairs here is very desperate", that the Mahdi was "assembling a great army to attack us", and that "in three days the town may be in the hands of the rebels". On 7 January a telegram arrived from Coetlogon to the Khedive strongly urging the necessity for an immediate order to retreat being given. "Were we twice as strong as we are we could not hold Khartum against the country, which without a doubt are one and all against us." On 9 January Power telegraphed to *The Times* that the telegraph lines between Khartum and Sennaar had been cut and that rebel forces were within a few hours of the capital. On 14 January he reported that all communication with Sennaar had been cut off and that the tribes on both banks of the Blue Nile had declared for the Mahdi.

Baring, who seems to have grasped the difficulties of evacuation after talking to Abdul Qadir, wrote a private letter to Granville on 14 January[29] describing the great distances to be traversed, the scarcity of provisions, the difficulties of navigating the Nile at low water and the certain expense of the whole operation. Nevertheless, on 16 January, orders were sent by the Egyptian Government to the Acting Governor-General in Khartum ordering a withdrawal of the Sennaar garrison on Khartum pending the evacuation of Khartum itself, and instructing that the Governors of Bahr-al-Ghazal and Equatoria should be informed of the situation and told to make whatever arrangement they could at their discretion. On the following day orders were given authorising the Sennaar garrison to evacuate to Abyssinia instead of Khartum if the Sennaar garrison commander thought fit. The Acting Governor-General was also instructed to evacuate to Berber "civilians and non-combatants who might wish to leave and for whom transport could be found", and to make arrangements for the garrison to be evacuated at his discretion either via Berber and the Nile route, or via Abu Haraz, on the Blue Nile, to Suakin, in accordance with a suggestion just received from Baker Pasha at Suakin. He was warned that the Berber–Suakin route was probably closed.

By that time Coetlogon was in a more optimistic mood and telegraphed Fraser, Sir Evelyn Wood's C.O.S., that they were not taking any steps to evacuate Khartum but trying to arrange for the withdrawal of the Sennaar garrison to Khartum. When that had been done he thought it would be possible to hold out in Khartum for as long as supplies lasted.[30] In the event no action was taken about evacuation until after Gordon's arrival at Khartum in February, although a number of civilians made their way from Khartum to Berber by their own arrangements.

On 16 January Baring, having failed to persuade Abdul Qadir to conduct the evacuation, informed Granville that "The Egyptian Government would feel obliged if Her Majesty's Government would send at once a qualified British officer to go to Khartum with full powers, military and civil, to conduct the retreat."

CHAPTER THREE

THE SELECTION OF THE MISSIONARY

SINCE THE BEGINNING of 1882 the Egyptian question had been one of the most explosive issues in British politics. It had presented Gladstone's Liberal Government with a series of problems, and the necessity for a series of decisions, which menaced its cohesion, tormented the consciences of many of its supporters, complicated relationships with foreign Powers, and provided material for attack both from the Tory opposition and from the Press. Among the members of the Government there was nothing like unity of opinion about the policy to be pursued. The Radical wing, led by Harcourt, the Home Secretary, considered that the main object of the Government's Near Eastern policy should be to reverse the "Imperialism" of the preceding Tory administration. They would have liked to avoid occupying Egypt altogether and, after the occupation, wanted to evacuate Egypt as soon as possible. Bright, one of the members of the Government, resigned in protest against the occupation, which had come about mainly because of the fears of the Admiralty and the War Office about the safety of the Suez Canal, and because the Foreign Office, primed by Malet, the British Agent in Cairo, and Colvin, the British Controller-General, were representing the nationalist movement as fanatical, anarchical and xenophobic.

After the occupation both Government and Opposition were officially in favour of an early evacuation after the restoration of order and security. But there were numerous undercurrents which began to ruffle the surface as it became apparent that this restoration was likely to be a long and difficult process. The immense difficulty, the apparent impossibility, of effecting any reforms in Egypt within the inefficient and discredited instruments of the Khedivate, the Pashas, Ottoman suzerainty and the hotch-potch of international organisations and controls in which Egypt was entangled, led to an increasing demand for annexation and the direct administration of Egypt by British officials, who would sweep away all the indigenous and international paraphernalia of misgovernment and start with a clean sheet on the work of rehabilitation. The annexationists were actuated by varying motives. Many civil and military officials on the spot were frustrated by the limitations on their authority imposed by the existing system. Many humanitarians, including, up to a point, Gordon, horrified at the inefficiency and oppressiveness of Pashadom, thought that annexation would be in the best interests of the Egyptian masses. Many financial and business interests saw in annexation the best prospect for existing, and security for future, investments. The soldiers and sailors tended to believe that annexation was the best solution from the point of view of security of communications with India. The rising generation of Imperialists, who believed in expansion for expansion's sake, and who were already becoming interested in staking out British claims in Central Africa, were naturally in favour of annexation. This Imperialist opinion was not yet strongly represented on either side of the House in an economy-conscious Commons. But it was a force with which any Government had to reckon. It was strongly represented in the Press and tended to be used as a stick to beat the Government by those to whom Liberalism, and particularly Gladstonian Liberalism, was synonymous with weakness, pusillanimity, truckling to foreigners and a disregard for British interests. On the other hand there were those who were moved to diametrically opposite conclusions by the chaos and inefficiency of affairs in Egypt during the first year or two of the occupation. Radicals, who had disapproved of the occupation, and who saw it as a device for propping up an oppressive and discredited system of government, wanted to get out of Egypt as quickly as possible in order to leave the field free for popular indigenous forces to assert their supremacy. Others, who were mainly concerned with public economy, avoiding foreign commitments and keeping out of trouble generally, and who saw the Egyptian imbroglio only as a source of financial expense and international discord, were also in favour of getting out as quickly as possible and leaving the Egyptians to stew in their own juice.

There was therefore a mixture of materialism and idealism

on each of the two wings of opinion. And in the middle was the Government, with its right wing touching the annexationists and its left wing touching those who advocated an immediate withdrawal. It was dominated, in its approach to the Egyptian problem, by two preoccupations: first by the necessity to arrive at some consensus representing the highest common factor of the diverse views of its members, secondly by the necessity to translate this into action relevant to the realities of the situation. Its resultant Egyptian policy was a compromise in which no consistent thread of principle was observable at the time or has been discernible since. What the Government did, in effect, was to remain in Egypt without annexing it, proclaim their intention of withdrawing without making any preparations for doing so, and limit as far as possible the assumption of administrative responsibilities. This involved giving as much countenance and authority as possible to the Egyptian Government. Since the annexationists and the advocates of withdrawal were both agreed on the inefficiency and corruption of the Khedive and the Pashas, this policy infuriated both wings of the Government's critics. It also militated against popular acceptance of the occupation in Egypt itself, since it irritated the ruling classes on the one hand and produced no observable benefits for the masses on the other.

Any active intervention against the Mahdist rebellion, apart from the expense involved (and it is sometimes forgotten how diffident Governments used to be about asking Parliament for money), would have been a step towards annexation and made the prospect of a speedy withdrawal still more remote. It is not surprising that the Government, which wished to keep the option of withdrawal open, and which probably did not contain any convinced annexationists, rejected Sir Charles Wilson's advice, given in the closing months of 1882, to assume some direct responsibility in the Sudan. They also took no notice of Stewart's prescient warnings about the desirability of the Egyptian Government abandoning the outlying parts of the Sudan in order to concentrate on improving the administration and defence of the Red Sea coast and the Nile Valley as far south as Sennaar.

The attitude of the two extreme wings of British opinion

towards the Mahdist rebellion was predictable. The annexationists wanted to take over the Sudan together with Egypt, although most of them agreed with Stewart that the outlying parts of the Sudan should be abandoned and the rest governed by British officials under some system of indirect rule. The Radicals tended to regard the rebellion as an extension of the Arabi rebellion—as a protest against the misgovernment of the Pashas, as a war of liberation by people "rightly struggling to be free", and concluded that it would be just as wrong for the British to intervene in the Sudan as it had been wrong for them to occupy Egypt. The soldiers and sailors were unanimous for holding Suakin and the Red Sea ports but reluctant to commit British or Indian troops to any campaign in the interior.

During the spring and summer of 1883 the Sudan rebellion "went to sleep" as far as British Parliamentary and public opinion were concerned. Malet made a few faint warning noises from Cairo about the possible implications of the Hicks expedition, but the British Government, "resolute for drift", persisted in their policy of non-interference to the extent of refusing to advise the Egyptian Government against a course which Stewart had warned them might be disastrous.

The death of Moncrieff on the Tokar relief expedition, at the beginning of November, and the news of the annihilation of the Hicks expedition, which was received later in the month, stirred public and Parliamentary opinion and imposed upon the Government the necessity for a reconsideration of the whole Sudan question. Moncrieff had had no authority to proceed on the Tokar expedition, and Hicks and the British officers killed with him were retired officers for whose employment in the Sudan the British Government had expressly disclaimed responsibility. But British public opinion saw that British-led forces had been defeated and regarded British honour and British interests as being involved. From the end of November onwards, the Sudan became front-page news in the British Press.

Parliament was not in session when news of the Hicks disaster was received, but there was much criticism of the Government in the Press. Members of the Government were divided in their views. Dilke, lately Under-Secretary of State at the Foreign Office and, at this time, President of the Local Government Board, admitted privately that the Government should have taken Stewart's advice and compelled the Egyptian Government to abandon the Kordofan expedition and give up the outlying parts of the Sudan.[1] Others, like Childers, the Chancellor of the Exchequer, thought that the Government should have been even stricter about non-involvement and forbidden the employment of any British officers, retired or otherwise, in the Sudan.[2] All were unanimous in their determination not to become involved in the Sudan, and were advised by Baring, who had replaced Malet in Cairo in September, that this would probably not be necessary, although it was impossible to "separate the Egyptian question from the Sudan question altogether". The main anxiety, after the Hicks defeat, was the defence of "Egypt proper" from a possible Dervish invasion. The great question was—what part of the amorphous area known as the Sudan could be regarded as "Egypt proper" in that its retention was essential to the defence of the Nile Delta and the Suez Canal? Baring, in a telegram to Granville on 19 November, gave no answer to this question except to express the opinion that the Egyptians should "withdraw to whatever position on the Nile they can be sure of defending". In the same telegram he suggested that the British Government might help the Egyptian Government to obtain the services of some British officers not on the active list. In other words, a repetition of the not very successful Hicks experiment.

After the news about Hicks had been confirmed, the British military authorities, in London and Cairo, began an urgent consideration of the military implications from the point of view of the defence of Egypt. The British Government agreed, on the recommendation of Baring, Stephenson and Wood, that the existing strength of British forces in Egypt should be maintained for the time being and that the impending evacuation to Alexandria of the British garrison in Cairo, which had been publicly announced in London a month before, should be postponed indefinitely. On 23 November, Wolseley, the Adjutant-General, submitted a note to Hartington, the Secretary of State for War, in which he recommended that the whole of the Northern Sudan east of the Nile should be held, and that

British-officered Egyptian troops should be immediately sent to reinforce the Egyptian garrisons at Khartum, Berber and Suakin. This was in opposition to the views of Baring and of Wood, who were against sending units of the new Egyptian Army out of Egypt, or on active operations, until they had been properly trained. Wolseley also recommended the garrisoning of Aswan by British-officered Egyptian troops in order to convince the inhabitants of the intention to defend them against the Dervishes if necessary, and stated that he opposed withdrawal from the Sudan on account of the extreme military difficulty of such an operation.[3] Hartington, in forwarding Wolseley's note to Granville, expressed his general agreement with its contents.

It was at this point that the possibility of Gordon's being sent to the Sudan was once more taken up. Almost exactly a year before, Sir Charles Wilson, Military Adviser to the British Agent in Cairo, had recommended the appointment of Gordon as Governor-General of the Sudan. The Egyptian Government had objected and Malet had been unenthusiastic. Granville had interviewed Gordon in November 1882, after having received Wilson's recommendation, and had discussed the affairs of the Sudan with him. In this interview Gordon had minimised the importance of the rebellion, recommended the appointment of Wilson as Governor-General and expressed the view that, with the moral support of the British Government, he would have no difficulty in restoring order. After this interview there was some discussion between members of the Cabinet about the possibility of Gordon's appointment. Northbrook, First Lord of the Admiralty, doubted whether it would be wise, thought that Gordon would not go anyway, and advocated the appointment of Wilson as Gordon had suggested.[4] The Queen thought that either Sir Samuel Baker or Gordon might settle things in a couple of months.[5] In the end, partly because of the Egyptian Government's objections and Malet's lack of enthusiasm, the matter was allowed to drop. But Gordon's view about the comparative unimportance of the rebellion no doubt encouraged the Government in their policy of non-intervention in the Sudan. For the first time Gordon had given advice which happened to chime with the

Government's own inclinations. Accordingly, his stock rose and he was no longer regarded as "not being clothed in the rightest of minds".

Nothing more was heard about Gordon in British official circles until the middle of October 1883 when he asked the War Office for permission to serve under King Leopold in the Congo. After this had been turned down and before the British Government knew of Gordon's intention to take up the post offered by Leopold, which would have involved resigning his commission, the possibility of Gordon's employment in the Sudan was once more raised in rather a circuitous way. Colonel Bevan Edwards, who had served under Gordon in China, and who was later to become an M.P., wrote to General Sir Andrew Clarke, Inspector-General of Fortifications at the War Office, suggesting that Gordon should be employed by the British Government to deal with the situation in the Sudan. The letter stated that, although Gordon would be unwilling to serve under the Khedive, he would probably be willing to assist the Khedive if he were employed by the British Government. Edwards suggested that he be given supreme power in the Sudan with the rank of Lieut.-General in the British Army and have put at his disposal a division of troops from India consisting of two British brigades and four or five native battalions. "By making Gordon supreme he will settle the matter for them in a way that no one else would." On 24 November, Sir Andrew Clarke, perhaps because he was not on good terms with Wolseley, sent Edwards' letter to Childers, the Chancellor of the Exchequer, who had previously been Secretary of State for War, with a covering letter warmly supporting his suggestion.[6] Childers sent the two letters to Granville, who received them a few days after he had received Baring's telegram of 19 November with his suggestion about helping the Egyptian Government to obtain the services of some British officers not on the active list, and just after he had received a telegram from Baring dated 23 November telling him about the Egyptian intention to hold Khartum and to dispatch the Baker–Zubair force to Suakin to try and open the Suakin–Berber road. Granville asked Gladstone whether he had any objection to Gordon's being employed in the Sudan.

"He has an immense name in Egypt. He is popular at home. He is a strong but sensible opponent of slavery. He has a small bee in his bonnet."[7] Gladstone raised no objection and Granville, on 1 December, telegraphed Baring: "If General Charles Gordon were willing to go to Egypt would he be of any use to you or to the Egyptian Government and if so in what capacity?" Baring, in his recollections on the subject twenty years later, wrote: "I did not at the time know General Gordon well, but I had seen a little of him and I had of course heard much of him. My first impression was decidedly adverse to his employment in the Sudan. Moreover, when I spoke to Sherif Pasha on the subject, I found that he entertained strong objections to the proposal. I was unwilling to put forward my own objections, which were in some degree based on General Gordon's personal unfitness to undertake the work in hand. In replying to Lord Granville therefore I only dwelt on the objections entertained by the Egyptian Government."[8] His reply, sent on 2 December, read: "The Egyptian Government are very much averse to employing General Gordon mainly on the ground that, the movement in the Sudan being religious, the appointment of a Christian in high command would alienate the tribes who remain faithful. I think it wise not to press them on the subject."

There is no reason to suppose that Baring was exaggerating the Egyptian Government's objections in order to avoid expressing his own opinion. Sherif had been in office while Gordon had been Governor-General and, like many other Pashas in the Egyptian ruling class, had suspected Gordon of trying to detach the Sudan from Egypt, and may have suspected that he was doing so under instructions from the British Government. There was, both before and after the occupation, a considerable suspicion of British intentions in the Sudan and Egyptian reluctance to withdraw from the Sudan was partly due to a belief that the British were planning to take it over themselves. Sherif had rejected Wilson's recommendation for Gordon's employment in October 1882; he had been extremely suspicious about Stewart's mission to the Sudan two months later, and he had ignored Stewart's recommendations about withdrawing from the west and south of the Sudan. And, in December 1883, when the pressure of events had compelled him belatedly to act upon that recommendation and when he would have been prepared to welcome British military assistance if it had been offered, he was still unwilling to accept Gordon in a position which, although it was not specifically mentioned, could not have been other than that of Governor-General. (There was, as yet, so far as the Egyptian Government were concerned, no question of evacuating the whole of the Sudan.)

The British Government's reasons for putting Gordon's name forward were rather more complex. On the one hand they were confronted with the Egyptian Government's expressed determination to hold on to Khartum and Baring's opinion that they would be unable to do so. On the other hand they had the opinion of Wolseley, their principal military adviser, that Khartum should be held, because of the military difficulty of evacuating it, and that the garrison there should be reinforced by British-officered Egyptian troops. They were opposed to this themselves. They knew that Baring and Wood were opposed to it. Nobody seemed to know whether Khartum could be held without the British or Indian reinforcements which the British Government were determined not to send. Nobody seemed to know whether the retention of Khartum was necessary for the defence of "Egypt proper" and whether its retention depended on the re-opening of the Suakin–Berber road. In so far as there was a consensus of opinion it seemed to be that the defence of "Egypt proper" could only be secured by some sort of British committment to the defence of some part of the Sudan. The prospect was most unwelcome to a Government which disliked the prospect of undertaking financial, or increasing existing political and military, committments in Egypt, and which was publicly committed to and, for the most part, anxious for a speedy withdrawal from Egypt. Might it not be that everyone was exaggerating the seriousness of the rebellion and that Gordon who, in his interview with Granville, had shrugged it off as a "little local difficulty", and who was reputed to know the Sudan better than anyone, had taken the correct view of the matter? And, even if it were as serious as Wolseley and Baring made out, was not Gordon, who had put down the Taiping rebellion in China almost single-handed, capable of dealing with the situation? Many people seemed to think so.

But it was necessary that he, if employed at all in the Sudan, should, like Hicks, be employed by the Egyptian and not by the British Government, so that, if he shared Hicks' fate, the British Government should not be held responsible. But the Egyptian Government were unwilling to employ him. And Baring, like Malet a year before, was obviously unenthusiastic. So the proposal was, once more, allowed to drop.

There is no doubt that the possibility of employment in the Sudan was very much in Gordon's mind at this time. It is probable that Edwards' letter to Clarke was the product of confabulations among Gordon's friends, and not unlikely that it was written with Gordon's knowledge and approval. He may well have learned of Granville's approach to Baring. Rumours of it had appeared in *The Times*, in a message from their Cairo correspondent published on 3 December, which stated that "Gordon Pasha's name has again been brought forward, but no final decision has been taken". At all events, he did not immediately resign his commission on learning that the War Office had refused permission for him to serve in the Congo, even though he had apparently determined to accept Leopold's offer. He seems to have been half-expecting, and certainly hoping for, the summons which eventually came.

Gordon arrived in Brussels from Palestine on New Year's Day 1884. He saw King Leopold, told him that the British Government had refused him permission to go to the Congo, and explained that, if he did so, he would have to resign his commission and lose his pension. Leopold immediately agreed to compensate him for loss of pension by a cash payment and Gordon agreed to go to the Congo at the end of the month as Stanley's deputy. His principal object in taking up the appointment was concern for the abolition of the slave trade. In a note written for publication to the Secretary of the Anti-Slavery Society on 5 January, while he was still in Brussels, he told him: "We may abandon all idea of doing anything in the Sudan for the present. . . . Until we cut off the slave trade at the source of its existence no measures can be efficacious. . . . Now that General Gordon is going out as second-in-command to Stanley . . . we expect that their joint efforts will deal a fatal blow to the slave hunters . . . whatever may be the end of the Sudan revolt."

He returned to England on 7 January and, on that same day, wrote officially to the War Office resigning his commission.

Meanwhile, there had been important developments over the Sudan. Militarily, nothing much had happened. Another Egyptian attempt to relieve Tokar early in December had been defeated. The Suakin–Berber road was still closed. Sennaar was still besieged and Coetlogon was still sending agitated telegrams from Khartum. The Mahdi with most of his forces was still in Kordofan and communications between Cairo and Khartum via Korosko and Berber were still open. But, politically, things had been moving. The British Government, on Baring's recommendation, had insisted on an Egyptian withdrawal from the Sudan to as far north as Wadi Halfa on the understanding that they would make themselves responsible for the defence of the Nile valley north of Wadi Halfa and the Red Sea ports. The Khedive had accepted what amounted to a British ultimatum on the subject; Sherif and his Government had resigned and Nubar Pasha had formed a Government on the understanding that he accepted and would implement the policy of withdrawal. Sherif and his Government resigned on 7 January, the day on which Gordon landed in England, and Nubar took office as Prime Minister the next day.

Baring's insistence on the necessity of an Egyptian withdrawal to Wadi Halfa, which was accepted by the British Government and imposed by them on the Khedive, derived from the views of Generals Stephenson and Wood, and was based on the assumption that no military reinforcements for the Sudan were available either from Egypt or from elsewhere. The British Government had made it clear that neither British not Indian troops would be made available. They had also expressed their opposition to the idea of asking the Sultan to supply Turkish troops, although they had not expressly forbidden it. It is improbable that any adequate Turkish force would have been forthcoming in time even if it had been asked for. General Wood was averse to using the new Egyptian Army which he was building up. Neither Baring, nor his military advisers, had any confidence in the ability of Baker's force to open the Suakin–Berber road, particularly after the British Government's veto on the employment of Zubair. It was generally considered that the possession of this road was an essential condition of the continued possession of Khartum. It was not so generally recognised that its possession was also an all-but-essential condition for the successful evacuation of Khartum. Baring, in recommending evacuation, does not seem to have given any consideration to the military difficulties. In his telegram of 22 December, in which he recommended insistence on evacuation, he simply stated that "It would be necessary to send an English officer of high authority to Khartum with full powers to withdraw all the garrisons in the Sudan and to make the best arrangements possible for the future government of the country."

There was at this time, and later, much uncertainty and confusion, both in Cairo and in London, as to what was involved in the term "evacuation". Did it mean only the evacuation of the garrisons of Egyptian troops at Khartum and elsewhere in the Sudan? Did it mean the evacuation of Egyptian civilian employees and their families as well as the garrisons? Or did it mean the evacuation of all Egyptian and foreign communities and of all those Sudanese who, compromised by their support of the Egyptians, might wish to leave? The moral problem depended on the sort of treatment likely to be meted out to these various categories if they surrendered to the Mahdist forces. When the two Kordofan garrisons—Bara and el Obeid—had surrendered a year before they had been treated with reasonable leniency. The troops, who were mostly Sudanese, had been recruited into the Dervish forces; the Egyptian officers and officials and their families, and the European inhabitants, had been stripped of their property and taken into captivity. There had been a few executions, but nothing in the way of a general massacre. The practical problem was the difficulty of evacuating anyone at all owing to the vastness of the country, the shortages of food, water and means of transport, and the increasing dominance of the enemy.

The problem of the garrisons, composed of about half Egyptian or Turkish and half Sudanese soldiers, was measurable and clear-cut. Those in Kordofan had already surrendered. Those in Darfur were isolated and the only alternatives before them were—surrender to the Mahdi, evacuation as part of an arrangement with the Mahdi, or relief as a result of successful hostilities against the Mahdi. The third alternative seemed to be ruled out owing to the policy of withdrawal which had been adopted. The garrisons in Bahr-al-Ghazal and Equatoria were cut off from Khartum by the Mahdist occupation of both banks of the White Nile. Single armed steamers might have fought their way through but there was not enough armed river transport to evacuate the entire garrisons. There was a possibility of evacuation through the Congo or East Africa. Owing to the nature of the terrain and the availability of food and water, it was not impossible that these garrisons might hold out almost indefinitely provided that the troops remained loyal. One of the principal difficulties was the virtual impossibility of giving instructions to, or receiving information from, the garrisons in Darfur, Bahr-al-Ghazal and Equatoria. They had to be left to their own initiative and devices. Each of these provinces had a European Governor—Slatin in Darfur, Lupton in Bahr-al-Ghazal and Emin in Equatoria. In the event, the Darfur garrisons surrendered during 1884 as a result partly of starvation and partly of desertions to the Mahdi. The Bahr-al-Ghazal garrisons surrendered, also during 1884, almost entirely as a result of desertions to the Mahdi. The Equatoria garrisons, which were not seriously threatened militarily, held out until Emin was "rescued" by Stanley in 1887. The Sennaar garrison was besieged from the middle of 1883 onwards, but there was intermittent communication between it and Khartum, a distance of about 200 miles by the Blue Nile, and no problem over food supplies as Sennaar was in the middle of a grain-growing area. Failing any agreement with the Dervishes, the garrison, with the aid of sorties and river transport from Khartum, might have been able to fight their way down the Blue Nile to Khartum between May and September while the river was navigable. Alternatively they might have been able to fight their way to the Red Sea coast at Massawa via Abu Haraz and Kassala, or via Abyssinia. In the event the garrison held out until August 1885, eight months after the fall of Khartum, when it capitulated after a most gallant defence in which the Egyptian commander, Hasan Sadiq, was killed.

There were several Egyptian garrisons along the Abyssinian

frontier—Qallabat, Gera, Amadib, Senhit, Gedaref and Kassala. They were all cut off from Khartum; Gedaref and Kassala were besieged by Osman Digna's forces. During the course of 1884 all these garrisons except Gedaref and Kassala were successfully evacuated via Abyssinia as the result of an agreement arrived at between the Abyssinian and Egyptian Governments with the assistance of Admiral Hewett, the British Admiral commanding in the Red Sea. The Gedaref garrison surrendered in April 1884 before the signature of the agreement. The Kassala garrison, closely invested and cut off both from the Red Sea coast and Abyssinia by Osman Digna's forces, held out until July 1885, when it was forced to surrender by starvation. The garrisons of Tokar and Sinkat, near the Red Sea coast, were, as we have seen, closely invested at the end of 1883. After the various attempts to relieve them had failed, the Sinkat garrison was annihilated during February 1884 in an attempt to break out and gain Suakin, and Tokar surrendered shortly afterwards.

By the beginning of January 1884 it was, or should have been, clear that the evacuation of all these garrisons—except possibly those in Bahr-al-Ghazal and Equatoria—was a military or diplomatic, and not an administrative, problem. On the other hand, the problem of evacuating the garrisons at Khartum, Berber and points north on the Nile was still largely an administrative one. Both the land and the river routes between Khartum and Berber were still open. The Berber–Suakin road was closed but the desert route Berber–Abu Hamed–Korosko was open. It was mainly a matter of transport and food and water supplies. If it had simply been a question of evacuating troops, of which there were about 6,000 in Khartum, apart from a few hundred sick and wounded, if it had been tackled at once, before the enemy had begun to close in on the Nile north of Khartum, and if it had been decided to leave to its fate the garrison of Sennaar (which, leaving the possibility of negotiation aside, was the only one which might have been withdrawn into Khartum), the problem might have been manageable. Most of the Sudanese soldiers, who comprised about half the garrisons, might well have preferred to remain where they were and join the Mahdi's forces, which would have meant less people for whom to provide food and transport. But the problem was complicated and magnified by the presence of between 10,000 and 15,000 mostly Egyptian civilians—men, women and children—in Khartum, and a lesser number in Berber, who wanted to leave with the garrisons and who, it was feared, might be exposed to Mahdist vengeance if they remained. The evacuation of such large numbers of non-combatants, in face of possible enemy attacks, posed intractable problems of supply, transport and protection which do not appear to have occurred to Baring or to the British Government when they imposed the policy of evacuation on the Khedive.

The Khedive only accepted the evacuation policy reluctantly. At one time it seemed likely that no Egyptian Ministry could be formed to implement it. The Khedive told Moberly Bell, *The Times* correspondent, that no Minister would accept office if it meant giving up Khartum.[9] It seems likely that this reluctance was due, not so much to considerations of prestige, obligations to the Suzerain Power, etc., which Sherif had advanced to Baring, as to a belief that the policy being imposed was impracticable in terms of a controlled evacuation and amounted to a total and unconditional abandonment to what they regarded as a merciless and barbarous enemy of all the Egyptians in the Sudan, both military and civilian.

There was also some dissent in England over the evacuation policy. Wolseley, in his note to Hartington on 23 November, had expressed himself as being in favour of holding on to Khartum because of the difficulties of evacuation, and had advocated strengthening the garrisons at Khartum, Berber and Suakin with British-officered Egyptian troops. It is unlikely that his opinion had been changed by the British Government's subsequent insistence on evacuation, which had been adopted on the advice, not of the War Office, but on that of Baring, advised by Stephenson and Wood, of whose military capacities Wolseley had a poor opinion. Public opinion was also beginning to become interested. On 26 November a message appeared in *The Times* from their Egypt correspondent stating that the object of sending Baker's force of 2,000 Gendarmes and 6,000 blacks to Suakin was to open the Berber road "as a means of retreat for the Khartum garrison which the bulk of opinion deems it inadvisable to defend". Moberly Bell, *The Times* correspondent, was being used by Baring, who was already convinced of the necessity for abandoning Khartum, to commend evacuation both to the Egyptian authorities and to the British public, and this message—the first public intimation that the evacuation of Khartum was being contemplated—was undoubtedly inspired by Baring to this end. During December Sir Samuel Baker, the explorer, a brother of Valentine Baker, and a leading unofficial pundit on the Sudan, wrote a series of letters and articles to *The Times* from his Devonshire retreat, of which the general theme was that Khartum must be held, that the British must assist in holding it, that the Suakin–Berber road must be opened and the Berber garrison reinforced by Indian troops, that British troops must be sent to garrison Dongola in replacement of Egyptian troops sent from Dongola to reinforce Berber, and that Arab troops must be raised round Korosko to keep open the desert route between Korosko and Berber. "The Sudan will be lost unless England should at once assume power. Khartum may quickly be rendered impregnable. . . . There is no important difficulty if the organisation is put in the hands of a capable man." Baker also, assuming, or having been informed, that Gordon was of much the same opinion as himself, suggested, in a letter which reached Gordon in Brussels on 1 January, that he too should write to the Press stating his views. Gordon replied next day that his "inner voice" warned him against doing so, and added: "I will not go to the Sudan for I feel it is too late." This was presumably with reference to a letter from Baker which appeared in *The Times* on 1 January advocating the policy which he had put forward in December and suggesting that Gordon should be "invited to assist the Government".

The faint murmurings which were being expressed in England against the policy of evacuating the Sudan were of a piece with the discontent of the annexationists against what they regarded as the hesitancy of British policy in Egypt. They regarded insistence on evacuating the Sudan as deriving from a deplorable reluctance to assume responsibility in Egypt, and realised that a commitment to defend the Sudan would impose the necessity for assuming a greater measure of control over Egypt.

The Times, in a leader published on 1 January, the same day on which Baker's letter appeared, put the point succinctly, if rather optimistically: "It only needs to be known in the Sudan that we have really taken Egypt in hand; that knowledge would put an end to the Mahdi's power north of the desert." (For "desert" presumably read "Kordofan".)

The Government's decision to insist on an Egyptian evacuation of the Sudan became known in England on 7 January, the day of Sherif's resignation and the day of Gordon's arrival in England. There was, on the whole, more interest expressed in the Press on the prospects of firmer British control in Egypt than on the specific question of whether or not to evacuate the Sudan. The Sudan rebellion was looked on principally as an additional reason for an indefinite occupation of, and increased British control in, Egypt, since it was generally recognised that a British military presence in Egypt was necessary to defend that country from a possible Mahdist invasion. There was some opposition to the evacuation policy when it was announced—or rather when it leaked out, for no official announcement was made—including a letter in *The Times* attacking it from Mr Ashmead Bartlett, a Conservative M.P. and prominent annexationist. But there was a general tendency to accept it as inevitable.

Then, on 9 January, the *Pall Mall Gazette* published the celebrated interview which W. T. Stead, the editor, had had with Gordon at Southampton the previous day. This interview, which was arranged by Captain Brocklehurst, a friend of Gordon's in the War Office who accompanied Stead to Southampton, took place the day after Gordon had written to the War Office resigning his commission. The promptings of his "inner voice" had presumably changed since his letter to Baker a week earlier. In the published account of the interview Gordon was quoted as making the following points:

(i) That the eastern Sudan—meaning the provinces lying east of the White Nile and north of Sennaar—were indispensable to Egypt and that their retention would, in the long run, cost less than their abandonment.

(ii) That the danger to be feared from the Mahdi was, not that he would march into Egypt, but in the influence on Egypt and the rest of Islam of a Mahdist conquest of the Sudan.

(iii) That evacuation was impracticable because of transport difficulties: "How will you move your 6,000 men in Khartum —to say nothing of other places . . . through the desert to Wadi Halfa? Where are you going to get the camels to take them away? . . . Whatever you decide about evacuation, you cannot evacuate because your army cannot be moved. You must either surrender absolutely to the Mahdi or defend Khartum at all hazards."

(iv) That the eastern Sudan could be saved "if there is a firm hand in Egypt". Nubar should be placed in power and given a free hand. (It had been announced in the Press that morning that Nubar was forming a Government.) "Nubar should be left untramelled by any stipulation about the evacuation of Khartum. I imagine he would appoint a Governor-General with full powers and furnish him with £2 million, which would be needed to relieve the garrisons and quell the revolt."

(v) That, once this had been done, a "permanent constitution" should be granted to the Sudan by which "no Turks or Circassians would be allowed to enter the province to plunder its inhabitants". Darfur should be returned to the deposed ruling family and various territorial concessions made to Abyssinia. If all this were done, he estimated that the Sudan could be administered at the cost of a temporary subsidy of £200,000 p.a. . . . "The Sudan will never be a source of revenue to Egypt, but it need not be a source of expense."

(vi) That the cause of the rebellion was Egyptian misgovernment. "That the people were justified in rebelling nobody who knows the treatment to which they were subjected will attempt to deny. . . . It is an entire mistake to regard the Mahdi as a religious leader. . . . He personifies popular discontent. . . . The movement is not really religious but an outbreak of despair. . . . The egg of the present rebellion was laid in the three years during which I was allowed to govern the Sudan on other than Turkish principles."

(vii) That it ought to be possible to "come to terms with the Sudan, to grant them an amnesty for the past and security for decent government in the future. If this were done and the government entrusted to a man whose word was truth all might yet be re-established."

(viii) The account of the interview concluded with a warning about the "impolicy of announcing an intention to evacuate Khartum. . . . The moment it is known that we have given up the game, every man will go over to the Mahdi."

Gordon afterwards told Sir Andrew Clarke that he would not have expressed these opinions if he had known that the policy of evacuation had already been decided upon.[10] But he did know. He was a voracious reader of newspapers and was, of course, deeply interested in the Sudan. The news of Sherif's resignation, and the reason for it, had appeared in *The Times* that morning and in the *Pall Mall Gazette* the previous evening. It is not believable that Gordon did not know. The probable explanation is that he had by that time given up hope that the Government would employ him. As he wrote in the same letter to Clarke: "Things are too mixed in Egypt and the Sudan for me to think of it and you know this well enough. As to Taufiq I could never serve him, for he would never forgive my letter (presumably a letter he had written to *The Times* about Taufiq a year before), so that is that."

Publication of the interview in the *Pall Mall Gazette* on 9 January was accompanied by a leading article by Stead headed "Chinese Gordon for the Sudan". Stead, on Gordon's authority, attacked the whole policy of evacuation. "If General Gordon is right . . . the task is not merely difficult, it is impossible. The means of transport are altogether lacking and without camels it is as absurd to talk of crossing the desert as to propose to cross the sea without ships. If this be so, then there is no alternative but to hold on to Khartum as hard as we can and as long as we can and trust to time and tribal jealousies to open a way of escape for the endangered garrisons." He then went on to advocate sending Gordon to Khartum with full powers. "We cannot send a regiment to Khartum, but we can send a man who on more than one occasion has proved himself more valuable in similar circumstances than an entire army. Why not send Chinese Gordon with full powers to Khartum, to assume absolute control of the territory, to treat with the Mahdi, to relieve the garrisons, and to do what he can to save what can be saved from the wreck of the Sudan?"

The article did not explicitly advocate a reconquest of the Sudan, and even mentioned the possibility of a negotiation with the Mahdi. It attacked the policy of evacuation on the ground not of its undesirability but of its impossibility. In this, Stead was in agreement with Gordon, with Wolseley, and indeed with almost everyone who had devoted any serious thought to the question.

The publication of the interview was a great journalistic "scoop" and created a great sensation. Gordon had for many years been a well-known figure and any news about him was always good for a paragraph or two in the Press. Many of his friends and relatives, and even Gordon himself, were not unwilling to satisfy the public curiosity. There had been several books published about him. The latest of these—*Chinese Gordon* by his relative Egmont Hake—had been published about Christmas time. The previous suggestions about his employment in the Sudan had, by design or otherwise, not been kept secret. His intention of going to the Congo, and the British Government's refusal to permit him to do so, which would have meant his leaving the British Army, had been "leaked" to the Press. During the first few days of January, both *The Times* and the *Pall Mall Gazette* had referred to the subject, expressing regret that the "ablest leader of irregular forces England has produced" could not be found employment by the Government "when so much other work is urgently waiting to be done in Egypt and elsewhere".

There was a great public interest in, and growing unease about, the situation in the Sudan. The opinions expressed by Gordon in his interview with Stead contained something to confirm the prejudices and relieve the fears of almost everyone, including those of the Government whose policy of evacuation had been ridiculed. He minimised the seriousness of the rebellion and conveyed the impression that the Government had been stampeded by panic-stricken advice from Cairo and Khartum. Although he opposed evacuation on the ground that it was impracticable, he seemed to imply that the object of evacuation—the relief of the garrisons—could be achieved, and the danger of evacuation—a threat to "Egypt proper"—

averted without much expenditure of money or force, and that it was possible for a "man whose word was truth" to "come to terms with the Sudan". He pleased the annexationists by demanding a "firm hand" in Egypt and by adumbrating the possibility of a peaceful Sudan, nominally attached to but virtually separated from Egypt and governed by a British Governor-General whose moral influence would open up the country to the influences of European civilisation and British trade. He held out simultaneously to the Egyptian Government the hope of relieving the Egyptian garrisons without the danger and humiliation of evacuating them, to the British Government the hope of a peaceful and inexpensive settlement, and to the Imperialists the hope of a British-controlled highway into Central Africa. In short, he offered all things to all men, with the unspoken proviso that the whole matter should be put into his hands. Certainly, he had proposed Sir Samuel Baker as a suitable Governor-General, but implicit in the interview was the suggestion that he himself was the "man whose word was truth" and who, given the opportunity, could put everything to rights.

Although the Cabinet, on Baring's recommendation, had agreed on evacuation, Hartington, and probably some other members, were uneasy about its practicability. They had adopted the policy against the advice of Wolseley, whose view coincided with that of Gordon. The adoption of this policy, whether they liked it or not, involved some responsibility for its successful execution, and there seemed to be some doubt as to whether it could be successfully executed. They had been induced to insist on evacuation because the only alternative seemed to be sending British or Indian troops to the Sudan, with the probability of a troublesome military campaign there, followed by a garrisoning of the country. Apart from the loss of life and sacrifice of Liberal principle which this would have involved, the financial cost would either have added another complication to the Egyptian financial imbroglio or would have to be borne by the British taxpayer. In these circumstances, the appearance of a *deus ex machina* who, in effect, claimed to be able to arrange the whole business without tears, could not have been without its attractions. Even if he tried and failed, nothing very much would be lost. And there did not seem to be very much difference in principle between the evacuation of the garrisons insisted upon by the Government and their relief as adumbrated by Gordon. The only difference seemed to be, that their relief, as seen by Gordon, would be preceded by a non-violent pacification of the country, which would enable evacuation to be carried out as an agreed part of a constitutional settlement instead of by means of an opposed, humiliating and possibly unsuccessful retreat. There may be some substance in the belief that Gordon's employment in the Sudan was due to the Press agitation which followed the publication of the *Pall Mall Gazette* interview. But the truth of the matter probably is that the Cabinet were influenced, not by popular agitation, but by the tempting, although illusory, possibility of extricating themselves from an awkward situation by handing the problem over to Gordon.

The campaign which developed in the Press concentrated on Gordon's (and Wolseley's) point about the impracticability of evacuation and carried the argument to its logical conclusion. If evacuation was impossible, the choice lay between abandonment on the one hand and reconquest and rehabilitation on the other. Abandonment would discredit the British position in Egypt, both with the Egyptians themselves and with the Powers, and probably expose Egypt to invasion from the Sudan. Hence the necessity for reconquest and rehabilitation, providing for the relief of the garrisons, or some of them, and the setting-up of a friendly and subservient buffer-state in the Sudan to protect the southern frontier of Egypt. If this could be done by peaceful means through the influence of British officers on the tribes and so on, so much the better. An essential element would be the security of the Suakin–Berber route. This would necessitate the construction of a railway between the two points—a project in which an English capitalist group was, incidentally, interested. A railway would open up possibilities of trade both to sustain the economy of a pacified Sudan, and assist in the opening up of Central Africa via the Nile by British enterprise in competition with the suspiciously regarded attempts of King Leopold and his coadjutors to do the same thing by international enterprise via the Congo. It would help to put an end to the slave trade. It was undesirable that the work of pacification and subsequent rehabilitation should involve the employment of large numbers of British troops or the expenditure of large sums of British money. It was also undesirable that these should be used merely to provide for the restoration of that Egyptian misgovernment which, it was believed, was the cause of all the trouble. But, by the employment of Englishmen of the right type, it might be possible to introduce some form of indirect rule, free of Egyptian influence and buttressed by locally-recruited black troops. One possible method of procedure might be, in the words of the *Pall Mall Gazette*, to "Sarawak the Sudan"—to get some Englishman like Gordon to establish himself as a dictatorial and quasi-independent ruler. There was no end to the romantic notions of the Imperialists, who were interested, not in retaining the Sudan for Egypt, but in separating the Sudan from Egypt and using it both as a buffer-state securing the southern frontier of a British-controlled Egypt and as a field for British exploitation in the impending European "Scramble for Africa". In this context, "evacuation" simply came to mean the removal of Egyptian influence from the Sudan and, as such, ceased to be a bone of contention.

Gordon's letter of resignation reached Hartington's desk on the afternoon of 10 January, the day after the publication of the *Pall Mall Gazette* interview. On 8 January he had told Granville that Gordon, if he accepted service in the Congo, would have to resign his commission, and lose his pension. He confessed that "if he declines to retire we ought to remove him, but it will be awkward".[11] Gordon's resignation relieved Hartington of the possible awkwardness of having to "remove" him. But, in the meantime, the *Pall Mall Gazette* interview and the "Chinese Gordon for the Sudan" article had been published. If the Government changed their mind and let Gordon go to the Congo without resigning and losing his pension, they would be criticised for not using him in the Sudan. If they refused to agree to his going to the Congo, and accepted his resignation, without offering him responsible employment elsewhere, they would be criticised even more. Hartington, although he had agreed in Cabinet to the evacuation policy, was, privately, against it, on the ground, advanced by Wolseley, and now publicly supported by Gordon, of its impracticability. Although there is probably no substance in W. S. Blunt's belief that the *Pall Mall Gazette*'s "Chinese Gordon for the Sudan" leader and Stead's interview with Gordon were inspired by the War Office to defeat the evacuation policy,[12] it is clear that, about this time, Wolseley pressed upon Hartington the desirability of employing Gordon in the Sudan. On the morning of 10 January, the day after the publication of the *Pall Mall Gazette* interview, but before he had seen Gordon's letter of resignation, Hartington, referring to the fact that Nubar had replaced Sherif as Prime Minister, wrote another note to Granville about Gordon: "I believe that Nubar is a friend of Gordon's and therefore may be more disposed than Sherif to employ him . . . Wolseley thinks that his employment would be most desirable."[13] Later in the day, after he had seen Gordon's letter of resignation, Hartington wrote Granville a third note about Gordon. "Gordon has now formally sent in his resignation. I do not think that there is now any possible compromise between accepting it and approving his employment . . . I don't know how long it is since Baring expressed an opinion adverse to his employment in the Sudan. Present circumstances might alter his opinion. I understand that Gordon would probably postpone his Congo employment if asked to go to the Sudan. I believe that some people think highly of the value he would be of [*sic*] there. Do you think it would be worth while asking Baring again? I have directed that his resignation is not to be accepted till we hear again from you."[14]

The request made in Baring's telegram of 22 December for "a British officer of high authority with full powers to withdraw all the garrisons in the Sudan and to make the best arrangements possible for the future government of that country" had not been dealt with in Granville's reply and Baring had not referred to it again. But the Queen, who had seen Baring's telegram, had remembered it, and on this same 10 January sent a note to Granville regretting that "Sir Evelyn Baring's repeated requests for an answer on the employment of British officers are not noticed".[15] Granville must have received the Royal communication at about the same time as he received Hartington's second note of 10 January. On the evening of that day, presumably acting under this combined pressure, he telegraphed Baring asking whether Gordon or Sir Charles Wilson would be of assistance "under altered conditions in Egypt".

Baring later related his reactions to this telegram.[16] "I had had further time to think over this proposal (i.e. to send a British officer to Khartum) since sending my telegram of December 22. The more I thought of it, the less was I inclined to send General Gordon, or indeed any Englishman, to Khartum. I discussed the matter with Nubar Pasha and we both came to the conclusion that the best plan would be to send Abdul Qadir Pasha. . . . It was under these circumstances that on January 11 I telegraphed to Lord Granville: 'I have consulted with Nubar Pasha and I do not think that the services of General Gordon or of Sir Charles Wilson can be utilised at present.'"

Abdul Qadir, a previous Governor-General of the Sudan, who had been appointed Minister of War in the Nubar administration, at first agreed to go, although he impressed Baring, who does not seem to have realised it before, with the difficulties of the task, from the point of view of transport and supplies, and with the length of time it would take. But, on 15 January, disagreeing with Baring's insistence (later abandoned) that the Egyptian Government's intention to evacuate the Sudan should be publicly proclaimed, he changed his mind on the ground that this insistence made a difficult task impossible. Baring, faced with Abdul Qadir's refusal, and having received from Granville a telegram dated 14 January asking for "further news as to prospects of retreat for army and residents at Khartum", and inquiring whether anything further could be done, telegraphed on 16 January stating that the subject, "which is one of very great difficulty", was being discussed and that "in the meantime the Egyptian Government would feel obliged if Her Majesty's Government would send out at once a qualified British officer to go to Khartum with full powers civil and military to conduct the retreat". He thus repeated, in a more urgent form, his request of 22 December.

Meanwhile Gordon, affecting surprise at the sensation caused by the *Pall Mall Gazette* interview, had retreated to Devonshire to stay with the Rev. Mr Barnes at his rectory at Heavitree. While there he paid a visit to Sir Samuel Baker who lived nearby at Newton Abbot. As a result, presumably, of this meeting, he sent Baker a letter, obviously intended for publication, which Baker duly sent on to *The Times*, where it was published on 14 January. It repeated the general thesis which had been developed in the *Pall Mall Gazette* interview and recommended Baker, "should it be decreed that you are invited to go to the Sudan", to exercise patience and diplomacy, to obtain from the Sultan of Turkey permission to engage 4,000 of his reserve troops to be placed under the command of Valentine Baker at Suakin, to recruit 2,000 troops in India and to ask the British Government for assistance with animals and military stores.

These recommendations seemed to show that Gordon regarded the pacification of the Sudan as being more difficult than he had indicated in the *Pall Mall Gazette* interview. Or possibly he wished to imply that the only alternative to using force was to employ him.

In the same issue of *The Times* there appeared a first leader stating that "it is worthy of remark that General Gordon's resignation has not yet been accepted by the War Office. This is in itself a proof that Her Majesty's Government are unwilling to lose his services. . . . It is not improbable that Gordon's capacity and experience may be made available for the defence of Egypt, if not for the restoration of the Khedive's authority over part of the Sudan." There was obviously something in the wind, in spite of the facts that Baring had again rejected Granville's suggestion and that Abdul Qadir was still intending to go to Khartum.

After Baring had turned down Granville's suggestion, Granville asked Hartington to leave the matter of Gordon's resignation open until 21 January. Hartington replied that he did not think that a decision could be delayed for so long and suggested that Gordon should be given permission to go to the Congo.[17] But, on the next day, 12 January, Wolseley, after consultation with Hartington, telegraphed Gordon asking him to come and see him at the War Office on the 15th, ostensibly about his pension. What had happened was that Hartington and Granville had agreed that Wolseley should sound out Gordon about going to the Sudan. This is clear from a letter sent by Granville to Gladstone, who was at Hawarden, on 14 January.[18] "There is rather a mess about Chinese Gordon.

In the autumn Hartington asked for a Foreign Office opinion whether he was to give him leave to act in the King of the Belgians' African Association. I gave my opinion against an officer on full pay being connected with this non-descript Association . . . Hartington accordingly telegraphed 'The Secretary of State declines to sanction the appointment.' Gordon came from Syria and agreed with the King. The result is that Gordon loses his rank and pay in the English army. On the other hand people are clamouring for Gordon to be sent to Egypt. I have twice asked Baring whether Gordon would be of use. He has agreed first with Sherif and now with Nubar to answer in the negative. But it is said that there has been an old quarrel between Baring and Gordon. Wolseley is to see Gordon to-morrow and will ask him as a friend what are his views. If he says that he cannot go to Egypt, or that he cannot go without a considerable force such as he mentions in a rather foolish letter in *The Times* of to-day, we shall be on velvet. If he says he believes that he could by his personal influence excite the tribes to escort the Khartum garrison and inhabitants to Suakin, a little pressure on Baring might be advisable. The destruction of these poor people would be a great disaster. . . . If he does not go to Egypt Hartington and I are inclined to tell him . . . [that] . . . I have withdrawn my objection [i.e. to his serving in the Congo]." On the following day—15 January—Gladstone telegraphed to Granville that he agreed with his proposal.

Granville's letter is very revealing. Egged on by Hartington, who was himself being egged on by Wolseley and, probably, by Brett, his private secretary, Granville had become convinced, in the light of the growing Press agitation for Gordon's employment in the Sudan, and in the light of Gordon's apparent determination to go to the Congo with or without the British Government's permission, that it had become necessary to offer Gordon employment in the Sudan provided that he was prepared to accept the evacuation policy and provided it was understood that he would receive no armed assistance. It is apparent that Granville hoped that Gordon would get him "off the hook" by refusing employment on these terms and so enable the Government publicly to justify giving him permission to go to the Congo. It is also apparent that, so far as

Granville was concerned, Gordon was to be offered the executive mission of arranging evacuation.

Gordon duly appeared at the War Office on 15 January. Wolseley started by telling him that the Foreign Office had decided to withdraw their opposition to his going to the Congo and that there was therefore no necessity for him to resign his commission. But, as an officer in H.M.'s service, it would be his duty to postpone taking up service under a foreign monarch until the claims of his own country had been satisfied. Would he be prepared to "go to Suakin to inquire into the condition of affairs in the Sudan?"[19]

The rest of the interview was described by Wolseley in a note to Hartington on 14 February.[20] (This note is rather confused in that it combines what Gordon said at the first meeting on 15 January and at a second meeting on 18 January.) According to this note, Gordon stated (*a*) that it would be far better to evacuate the Sudan than to reconquer it, "if such reconquest was to entail again handing it over to the government of the Egyptian Pashas"; (*b*) that the Mahdi's "power and strength would soon melt away" if it were made known to the people of the eastern Sudan that it was henceforth to be governed by English officers instead of Egyptian Pashas; (*c*) that the tribes now gathered round the Mahdi would not long hold together nor undertake distant expeditions and that for this reason he did not fear an invasion of Egypt. He went on to suggest to Wolseley that the Government send him to Suakin to study the situation and report. He might find that the best course was complete evacuation; on the other hand he might recommend that an attempt should be made to "constitute some settled government before we come to any final determination." . . . In this latter case he might recommend his own reappointment as Governor-General. Wolseley then appears to have asked Gordon to draft his own suggestions for instructions to be given him in the event of his being sent on a reporting mission to Suakin. Gordon's draft read as follows:

(1) To proceed to Suakin and report on military situation of Sudan and return. Under Baring for orders and to send through him letters, etc., under flying seal.

(2) Government not indebted beyond passage money and £3 *per diem* travelling expenses.

(3) Notify public.

(4) Nubar and Baring to be notified so as to give all assistance.

(5) Admiral Hewett (Admiral commanding in the Red Sea) to give me £500 to be accounted for.

(6) Letter to Brussels saying leave is given me to go to Congo after my mission to Suakin.

(7) Government only wish me to report and are in no way bound to me.

(8) Telegraph Egyptian Government to send Ibrahim Bey Fauzi (his former secretary) to meet me at Suez with a writer to attend on me.

That same evening—15 January—Granville telegraphed Baring: "I hear indirectly that Gordon would be prepared to go to Suakin without passing through Cairo on the understanding that the only object of his mission is to report on the military situation in the Sudan, after which he would return and his engagement towards H.M.G. would cease. He would take his instructions from you and send his reports through you under flying seal while you would in conjunction with Nubar Pasha afford him every assistance in telegraphing, etc." He asked Baring to give him his "real opinion" after discussing the matter with Nubar.[21] Granville sent a copy of this telegram to Gladstone with the comment that it was "not very satisfactory" (presumably because it was not in accordance with the plan described to Gladstone the previous day). Gladstone concurred with the telegram but expressed anxiety lest the Government might find themselves committed to act on any advice which Gordon might give.[22]

The proposal sent to Baring was quite different both from Baring's request on 22 December (and shortly to be repeated) for a British officer to superintend the evacuation and from Granville's suggestion to Gladstone that Gordon might use his influence with the tribes to facilitate an evacuation. It seems to have derived, not from Gordon, but from Wolseley, who had asked Gordon whether he would be prepared to "inquire into the condition of affairs in the Sudan".

Baring received Granville's telegram on 16 January, a few minutes after he had dispatched the Egyptian Government's request for "a qualified British officer . . . to conduct the retreat". For some reason, he chose to regard Granville's proposal as a reply to the request he had just sent on behalf of the Egyptian Government. Three-quarters of an hour after he had sent this request[23] he telegraphed, referring to his request earlier in the day and to the telegram he had just received: "General Gordon would be the best man if he will pledge himself to carry out the policy of withdrawal from the Sudan as soon as possible. . . . He must also fully understand that he must take his instructions from the British Representative in Egypt and report to him. . . . I would rather have him than anyone else provided that there is a perfectly clear understanding with him as to what his position is to be and what line of policy he is to carry out."[24] Gladstone, sent a copy of Baring's telegram, expressed his agreement with Baring's insistence that Gordon should be under his orders and report to him.[25]

From this point on, the preparations for Gordon's mission became involved in an almost unbelievable muddle. On the one hand the British Government ignored Baring's requests for a British officer to conduct the evacuation and proposed, at Wolseley's suggestion, that Gordon should go to Suakin and make a report. On the other hand Baring equated the proposal for Gordon's reporting mission to Suakin with his own request for an officer to go to Khartum to conduct the evacuation, and accepted Gordon, whom he did not really want, for a mission for which he had not been proposed. The only link between Baring's request and the British Government's proposal, contained in Granville's telegram of 15 January, was Granville's suggestion to Gladstone, on 14 January, that Gordon's supposed influence with the tribes should be used to facilitate the evacuation.

On 16 January, the day after his interview with Wolseley, Gordon crossed over to Brussels to explain to King Leopold that he might have to postpone his departure to the Congo as a result of the British Government having reversed themselves over his resignation and indicated that they might require him to go on a temporary mission to Suakin. On 17 January, after Baring's telegram accepting him had been received in London, the War Office telegraphed to him in Brussels asking him to return to London by the night boat and report to the War Office next morning.

CHAPTER FOUR

THE OBJECT OF THE MISSION

GORDON ARRIVED IN London from Brussels at 6 a.m. on 18 January. At 8 a.m. he saw Wolseley who told him what had happened and arranged with him to go to the War Office that afternoon to receive his instructions from a committee of the Cabinet. He met Wolseley again at the War Office at 12.30 p.m. to be briefed before his meeting with the Cabinet committee at 3.30 p.m.

Parliament was not sitting and most of the Cabinet, including the Prime Minister, were out of London. But Hartington and Granville, the two principal Ministers concerned, were in London and in close touch with each other. After Granville, on 17 January, had received Baring's qualified approval to his proposal, Gordon had been sent for and a Cabinet committee meeting, to be held at the War Office, hastily convened for the following afternoon. Apart from Hartington and Granville, it was found possible to get hold of only two Cabinet Ministers—Lord Northbrook, First Lord of the Admiralty, and Sir Charles Dilke, President of the Local Government Board—in time for the meeting, although Lord Kimberley, Secretary of State for India, and Lord Derby, Secretary of State for the Colonies, were both in London.[1] Lord Northbrook was an ex-Viceroy of India and a cousin of Baring, who had acted as his Private Secretary during his Viceroyalty. Sir Charles Dilke had been Under-Secretary of State for Foreign Affairs at the time of the occupation. He was a close political associate of Joseph Chamberlain on the Radical wing of the Cabinet. All four Ministers, together with Lord Carlingford, were members of an informal Cabinet committee dealing with the Sudan.[2] They had all been in favour of the occupation of Egypt. All of them except Hartington agreed with the Cabinet decision about the evacuation of the Sudan, partly because of their confidence in Baring, partly because they dreaded the idea of British involvement in the Sudan. Hartington, who was greatly under Wolseley's influence in military matters, shared Wolseley's doubts about evacuation. Neither Northbrook nor Dilke had been consulted, or even knew, about Granville's latest proposal to Baring concerning Gordon, which had been inspired by Hartington. Dilke later recorded that, on 16 January, he had protested to Granville against Baring's request to send a British officer to Khartum "to conduct the retreat".[3]

Gordon saw the four Ministers at the War Office at 3.30 p.m. and received his instructions. All the five people at this meeting recorded their accounts of it. The differences between them cannot be accounted for entirely by defective memory. There is some mystery here. At the heart of the mystery is the intention of the Cabinet committee. Did they intend to send Gordon to Suakin to report in accordance with the proposal made to Baring? Or did they intend that he should go to Khartum to conduct the evacuation in accordance with the request made by Baring? Gordon wrote three accounts of the meeting within a few days of its having taken place. The first, to the Rev. Mr Barnes, written the following day, simply stated: "Ministers said they were determined to evacuate and would I go and superintend it. I said yes." The second, to his sister, written also on the following day, read: "At 12.30 p.m. Wolseley came for me. I went with him and saw Granville, Hartington, Dilke and Northbrook. They said, 'Had I seen Wolseley and did I understand their ideas?' I said 'Yes', and repeated what Wolseley had said to me as to their ideas, which was, '*they would evacuate the Sudan*'. They were pleased and said, 'That was their idea, would I go?' I said, 'Yes'. They said, 'When?' I said, 'Tonight', and it was over." The third account, also to the Rev. Mr Barnes, was written on 22 January; "Wolseley came for me and took me to the Ministers. He went in and talked to the Ministers and came back and said, 'H.M.G. want you to understand that they are determined to evacuate the Sudan, for they will not guarantee future government. Will you go and do it?' I said, 'Yes'. He said, 'Go in'. I went in and saw them. They said, 'Did Wolseley tell you our ideas?' I said, 'Yes, he said you will not guarantee future government of Sudan and you wish me to go and evacuate it.' They said, 'Yes', and it was over and I left at 8 p.m. for Calais."

These three accounts are consistent. Although, clearly, summarised versions of what took place, they show Gordon to have been under the impression, unless he was deliberately deceiving his correspondents, that he was being sent to the Sudan in answer to Baring's request for "a qualified British officer . . . to conduct the retreat".

The accounts of the four Ministers differ from Gordon's version. Northbrook, in a private letter to Baring immediately after the meeting, wrote: "I got a summons to-day to the War Office to meet Chinese Gordon with Granville, Hartington and Dilke. The upshot of the meeting was that he leaves by to-night's mail for Suakin to report on the best way of withdrawing the garrisons, settling the country, and to perform such other duties as may be entrusted to him by the Khedive's Government through you. He will be under you and wishes it. He has no doubt of being able to get on with you. He was very hopeful as to the state of affairs, does not believe in the great power of the Mahdi, does not think the tribes will go much beyond their own confines and does not see why the garrisons should not get off. He does not seem at all anxious to retain the Sudan and agreed heartily to accept the policy of withdrawal."[4]

This account agrees with the telegram drafted by Granville on War Office paper immediately after the meeting, embodying the instructions to be given to Gordon, which was sent to Baring that same evening.[5] In this telegram Granville stated that Gordon was being instructed to "proceed to Suakin to report on the military situation in the Sudan and on the measures to be taken for the security of the Egyptian garrisons still holding positions in that country and of the Egyptian population at Khartum. He will consider the best mode of evacuating the interior of the Sudan and of securing the safety and good administration by the Egyptian Government of the ports of the Red Sea coast. He will pay special consideration to what steps should be taken to counteract the possible stimulus to the slave trade which may be given by the revolution which has taken place. Colonel [*sic*] Gordon will be under the orders of H.M.'s Minister at Cairo and will report through him to H.M.'s Government and perform such other duties as may be entrusted to him by the Egyptian Government through Sir

Evelyn Baring." These instructions were not given to Gordon at the time in writing but were incorporated into an official letter, sent to Gordon through Baring and delivered to him at Port Said. In these instructions he was informed that "You will consider yourself authorised and instructed to perform such other duties as the Egyptian Government may desire to entrust to you and as may be communicated to you by Sir Evelyn Baring."

Granville also wrote a private letter to Baring immediately after the interview with Gordon. In this letter[6] he expressed his pleasure at Baring's approval of Gordon's appointment which "would be popular with many classes in this country" and told him that Gordon had praised him very highly and expressed a wish to be placed entirely under him. He also told him that Gordon had at first wanted to be allowed to report in favour of the retention of the Sudan should it appear more desirable than an early evacuation, "but he now perfectly understands that our decision is final". He made it clear that Gordon did not wish to see the Khedive, although he had spoken well of Nubar. Assuming that he would go to Suakin, he expressed a fear lest Gordon and Valentine Baker should quarrel and asked Baring to arrange that Gordon was placed in the more commanding position. He also asked Baring to discuss with Gordon the slavery question.

Dilke, in a memoir drawn up from his diary notes some years after the event, wrote: "On the 18th I was summoned suddenly to a meeting at the War Office in Hartington's room at which were present before I arrived Hartington, Lord Granville, Lord Northbrook and Colonel [*sic*] Gordon. Gordon said that he believed that the danger at Khartum had been exaggerated and that the two Englishmen there had too much whisky; he would be able to bring away the garrisons without difficulty. We decided that he should go to Suakin to collect information and report on the situation in the Sudan. This was the sole decision taken but it was understood that if he found he could get across he should go on to Berber. Gordon started at night on the same day."[7]

Hartington, who was the prime mover in the whole operation, and who did not really believe in the evacuation policy, wrote two notes about the meeting immediately afterwards. One was to Granville, forwarding copy of a note which Gordon had written about various administrative points connected with his mission. Seven of these points dealt with pay and allowances for himself and Colonel Stewart, who was to accompany him as Military Secretary, with the cipher for communication with Baring, with a request that he might go to the Congo after completion of his mission in the Sudan and remain on the active list, with the request previously made to Wolseley about Ibrahim Bey Fauzi and a writer, with a request for a naval vessel to transport him from Port Said to Suakin, and with a request for Baring to meet him at Ismailia on his way through the Suez Canal. The eighth point read: "I wish the appointment to be announced in Egypt that I am on my way to Khartum to settle future settlement of Sudan to the best advantage of the people." Hartington asked Granville to make arrangements with Baring about this last request and about Baring meeting him at Ismailia.[8]

The same evening Hartington wrote a letter to Gladstone which purported to be an account of the interview with Gordon that afternoon, but which was in fact an account of Gordon's conversation with Wolseley on 15 January. "Gordon, on being pressed by Lord Wolseley as to what he would do if he had the direction of affairs, said that he would send himself out direct to Suakin without going to Cairo. The enclosed notes written by himself sketch the terms on which he would be willing to go. He was unable to indicate the nature of the advice which he would give to the Government until he had learned the state of things on the spot. He might recommend the Government to appoint him Governor-General of the Sudan. The expenditure of a large sum of money was not an absolute necessity. Some money no doubt would be required but time would probably do much. Or he might recommend absolute and immediate withdrawal. He could give no opinion without seeing state of affairs on the spot. If anything were to be done it should be done at once." Enclosed with this letter was a copy of the draft instructions which Gordon had made out for Wolseley on the 15th.[9]

On this same evening of 18 January Granville telegraphed

Gladstone: "As Gordon was ready to start to-night, Hartington, Northbrook, Dilke and I settled that he should go accompanied by Colonel Stewart. He has instructions." Gladstone telegraphed in reply: "I see no reason to doubt that you have done right."[10] When he received Hartington's letter Gladstone may have assumed that Gordon was going on the reporting mission adumbrated in Granville's telegram to Baring of 16 January. He may also have assumed that the question of evacuation was regarded by the four Ministers as open pending a report from Gordon.

Thus, even before Gordon left, the Cabinet was enmeshed in an intricate network of double-talk about his mission.

(1) There is no doubt that Gordon was under the impression that he had been instructed to go to the Sudan to conduct an evacuation, that he regarded himself as having accepted these instructions and expressed his confidence at being able to carry them out.

(2) Hartington, deliberately or otherwise, had given the Prime Minister the impression that Gordon was going on a reporting mission and that the question of evacuation was still open pending Gordon's report.

(3) Northbrook and Dilke both professed to be under the impression that Gordon's mission was for the purpose of reporting on the best means of effecting the evacuation.

(4) Granville, in his telegram to Baring conveying Gordon's instructions, attempted to link the reporting mission adumbrated in his telegram of 15 January with Baring's request for "a qualified British officer . . . to conduct the retreat" by instructing Gordon, in addition to reporting on "the military situation in the Sudan" and "the best mode of evacuating the interior", to "perform such other duties as may be entrusted to him by the Egyptian Government through Sir Evelyn Baring." The first part of these instructions was taken almost verbatim from the suggestion for a reporting mission made on 15 January with the significant omission of the words "after which he would return and his engagement . . . would cease". This omission, which must have been deliberate, clearly indicated Granville's intention that "such other duties as may be entrusted to him" should consist of supervising the evacuation,

and that this evacuation should take place under the Egyptian Government's responsibility and under Baring's instructions and proceed simultaneously with reports to London. What Granville seems to have been aiming at—and the other three Ministers may have been privy to this since the telegram to Baring was drafted by Granville while he was still at the War Office—was a form of words and a form of procedure which would avoid making the British Government formally responsible for the conduct of the evacuation.

The substantial points of controversy which arose later were concerned, not with any dispute as to whether it was a reporting or an executive mission, but (*a*) as to the meaning of the term "evacuation" and (*b*) as to whether or not it had been made clear that Gordon would not under any circumstances receive any armed support from the British Government.

With regard to (*a*); Gordon certainly accepted the evacuation policy, but the term "evacuation" did not exclude the conception of that gradual and peaceful transfer of power from Egyptian to Sudanese hands which Gordon apparently had in mind. One reason for employing Gordon was a belief that he might be able to accomplish this, and it is possible that Wolseley and Gordon, who had plenty of time to discuss the matter, agreed between themselves on a definition of evacuation which enabled Gordon, with a clear conscience, to accept the Cabinet's policy.

With regard to (*b*); all four Ministers were unanimous that it had been made clear to Gordon that there was no question of his receiving armed assistance in any circumstances. Hartington told the Commons on 19 February that "Gordon never suggested to anyone that the relief of the garrisons in the Sudan should be attempted by British forces" and that Gordon was engaged on "an essentially peaceful mission". Granville told the Lords on 4 April that "Neither in Gordon's instructions given in London or in Cairo was there the slightest question or indication that he was going to be backed up by a British army." Dilke and Northbrook, who professed to believe that Gordon had been sent on a reporting mission only, must have assumed that there was no question of armed reinforcement. Gordon, on the other hand, assumed that armed reinforcement was not absolutely precluded. In a note for Baring written during the voyage out he wrote: "I will carry out the evacuation as far as possible according to their [i.e. H.M.G.'s] wish and according to the best of my ability and with avoidance as far as possible of all fighting. I would however hope that H.M.G. will give me their support and consideration should I be unable to fulfil all their expectations." And, a week or so later, in a conversation with Professor Sayce at Luxor on his way to Khartum, he told him that he expected to be "supported by troops" if necessary.[11] The truth probably is that Wolseley, who did not believe in the possibility of a peaceful evacuation—however interpreted—and who had recommended, and continued to recommend, the dispatch of British or Indian troops to the Sudan, gave Gordon to understand that he would receive armed assistance if he got into difficulties, whatever Ministers might say.

There was great enthusiasm in the Press about Gordon's appointment, of which the fact, but not the detail, was immediately made public. The *Pall Mall Gazette*, which believed, with some reason, that it was responsible for the appointment, carried a jubilant leader on 19 January: "The whole Egyptian question has been revolutionised in an hour . . . one of the decisive steps which make or mar the destiny of Empires . . . H.M.G., having tardily decided to avail itself of Gordon's services . . . Gordon refused to serve under the orders of the Khedive. . . . If he went to the Sudan he would go under the orders of H.M.G. Otherwise he would not go. The Ministers accepted Gordon's conditions. Henceforth he will have full and undivided responsibility for affairs in the Sudan. Whether we evacuate the country or retain it, as soon as Gordon takes command and for as long as Gordon's command holds, England is directly responsible for whatever is done in the name of the Egyptian Government between the Third Cataract and the Equatorial Lakes . . . Gordon supreme in the Sudan necessitates the exercise of a similar authority by Baring in Cairo. . . . We may fairly assume that Gordon will have a free hand and that all his requirements will be loyally and promptly met." This was rather a large interpretation of Gordon's mission, and almost certainly came from Gordon himself, or from his friends.

There was already a feeling among some members of the Cabinet that Gordon had used the Press as a means of getting the appointment, and they now began to feel that he was using the Press as a means of securing acceptance for his own interpretation of his mission.

He was not the only one to do so. Baring, in Cairo, was similarly engaged. On 21 January, after he had received Granville's telegram of 18 January about Gordon's instructions, he wrote a private letter to Granville expressing satisfaction that Gordon had been placed under his orders, although doubting whether "a man who habitually consulted the prophet Isaiah when he was in difficulty" would obey anyone's orders. He also made a great point of Gordon's coming to Cairo, (*a*) because he was afraid he might quarrel with Baker in Suakin (*b*) because he doubted whether he could get to Khartum via Suakin, and (*c*) because he suspected that Gordon's real reason for avoiding Cairo was his desire to avoid seeing the Khedive, which was "rather silly". Baring made it quite clear that he regarded Gordon's mission as an answer to his own request for a British officer to conduct the retreat and told Granville that he thought Gordon would be of great use going to Khartum to organise the evacuation and leave some sort of government behind him under local tribal chiefs. He thought that this could be done if they did not worry too much about slavery, which could not in any case be abolished in the Sudan except by means of a British occupation. He thought there would be no difficulty about drawing up a suitable plan with Gordon but stressed that it would be necessary for him to come to Cairo.[12] He had already made the point about Cairo to Reuters correspondent, who sent a message to the London papers on 19 January that Gordon was going to Cairo and not to Suakin.

There ensued an entertaining little struggle by proxy between Baring and Gordon conducted in the columns of the Press. On 19 January the *Pall Mall Gazette* denied Reuter's report that Gordon would be going to Cairo and stated: "It was only on the distinct understanding that he was to be in no way responsible to the Khedive that he accepted the commission. His commission is very wide and leaves him practically free of any control save that of the Home Government. His influence with the tribes is so great that he may be able to detach them from the Mahdi and induce the Mahdi to accept the government of Kordofan. If it should be impossible to evacuate Khartum with safety, Khartum will probably be held. . . . A timely distribution of money will probably enable him to re-establish order in the Sudan." On 21 January (20 January was a Sunday) the *Pall Mall Gazette* carried a leader stressing the necessity for giving Gordon a free hand. "We do not believe that he will find any difficulty in coming to an understanding with Baring. . . . But the more distinctly it is understood that he is going to Khartum with absolute power to provide for the future government or for the immediate evacuation of the Sudan, the more likely that he will prove successful. . . . He will be controlled by Downing Street alone." In an Occasional Note in the *Pall Mall Gazette* the following day a less optimistic note was struck: "Gordon will not have a free hand and he will not be armed with full powers. He has been sent to do what he regards as impossible—to secure the evacuation of the whole country. In his own graphic phrase he is sent to 'cut the dog's tail off'. To render the process safe it may have to be postponed. After the breather thus afforded it may not be found necessary to abandon the hold which the commerce of the world has on the great north-east waterway of the Dark Continent."

The same number of the *Pall Mall Gazette*, as if to emphasise the fact that they were representing Gordon's own views, carried a signed article by Stead headed "Chinese Gordon's Policy for the Sudan." "Gordon believed that he would have no difficulty in making his way without a single attendant through the Bisharin Arabs[13] and that when he arrived in Khartum he would not have much difficulty in organising an 'Ever Victorious Army' out of the tribes which would enable him to hold Khartum until the forces of the Mahdi split to pieces." Stead went on to summarise the policy which Gordon would pursue "if he were left absolutely free". He would institute a great scheme for the restitution of native autonomy. "As Mr Gladstone demanded Home Rule for Bulgaria, so Gordon advocates Home Rule for the various races of the Sudan". "He would withdraw the authority of Egypt from the tribes. . . . Gordon did not seem to contemplate any attempt to relieve the garrison under Lupton.[14] If it can hold its own until the Mahdi is dealt with well and good; otherwise it may cut its way to Zanzibar. Gordon is convinced that the whole of Equatoria Province should be abandoned. . . . As for the future of the new Sudan, Gordon would apply the bag-and-baggage policy very thoroughly. No Turks or Circassians would be allowed to remain in the Sudan."

All this was very embarrassing to the Cabinet and to Baring. Gordon made no attempt to deny that the *Pall Mall Gazette* was quoting his views with his authority and the implication was that he was determined to act, not in accordance with his instructions, whether from Baring or the Cabinet, but in accordance with his own views as publicised in the *Pall Mall Gazette*. At all events, there seems little doubt that Gordon and his friends, including possibly some officers and officials at the War Office, were using the Press as a means of applying pressure on the Cabinet to accept Gordon's, and their, idea of the object of the mission. Gordon himself, certainly, Stead, probably, and some of Gordon's friends, possibly, still believed that Gordon's policy, as spelt out in the *Pall Mall Gazette*, could be accomplished without the use of British or Indian troops. But it was clear that, if this policy were unsuccessful, the British Government would, willy-nilly, become committed to the use of troops, either to accomplish the policy which it was sought to thrust upon them, or to extricate Gordon.

It is not surprising that a good deal of irritation against Gordon was displayed by some members of the Cabinet. On 19 January Granville told Hartington that he thought they had committed a "gigantic folly" in sending Gordon at all.[15] On 21 January Dilke wrote to Granville: "I was alarmed at Gordon's hints to the newspapers, for I fear they must come from him. When I was at the War Office I heard nothing of his going to Khartum or anywhere except to Suakin. But if he goes up to Khartum and is captured and held to ransom we shall have to send a terrible force after him even though he should go without instructions." And in a second letter on 24 January he expressed doubts as to whether Gordon had really changed his mind about evacuation since the *Pall Mall Gazette* interview, even though he had accepted a Government mission.[16]

On 22 January there was a full meeting of the Cabinet which approved Gordon's mission and the instructions sent to Baring concerning it. The Cabinet also had before them copies of no less than eight telegrams which Gordon had started drafting, almost from the moment he left Charing Cross. (He posted them from Lyons on 19 January.) Four of these telegrams contained the suggested texts of four Proclamations. The first was to be issued by the Khedive to the people of the Sudan before Gordon's arrival stating that Gordon was going to the Sudan as the Khedive's Representative and as the British Government's Commissioner to arrange for the evacuation of the country and the restoration of its former rulers. It called on the people of the Sudan to lay down their arms and co-operate peacefully with Gordon for the accomplishment of their own independence. The second was the proposed text of a Proclamation by Gordon himself telling them much the same thing. The third and fourth telegrams contained proposed texts of Proclamations by Gordon to the shaikhs of tribes in the eastern Sudan asking them to meet him at Suakin to discuss the future government of the Sudan and arrangements for enabling the Egyptian garrisons to be withdrawn without bloodshed. The other telegrams contained a proposal about the reinstatement of a member of the Darfur royal family as Sultan of Darfur, a proposal for the recruitment of Sudanese troops into the Egyptian Army and a proposal to exile Zubair, who was resident in Cairo, to Cyprus in order to prevent him from sending emissaries to the Sudan.[17]

These telegrams, although quite incompatible with any suggestion of a reporting mission, were in accordance with what Granville intended, and what Baring wanted, and seemed, on the face of them, in strict accordance with the evacuation policy. Dilke, who was already very suspicious of Gordon's intentions, noted that Gladstone "did not object, although strongly opposed to our undertaking responsibility in the Sudan, because Gordon still spoke in every sentence of conducting the evacuation".[18] It was agreed that the telegrams should be forwarded to Baring with the comment that the Cabinet had not sufficient local knowledge to enable them to judge the worth of Gordon's proposals, but giving him discretion to act upon them either at once or after consultation with Gordon.[19]

Baring replied the following day (23 January) that "all General Gordon's suggestions are excellent and quite harmonise with the lines on which we have already been working". But he took no action on any of them until after Gordon's arrival in Cairo.

After this Cabinet meeting, there could no longer be any doubt in the minds of any of its members as to the nature of the mission which they had approved. It was, as Dilke described it in a letter to Granville on 24 January, a "diplomatic mission" with the object of arranging for a peaceful Egyptian evacuation of the Sudan and the setting up there of indigenous succession governments. The difference between this and the policy adumbrated by Gordon and his friends in the columns of the *Pall Mall Gazette* could still just possibly be regarded as one of emphasis rather than of principle, the main points at issue being (*a*) the extent to which Gordon was to be subordinated to Baring and (*b*) the relative importance to be attached to evacuation on the one hand and the setting-up of succession governments on the other. In the event, the Baring–Gordon position caused no difficulty in that the two men, whatever their personal antipathies, found themselves in almost complete agreement over the policy to be pursued. The real difficulty arose when it became apparent that a political settlement of the country was an essential condition of a successful evacuation.

Gordon's proposal for a Proclamation announcing the impending evacuation of the Sudan was in direct contradiction to the theme of his *Pall Mall Gazette* interview only ten days before, in which he had not only opposed evacuation but condemned in the strongest terms the folly of announcing any intention to evacuate. But, by this time, Gordon had, in his own mind, satisfactorily equated "evacuation" with the granting of independence to the Sudan, and had apparently satisfied himself that his prestige would enable him to accomplish this without any serious interference with the Mahdi, who could be bought off with the government of Kordofan.

On 21 January Gordon embarked at Brindisi for Port Said on s.s. *Tanjore*. Before sailing he posted a letter to Northbrook written on the train. He told him: "The Government's decision to evacuate the Sudan is based on the impossibility without inordinate effort of securing a good future government, and I think it is a good decision. . . . The slave trade can only be stopped through the Congo. . . . I apprehend no difficulty with evacuation *vis-à-vis* the Sudan, but I fear great distress to the Egyptian employees who want to go to Egypt, and for that and the removal of the troops I ought to have £100,000. . . . Colonel Stewart is a capital fellow and knows the Sudan well."[20]

Colonel Stewart had not been Gordon's choice as a Military Secretary. He told Baring that "They sent him with me to be my wet nurse."[21] He was the officer sent by Dufferin in November 1882 to the Sudan to report on the position there. After spending some five months in the Sudan he had recommended the abandonment by Egypt of the whole of the southern and western Sudan. If his recommendation had been adopted at the time the occasion for Gordon's mission would probably not have arisen. Baring had more confidence in Stewart than he had in Gordon and believed that "a better chance of success would have presented itself if Colonel Stewart had been sent without General Gordon".[22] Gordon and Stewart were not temperamentally well suited and it appears from several indications that they did not get on very well together. Gordon was one of those people who require his collaborators to act as disciples. Stewart did not do this and maintained his independent judgement, which usually, although not always, agreed with that of Gordon.

On board s.s. *Tanjore* Gordon devoted himself to writing a long memorandum for Baring.[23] Its theme was that the British Government had come to the "irrevocable decision" to restore independence to the peoples of the Sudan and, to that end, were sending him to the Sudan to arrange for the safe removal of the Egyptian Government's employees and troops. He elaborated his plans for accomplishing this. He would restore the "petty Sultans who ruled the country at the time of Mohamed Ali's conquests and whose families still existed". When these petty Sultans had assumed power they might accept the Mahdi's suzerainty or not according to their own wishes. He thought they would probably not do so; in that case there would be two factions—the Sultans trying to assert their independence, and the Mahdi and his supporters opposing them. It would be necessary to support the Sultans by denying all military equipment to the Mahdi and handing it over to the Sultans. In the towns such as Khartum, Kassala and Dongola which had grown up since the Egyptian conquest, and where there were no traditional rulers, other arrangements would have to be made. One had to take into account the possibility that it would be necessary to support the Sultans in fighting the Mahdi and in providing for the evacuation of the Egyptian soldiers and employees. He thought that most of the Mahdi's followers would refuse to leave Kordofan and that only the Sudanese troops who had deserted to him would be prepared to follow him to the eastern Sudan. In that event it might be possible to bribe some of them to desert. But it was not unlikely that there would be some fighting in the process of establishing the successor government and evacuating the troops and employees. He realised that the policy was to evacuate the country with as little fighting as possible, and he was determined to carry out that policy and avoid any fighting as far as possible. "I would, however, hope that Her Majesty's Government will give me their support and consideration should I be unable to fulfil all their expectations."

Gordon arrived at Port Said on the morning of Thursday, 24 January. A cable from Granville was awaiting him: "Baring gives strong reasons why you should go to Cairo in which we hope you will concur." Also waiting for him was General Sir Evelyn Wood, the C.-in-C. of the Egyptian Army, with two letters, one from Baring, and another from an old friend, a fellow R.E. officer, Major-General Sir Gerald Graham, also urging him to come to Cairo. Baring, after assuring him of his "most cordial support and assistance", told him: "I think you had better go to Khartum and arrange for the withdrawal of the Egyptian garrisons, etc., as rapidly as is consistent with (i) the saving of life and, so far as is possible, property, and (ii) the establishment of some rough form of government which will prevent, as far as is possible, anarchy and confusion arising on the withdrawal of the Egyptian troops. The task, although very difficult will not, I believe, in your hands, be altogether impossible." Graham's letter was in more familiar terms, appealing to him to "throw over all personal feeling" and come to Cairo.[24] With Wood's verbal persuasions added, Gordon seems to have made no difficulty and got on the train for Cairo, arriving there the same evening.

He spent Friday and Saturday in Cairo, leaving there by train for Asyut on Saturday evening. They were two very busy days. On Friday morning, Gordon and Stewart, accompanied by Baring, were received in audience by the Khedive. According to Stewart, "Gordon apologised to Taufiq for his former brusque behaviour and the interview went off very well."

Later that morning a meeting was held at the British Agency. At this meeting Gordon, Stewart, Nubar, Wood and Baring were present. An account of the meeting was recorded in Stewart's diary.[25] It was agreed that Gordon was to receive a credit of £100,000, that the evacuation was to be gradual, that Firmans were to be prepared appointing Gordon Governor-General of the Sudan and announcing the Egyptian Government's intention to evacuate the country, that Baker was to be made Governor of the Eastern Sudan, that a visit to Abyssinia should be made by a British officer from Aden to report on the possibility of evacuating some of the Egyptian garrisons through that country, and that a member of the ruling family of Darfur should accompany Gordon to the Sudan. It was apparently agreed by all present that Granville's telegram authorised Baring to give Gordon instructions regarding evacuation in the name of the Egyptian Government, and nobody seems to have taken the "reporting" part of the mission very seriously. There seems also to have been no serious dispute about the nature of the instructions which Gordon was to receive. Baring recorded that "after a long discussion the meeting was adjourned till the following afternoon", and that, in the interval, he was to draft detailed instructions for Gordon on the lines which had been discussed.

The following afternoon, when the meeting was reconvened, the draft instructions were read out, discussed and "a few changes were made". These instructions,[26] after drawing attention to the last paragraph of Granville's instructions to Gordon, authorising Baring to give him such instructions as seemed necessary, pointed out that what was needed, from the point of view of the Egyptian Government, were (*a*) measures for the security of the Egyptian garrisons in the Sudan and for the safety of the Egyptian population in Khartum and (*b*) arrangements for "the best mode of effecting the evacuation of the interior of the Sudan". The instructions went on to point out that "these two points are intimately connected", and to estimate that "10,000–15,000 people will wish to come north from Khartum only when the Egyptian garrison is withdrawn. These people are native Christians, Egyptian employees, their wives and children, etc. The Government of H.H. the Khedive are earnestly solicitous that no effort should be spared to ensure the retreat both of these people and of the Egyptian garrison without loss of life." "As regards the most opportune time and the best method for effecting the retreat, whether of the garrisons or of the civil population, it is neither necessary nor desirable that you should receive detailed instructions. . . . You will bear in mind that the main end to be pursued is the evacuation of the Sudan. This policy was adopted after very full discussion by the Egyptian Government on the advice of H.M.G. It meets with the full approval of H.H. the Khedive and of the present Egyptian Ministry. I understand also that you entirely concur in the desirability of adopting this policy and that you think it should on no account be changed.[27] You consider that it may take a few months to carry it out with safety. You are further of the opinion that the restoration of the country should be made to the different petty Sultans who existed at the time of Mohamed Ali's conquest, and whose families still exist; and that an endeavour should be made to form a confederation of these Sultans. In this view the Egyptian Government entirely concur. It will of course be fully understood that the Egyptian troops are not to be kept in the Sudan merely with a view to consolidating the power of the new rulers of the country. But . . . you . . . are . . . given full discretionary power to retain the troops for such reasonable period as you may think necessary in order that the abandonment of the country may be accomplished with the least possible risk to life and property. A credit of £100,000 has been opened for you . . . and further funds will be supplied to you on your requisition when this sum is exhausted."

The instructions also summarised the existing position regarding evacuation, so far as it was known: "A short time ago the Khartum authorities pressed strongly on the Egyptian Government the necessity for ordering an immediate retreat. Orders were accordingly given to commence at once the withdrawal of the civil population. No sooner, however, had these orders been issued than a telegram was received from the Sudan strongly urging that the orders given for commencing the retreat immediately should be delayed. Under the circumstances and in view of the fact that the position at Khartum was represented as being less critical . . . it was thought desirable to modify the orders given for the immediate withdrawal of the civil population and to await your arrival." (On the following day—27 January—a telegram was sent by Nubar to the Acting Governor-General that "Pending Gordon's arrival you cannot do wrong in sending away from Khartum as soon as transport can be procured all those civil servants whose functions have ceased to exist, either in Khartum or elsewhere.")

The instructions concluded: "In undertaking the difficult task which now lies before you, you may feel assured that no effort will be wanting on the part of the Cairo authorities, whether English or Egyptian, to afford you all the co-operation and support in their power."

Gordon formally acknowledged receipt of these instructions two days later from Upper Egypt, confirming that he fully understood them and would act accordingly "as far as circumstances will permit, while keeping in view that the evacuation of the Sudan is the object of H.M.G."[28]

During the twenty-four-hour interval between the two meetings, Baring also arranged with Nubar for the drawing up, in Arabic, of the two Firmans agreed at the first meeting, and two Proclamations based on the Firmans.[29] The first Firman was a Firman of appointment: "Seeing that the present state of affairs . . . requires a person capable of grappling with the difficulties of the situation and of ameliorating the condition of the inhabitants by restoring tranquillity on a sure basis", it directed Gordon to "carry out our good intentions for the establishment of justice and order . . . (and) . . . assure the peace and prosperity of the peoples of the Sudan by maintaining the security of the roads open to commerce". The second

Firman instructed Gordon "to carry into execution the evacuation of those territories and to withdraw our troops, civil officials, and such of the inhabitants, together with their belongings, as may wish to leave for Egypt. We trust that Y.E. will adopt the most effective measures for the accomplishment of your mission in this respect and that, after completing the evacuation, you will take the necessary steps for establishing an organised government in the different provinces of the Sudan."

Baring later told Granville[30] that "General Gordon has authority and discretion to issue one or other of these Proclamations whenever he may think it desirable to do so." That is to say, in Baring's opinion, they were to be regarded as alternatives, according to whether or not Gordon considered it politic to proclaim the evacuation policy. The contents of the two Firmans and Proclamations were closely in accord with Gordon's view of his mission as communicated to Granville in the draft telegrams sent from Lyons and forwarded to Baring, with the authority of the Cabinet, to act upon them or not, at his discretion. According to this view, both Firmans were to be published, the first immediately, the second later.

Some disquiet was later expressed in the Commons about Gordon's appointment as Governor-General, partly on the ground that it would remove him from the effective control of the British Government. It also appears that the Cabinet were not entirely happy about this, although Gordon, both in London and in his telegrams en route, had clearly indicated this to be his intention and the Cabinet had raised no objection. On 7 February, in reply to a question in the Commons, Hartington asserted that Gordon was not in the Khedive's service and that "the mission upon which Gordon was sent is a mission upon which he was sent by Her Majesty's Government". He gave no reply when asked how he reconciled Gordon's appointment as Governor-General by the Khedive with his assertion that he was not in the Khedive's service. In fact, the Cabinet wanted it both ways. They wanted effectively to control Gordon, but they also wanted to throw the responsibility on the Egyptian Government if things went wrong. Hence the equivocal confusion in Granville's instructions between a "reporting" and an "executive" mission.

Although Gordon was, formally, Governor-General of the Sudan and a servant of the Khedive, he was also H.M.G.'s Commissioner. In practice, he was under the orders of the British Government and such orders as he received from the Khedive were instruments for carrying out his orders from the British Government. Any argument to the contrary is pure sophistry. The real significance of Gordon's appointment as Governor-General, and one which was ignored by the British Government, was that it made it morally impossible for him to leave the Sudan until or unless his mission had been successfully accomplished, or until or unless the Khedive gave him permission to do so. But his dominant instructions were those which he had received from Baring. These instructions were unfortunately vague and equivocal. (*a*) It was not made clear whether his mission included responsibility for the withdrawal of all the Egyptian garrisons and those who wished to leave or only for those in Khartum. (The Khedive's second Firman referred unequivocally to the whole of the Sudan.) Baker was trying to relieve Sinkat and Tokar and arrangements were about to be made, with Gordon's knowledge, for the attempted evacuation through Abyssinia of the garrisons near the Abyssinian frontier. But there was no specific reference in Gordon's instructions to the garrisons in Sennaar, Darfur, Bahr-al-Ghazal and Equatoria. (*b*) There was no reference to possible evacuation routes or to any assistance to be provided to keep them open. (*c*) There was no reference to the possibility of negotiation with the Mahdi. (*d*) No attempt was made to define "all the co-operation and support in their power" promised by the "Cairo authorities whether English or Egyptian".

Baring later expressed the opinion that "it mattered little what instructions General Gordon received because he was not the sort of man to be bound by any instructions".[31] What the cynical Nubar thought is not recorded. The whole problem was simply handed over to Gordon to make what he could of it on the understanding that he should try and get the Egyptian garrison and the 10,000–15,000 civilians who wished to leave out of Khartum and back to Egypt "without loss of life". This was the core of his instructions and he was provided with a credit of £100,000 in order to assist him to do so, with the indication that more would be available if necessary. Baring, and all the other authorities in Cairo, were well aware that the British Government had categorically refused to send any British or Indian troops to the Sudan. They were also aware that Baker's force at Suakin was almost certainly incapable of opening the Suakin–Berber road and that no other Egyptian force was available to send to the Sudan. The possibility of sending a Turkish force was not discussed during Gordon's stay in Cairo. The evacuation policy had been imposed on the Egyptian Government on Baring's advice and Baring, with a knowledge of all these limitations, had asked for a British officer to assist them to carry it out. He therefore evidently regarded Gordon's mission as a practicable one, although he would have preferred its being carried out by some officer more amenable to his instructions than Gordon was likely to be.

The case for sending Gordon was based on the belief that, by reason of his quite exceptional qualities, and by reason of the influence and prestige which he was believed (by most Englishmen) to have among the inhabitants of the Sudan, he would be able to accomplish what nobody else could. The case against sending him was a case either for doing nothing or for reconquering the Sudan. For nobody else claimed to possess the qualities which were claimed for Gordon by his friends and supporters and, to some extent, by Gordon himself. Abdul Qadir, the best qualified Egyptian, had refused to go. Wolseley did not believe that an orderly and peaceful evacuation was possible. If Baring had refused Gordon, it is probable that no other "qualified British officer" would have been made available. Gordon represented Baring's only chance of implementing the policy which he and his military advisers had recommended and, by implication, assumed to be practicable. At the time he recommended it, he had not considered the difficulties involved and he was in the position of being compelled, in spite of himself, to regard Gordon as a *deus ex machina.* The Cabinet, having accepted Baring's recommendation, were in much the same position. The implementation of the policy which they had accepted, as the only apparent alternative to an open-ended military committment which they were determined not to accept, depended on their accepting

Gordon's reputation at the inflated value put upon it by Gordon himself and his friends.

The Cabinet's and Baring's policy of "evacuation without tears" failed because Gordon's qualities were insufficient to overcome its basic impracticability. His diagnosis of the situation in the Sudan—his underrating of the Mahdi's religious influence, his conviction that the rebellion was a spontaneous uprising against Egyptian oppression, his belief in the possibility of setting up indigenous petty Sultans in opposition to the Mahdi—was erroneous. His belief, or rather the belief of his friends and supporters, in his influence over the peoples of the Sudan as compared with that of the Mahdi was exaggerated to the point of fantasy. "The British belief in Gordon's power to inspire devotion among the Sudanese was greatly exaggerated. . . . His influence on the Sudanese, even when it was at its highest, was far more limited than the British public realised. Furthermore, the temper of the Sudan had changed. In 1879 a foreign and Christian Governor-General might ensure them better conditions than his Turkish predecessors. By 1884 a divinely appointed ruler of their own stock had arisen among them to destroy the oppressors. On every point the Mahdi could outbid Gordon. Whereas British opinion saw in Gordon the liberator of the slaves, to the northern Sudanese he was the man who had sapped the foundations of their prosperity. . . . Gordon's popularity and prestige in 1884 depended directly . . . on the prospect of British troops coming to support him."[32] The justified belief in Gordon's qualities as a guerrilla leader was irrelevant to the purpose of his mission, which was dependent for its success on its being a peaceful one.

In retrospect, the idea of sending two men, foreigners and Christians, with a very rudimentary knowledge of the local language and only a limited knowledge of the country, alone, with a credit of £100,000 and an Egyptian secretary, to conduct the peaceful evacuation of a demoralised garrison of some 6,000 men, plus 10,000–15,000 unarmed civilians, including a large proportion of women and children, through some 500 miles of desert, in face of a victorious enemy, and through the midst of an armed, hostile and predatory population, does not seem to have been a very promising one. It could only have been achieved as a result of a prior pacification of the country, either by negotiation with the enemy, or by instigating a successful movement of counter-insurgence against the enemy, or by reconquest. The last of these was ruled out. The first seems to have been momentarily considered by Gordon but was decisively rejected by Baring. (While on the voyage out Gordon mentioned casually to one of his travelling-companions the possibility of his going to see the Mahdi. He does not appear to have mentioned this possibility in Cairo and when Baring heard about it after Gordon had left Cairo, he telegraphed to Gordon forbidding it, and Gordon never raised the matter again.) The third possibility—counter-insurrection—was implicit in Gordon's proposal about the petty Sultans and in his later proposal about Zubair. But the first proposal was never considered in detail and the second was only made, at the last minute, just before Gordon left Cairo.

Zubair ar-Rahmat had been living in Cairo in honourable exile for the last ten years. His position is one which it is difficult to understand in the West but which was common enough in the Ottoman Empire. He was under surveillance and was forbidden to return to the Sudan. But he was a person of considerable wealth and consequence, lived in some state and was on visiting terms with the Egyptian Ministers. He was in close touch with the Sudan through emissaries and was believed still to have great influence there. He had, at the Egyptian Government's request, raised, and been intended to command, a force of 6,000 Sudanese to fight in the Sudan with Baker's Gendarmes and had only been prevented from going to the Sudan with them at the insistence of the British Government who were worried about the effect on public opinion of Zubair's slave-dealing past. But many people believed that he was in close and sympathetic touch with the Mahdi. Gordon, on his way to Egypt, had suggested his exile to Cyprus in order to prevent him from communicating with the Sudan.

On the afternoon of Friday, 25 January, when paying a courtesy visit to Sherif Pasha, the former Prime Minister, Gordon accidently met Zubair, and the two men exchanged civilities. Immediately after this chance meeting, Gordon wrote a long letter to Baring[33] requesting that Zubair should be invited to accompany him to Khartum with the object of setting up a settled government in the Sudan. "Zubair without doubt was the greatest slave hunter who ever existed . . . [but he] is the most able man in the Sudan, he is a capital General and has been wounded several times. He has a capacity for government far beyond any man in the Sudan. All the followers of the Mahdi would I believe leave the Mahdi on Zubair's approach, for the Mahdi's chiefs are ex-chiefs of Zubair. . . . It cannot be the wish of H.M.G., or of the Egyptian Government, to have an intestine war in the Sudan on its evacuation, yet such is sure to ensue, and the only way which would prevent it is the restoration of Zubair, who would be accepted on all sides and who would end the Mahdi in a couple of months. My duty is to obey the orders of H.M.G., i.e. to evacuate the Sudan as soon as possible, *vis-à-vis* the safety of the Egyptian employees. To do this I want no Zubair. But if the addenda is made that I leave a satisfactory settlement of affairs, then Zubair becomes a *sine qua non*. Therefore the question resolves itself into this; does H.M.G. or the Egyptian Government desire a settled state of affairs in the Sudan after evacuation? If they do, then Zubair should be sent; if the two Governments are indifferent, then do not send him and I have confidence that we will get out the Egyptian employees in three or four months and will leave a cockpit behind us." Gordon told Baring that he was not worried about the possible effect of Zubair's employment on the slave trade, "for there will be slave trade always as long as Turkey and Egypt buy the slaves", and explained that the difficulty was the malice which Zubair might well bear him as the result of the execution of his son by Gordon's orders. He concluded: "I would willingly take the responsibility of taking Zubair up with me if, after an interview with Sir E. Baring and Nubar Pasha, they felt the mystic feeling that I could trust him and which mystic feeling I had for him when I met him at Sherif Pasha's house. In this affair my desire, I own, would be to take Zubair."

Baring, as he afterwards explained, had "no confidence in opinions based on mystic feelings".[34] But he was probably, like Gordon, beginning to have doubts about the "petty Sultans" and, in advance of Gordon, beginning to realise that a settlement of the country was a preliminary condition, and not an optional accompaniment, of evacuation. He therefore arranged the meeting Gordon had suggested, which took place on the afternoon of 26 January, a few hours before Gordon's departure for the Sudan. Zubair, Gordon, Baring, Nubar, Wood, Stewart, Colonel Watson, a friend of Gordon's and an officer in the Egyptian Army, and Giegler Pasha, a European ex-official in the Sudan, were present. After the meeting,[35] and in Zubair's absence, Gordon's recommendation was discussed. According to his own account, Baring was in favour of accepting it, but "the weight of authoritative opinion was decidedly against".[36] Apart from this authoritative opinion, Baring was impressed by the fact that "forty-eight hours before I received General Gordon's Memorandum proposing that Zubair Pasha should accompany him to the Sudan, I had received, through Lord Granville, a proposal, also emanating from General Gordon, that Zubair should be deported to Cyprus".[37] He therefore concluded that "it might eventually be desirable to employ Zubair Pasha, but it was necessary to give General Gordon more time to think over the matter before taking action". For the time being he contented himself with warning Zubair to "use his influence to facilitate the execution of the policy on which the Government was determined".

Gordon left Cairo by train for Asyut just before ten o'clock that evening. His personal staff consisted only of Stewart and Ibrahim Bey Fauzi. General Graham and his A.D.C. were to accompany him as far as Korosko. Also travelling with him was the Sultan of Darfur, with a numerous suite, the first of the "petty Sultans" whom it was planned to install in their previous dominions. The Sultan, Amir Abdul Shakur, was a son of the previous reigning Sultan who had been killed by Zubair. Gordon had requested that he should be invited to accompany him, and the Egyptian Government had hurriedly summoned him, waved aside his requests for delay, and given him "£2,000, a well-embroidered coat and the biggest decoration that could be found." His appearance at Cairo railway station lent a note of farce to Gordon's departure. Extra carriages had to be added to the special train to accommodate his numerous retinue and "at the last moment his gala uniform was almost forgotten and there was some confusion until it was found". Gordon was seen off by a large party, including Nubar, the Prime Minister, who embraced him, the Khedive's Chamberlain, Baring, in spite of a sore throat, Sir Evelyn Wood and a number of British officers in the Egyptian Army. One of these, Major Wingate, afterwards a Governor-General of the Anglo-Egyptian Sudan and a High Commissioner of Egypt, recorded that Gordon was still depressed at the rejection of his recommendation about Zubair, and that Baring promised him that if, on further consideration, he still, when he reached Khartum, remained of the same opinion, he would do what he could to back up his request.[38]

On 28 January, a couple of days after Gordon's departure, Baring wrote a private letter to Granville giving his impression of him:[39] "What a curious creature he is. He is certainly half cracked, but it is impossible not to be charmed by the simplicity and honesty of his character." He went on to tell Granville that the audience with Taufiq had gone off very well, and that Gordon was hopeful of completing his task in three or four months. "He wishes particularly to impress on you that he agreed entirely in the policy of abandoning the Sudan. Nothing could be more friendly and conciliatory than his conduct to everyone." He did, however, warn Granville that Gordon was "terribly flighty and changes his opinions very rapidly".

There is every reason to believe that, when he left Cairo, Gordon was entirely sincere in his intention of carrying out the evacuation policy and reasonably confident of his ability to do so. While in Cairo he had disagreed with his friend Graham, who was opposed to evacuation. Later, on the train to Asyut, when Graham pointed out the discrepancy between Gordon's present views and those he had expressed to Stead a fortnight earlier, Gordon refused to discuss the matter and pointed out that there was no alternative between annexation and evacuation.[40] He appears, in his own mind, to have equated "evacuation" with independence for the Sudan, which was what he really wanted, and to have reconciled himself, in the words of the note written on s.s. *Tanjore*, to "leaving them (i.e. the Sudanese) as God has placed them . . . no longer oppressed by men coming from lands as remote as Circassia, Kurdistan and Anatolia". He still hoped to set up some alternative form of government, although he was beginning to realise that the idea of restoring the "petty Sultans" was chimerical. But he still regarded this as a desirable adjunct to, and not a necessary condition of, evacuation. He still under-estimated the seriousness of the rebellion, maintaining the opinion he had expressed to Granville in November 1882—that it was a protest against Egyptian tyranny, that it had no serious religious content, that the Mahdi's influence was confined to Kordofan. On that assumption, all that was needed to quieten the country sufficiently to effect the evacuation was the redress of grievances, the restoration of confidence, a little firmness, a little bribery, a liberal application of the Gordon charisma, and, of course, the Divine guidance which he was confident of receiving. The inconsistencies between his instructions and his declared intentions on the one hand, and his recommendations and his actions on the other, which became manifest almost immediately after his departure from Cairo, and which were attributed both by Baring and most of the members of the Cabinet, either to bad faith or to deliberate disobedience, may well have been due to his increasing appreciation of the extent to which he had previously misjudged the situation in the Sudan.

The Cabinet had some reason to be doubtful of Gordon's good faith in view of the continuing newspaper campaign, which seemed to be based on information derived from Gordon, and which increasingly advocated a policy at variance with that of the Government. On 23 January a leader in the *Pall Mall Gazette* stated that Gordon was in disagreement with the Government about evacuation. "While we doubt the necessity of holding the whole of the eastern Sudan, we are more dubious than ever about the necessity for abandoning the Nile. Our interest is limited to the control of the Red Sea littoral and the security of the navigation of the Nile. The Upper Nile is best approached via the Sudan. The necessity for keeping it open necessitates a railway between Suakin and Berber. Egyptian sovereignty should be limited to the Red Sea littoral and the bed of the Nile and the route between them. This would include Khartum and all the stations on the Nile. At a time when all Europe is engaged in eager rivalry for the right to open the Congo we dare not acquiesce in the closing of the Nile." And, on 28 January, the *Pall Mall Gazette*, in a message from Cairo, quoted "a friend of Gordon" as saying; "He is going to the Sudan as an English soldier obeying the orders of the Queen and has no connection with the Egyptian Government which he would serve under no circumstances whatever. He has put aside his personal convictions in order to carry out instructions which all know to be contrary to his own ideas. His mission is thoroughly pacific and, though he hopes for success, he does not conceal misgivings." Subsequent articles developed the theme that Gordon's real purpose in going to Khartum was "the establishment of civilised government . . . which will hold open the waterway of the Nile and its approaches for the commerce of the world",[41] and that the "best solution would be to make General Gordon himself Dictator of Khartum and the Nile highway and let him reign on the Nile as Rajah Brooke reigns in Sarawak. If Gordon refuses it ought not to be impossible to find a capable successor."[42] On 20 February a *Pall Mall Gazette* leader announced that Gordon "may yet be installed as Lord Protector of Khartum and the Nile highway by the unanimous desire of the population of the Sudan. . . . He would keep the Nile open to commerce and closed against the slave trade from Berber to the Lakes. . . . He would be absolutely free both of Downing Street and Cairo and he would be able to repeat on a far grander scale the achievement of Rajah Brooke."

The Times, although less euphoric, seemed also to be acting as Gordon's mouthpiece in advocating a policy opposed to that of the Government. On 21 January a first leader stated that Gordon would be going straight to Suakin as the representative of the British and not of the Egyptian Government. "On reaching Suakin he will at once bring into play his knowledge of local characteristics and his personal knowledge of local chiefs. . . . He will proceed to Khartum under the escort of the Hadendowa.[43] Once there he will summon the chiefs of the neighbouring tribes and announce that he has come in the name of the British Government to restore their liberty." The article added that Gordon's views did not include the abandonment of Khartum. "When the matter comes to be closely investigated, Khartum can no more be thrown away than Suakin. It is not only the key of Lower Egypt but the key of the Sudan, whether for the development of commerce or the suppression of slavery. . . . If Khartum is not held by a just and wise government, it must become a den of thieves. . . . This does not hinder General Gordon from evacuating the Sudan south of Khartum. . . . If that were effected the Mahdi would become less formidable and an honest and capable administration at Khartum would win us the respect of the natives." On 23 January another *Times* leader stated that "Gordon . . . has accepted a commission which includes arrangements for the evacuation of the Sudan. The policy is not that which Gordon would desire to carry out. . . . It is to be hoped that he will be allowed to determine whether it is not possible and desirable to hold Khartum. It can hardly be doubted that Gordon would be in favour of this." The article went on to state that it was desirable that Gordon should go to Khartum via Suakin and that it would be better for him not to see Baring en route. On 25 January another *Times* leader expressed regret that Gordon was not going via Suakin, stated that he was "unwilling to be identified in the eyes of the people of the Sudan as the Representative of any Government than that of England", and went on to refer to the prospect of his "re-establishing at Khartum a barrier to barbarism and a centre of civilising influence on the Upper Nile".

Although Gordon, now that he was a public figure, could no more refrain from communicating with the Press, whenever it was available, than a dipsomaniac can keep off alcohol, and although he had almost certainly used the Press as a means of putting himself forward for the Sudan mission, it is not necessary to assume that the views attributed to him by the *Pall Mall Gazette* and *The Times* were derived directly from him. It is more likely that they were an interpretation of his views by various of his friends and colleagues, including probably some at the War Office, who had their own political axes to grind and who were using Gordon's name to advance their own views. But Gordon seems to have made no attempt to disavow the use which was being made of him (and he could hardly have been unaware of it), and there was some excuse for the suspicion towards him displayed by some members of the Cabinet. This suspicion was subsequently strengthened by Gordon's use, after his arrival in Khartum, of Power, the young *Times* correspondent there, as a mouthpiece for the direct communication of his views to the British public.

After Gordon had left Cairo, Baring cabled Granville telling him that he had left for Khartum fully understanding that "he is to carry out the policy of evacuation with which he expressed to me his entire agreement", and stating that he was mailing Gordon's instructions "which leave no doubt on this point and which were drafted at his request and with his full approval". On the same day—28 January—he mailed to London a copy of the instructions he had given to Gordon, without any mention of the two Firmans and Proclamations. On 1 February, after a cabled inquiry from Granville, he mailed the English translations of the two Firmans and Proclamations, explaining: "Gordon took with him two Firmans and two Proclamations; in one of these latter the evacuation of the Sudan is specifically referred to, while the other contains a less direct statement of the intentions of the Government. General Gordon has authority and discretion to issue one or other of these Proclamations whenever he may think it desirable. . . . He fully understands that he is going up to Khartum for the purpose of carrying out the policy of evacuation, but it was thought desirable that the widest discretionary powers should be given him as regards the manner of carrying out this policy and the best time and mode of announcing it at Khartum." Referring to the criticisms in the English newspapers, Baring emphasised that "Gordon's suggestions have been followed in every particular. . . . His views differ in no sort of way from those entertained by Nubar Pasha and myself."[44]

The mailed instructions to Gordon, together with copies of the Firmans and Proclamations and a copy of Gordon's Memorandum written on board s.s. *Tanjore*, reached London on 7 February, the day after the arrival of news from Suakin that Baker's force had been completely routed at el-Teb in an attempt to relieve Tokar. This disaster removed any remaining possibility that the evacuation of Khartum via Berber–Suakin could be accomplished without the intervention of a

British or an Indian or a Turkish force at Suakin. As far as Egyptian reinforcements were concerned, Baker's force was the bottom of the barrel.

When Parliament met on 5 February, two days before Baring's instructions to Gordon had been received by the Cabinet, and one day before the news of the disaster at el-Teb had been received in London, it was announced in the Queen's Speech: "I have . . . dispatched Major-General Gordon to report on the best means of giving effect to the resolution of the Khedive to withdraw from the Sudan and have permitted him to act in the execution of this measure." Although this placed rather undue stress on the "reporting" as compared with the executive aspect, there can have been little doubt, in the minds of anybody directly concerned, as to the intention of the mission.

The question is, whether or not Gordon genuinely attempted to carry out that intention. Baring, writing over twenty years after the event, expressed the opinion that Gordon "threw his instructions to the winds",[45] that "he tried to force the hand of the Government and oblige them to send an expedition to the Sudan",[46] and that he made "no serious effort to carry out the main ends of British and Egyptian policy in the Sudan".[47] Gladstone, in a Memorandum prepared for the Cabinet in April 1885, wrote: "It seems probable that Gordon, perhaps insensibly to himself, and certainly without our concurrence, altered the character of his mission and worked in a considerable degree against our intentions and instructions."[48] Later, in a letter to Granville written in July 1890, he referred to Gordon as "turning upside down every idea and intention with which he left England and for which he had obtained our approval".[49] Granville told Gladstone that he felt "deep and great regret, but no remorse" at his responsibility for sending Gordon, and particularly regretted not having pressed a proposal to the Cabinet to recall Gordon "when he changed his policy".[50] Northbrook, in January 1886, wrote: "Instead of doing as we wished, viz. withdrawing the garrison of Khartum, Gordon, on his arrival, hankered after the *ignis fatuus* of arranging for a settled government of a country which could not be settled excepting by a lengthened and possibly a permanent occupation in force."[51] Dilke wrote: "I could not but admit that he [i.e. Gordon] had defied every instruction which had been given to him",[52] that he was "little disposed to listen to us, although on some points, for a few days, he pretended to listen",[53] and that "we were evidently dealing with a wild man under the influence of that climate of Central Africa which acts even upon the sanest men like strong drink".[54]

Hartington, however, took the opposite view. On 24 September, in a letter to Granville, he wrote: "We have no proof that he [i.e. Gordon] could have done anything different from what he has done and is doing, or that he has wilfully disobeyed or disregarded our instructions. . . . It is not possible that . . . he could have left Khartum without sacrificing the lives of himself and those who followed him and also of those whom he left behind. He had no alternative but to hold on at Khartum and keep the insurgents at bay."[55]

So did Selborne, the Lord Chancellor. In a Memorandum circulated to the Cabinet on 29 July 1884 he wrote: "There is nothing whatever to show that the military operations which he [i.e. Gordon] has been carrying out have exceeded what was necessary for strictly defensive purposes. I cannot impute to him as a fault that he has been desirous of leaving behind him a settled government in Khartum. The accomplishment of that object, if possible by peaceful means, was contemplated at the commencement of his mission and it was in itself beyond all doubt desirable for the security and tranquillity of Egypt. The fact that General Gordon has been under the necessity of repelling force by force does not prove that he has sought to accomplish that object by other than peaceable means."[56]

In the following chapters we shall, in the light of Gordon's actions after leaving Cairo, consider the validity of the views expressed by Baring, Gladstone, Granville, Northbrook and Dilke on the one hand, and those expressed by Hartington and Selborne on the other, and try to answer the question as to whether or not Gordon disobeyed his instructions. On the answer to that question depends, first the extent of the Cabinet's political responsibility for the failure of Gordon's mission, and secondly the extent of their moral commitment to send an expedition to rescue Gordon.

CHAPTER FIVE

THE OUTSET OF THE MISSION

GORDON AND HIS party arrived at Asyut, where they were to embark on a Nile steamer for the next stage of the journey to Aswan, at nine o'clock on the morning of Sunday, 27 January. "The Sultan [of Darfur] stepped from his carriage in gorgeous array, a uniform bedizened with gold lace and with the broad ribbon and plaque of the Medjidieh slung across his shoulder. With long and rapid steps, followed by his motley crowd of ragged and dirty women and men, he passed us on the way to the steamer . . . [where] . . . he and his court took possession of the main deck-cabin, but were speedily and ignominiously expelled by Gordon Pasha,"[1] who told the Sultan to dress in civilian clothes and to behave himself. The first experiment with the "petty Sultans" was not turning out well. On the steamer the Sultan, although abandoning his pretensions to magnificence, took to drinking. He and his suite were left behind at Aswan to make their own way to Darfur. He never attempted to do so and eventually returned to Cairo.

As a result of the obvious inadequacy of Abdul Shakur, Gordon began to feel anxious about the position of Slatin and the Egyptian garrisons in Darfur. On the way to Aswan, he told Stewart that he had decided to send a message to the Mahdi in Kordofan offering him £10,000 for the safe-conduct of the Darfur garrisons to Khartum, adding that "he did not see why we should fight, that the Mahdi was Governor of Kordofan and he was Governor of Khartum and there was no reason why they should not remain at peace". This message was sent to the Mahdi from Aswan[2] but it is not certain whether it ever reached him. Gordon also spent some time trying to knock some sense into the Sultan of Darfur, "talking Arabic utterly regardless of grammar, as he does French, but he rarely seems at a loss for a word—when he is he refers to his interpreter—and he always seems to make himself understood".

The voyage to Aswan took three days. From each stopping-place Gordon sent a stream of messages to Baring, in spite of attempts by Graham and Stewart to dissuade him from putting forward any plans until he had had time to study the situation. The most important of these messages was an undated Memorandum, accompanied by a map, which he sent by mail from Farshut on 28 January.[3] In it he defined the areas of unrest in the Sudan into (*a*) Kordofan, where the rebellion was "too strong to be touched", (*b*) the Gezira (i.e. the area between the White and Blue Niles south of Khartum) where "raiding tribes" were "hemming in Sennaar" and (*c*) "the rebellion of the Hadendowas round Suakin" which he seemed to think had little or no connection with the Mahdist rebellion. He proposed (i) to get down to Egypt all Egyptian employees, their families and their belongings, (ii) "to replace these employees by native Sudanese officials under myself, thus forming the nucleus of the future government of the Sudan", (iii) to concentrate the neighbouring tribes against the Hadendowa and open the routes Suakin–Berber and Suakin–Kassala, (iv) to relieve Sennaar, (v) to send five steamers to carry down the families of the troops in Equatoria and Bahr-al-Ghazal and (vi) to arrange at Dongola for the exodus of those who remain in Darfur, "if they still exist". He told Baring that "for this programme I need five officers to assist me for six months. . . . They are not to lead troops or enter into active operations, but merely to hold together the well-disposed Sudanese tribes against the pillaging tribes. . . . The suppression of the rebellion will be the act of the Sudanese themselves." He added that if Baring thought the request for these officers would raise an outcry in England, he could do without them, but that his mission would take longer. He reiterated that "if fighting occurs it will be the Sudanese Conservatives against the Sudanese communists who desire to rob them" and "in the fighting, if it occurs (which is not certain and which I hope may be avoided) there is no idea of asserting the Khedive's authority over the Sudan, but only of forming a firm conservative Sudan Government, which I believe H.M.G. has in view". This message was followed by another, telegraphed, message from Aswan cancelling the request for the five officers.

At Luxor, Gordon had the conversation with Professor Sayce which has already been mentioned. He also had a short meeting with M. Marquet, who had been French Consul in Khartum and was on his way back to Europe. Marquet afterwards met Baring in Cairo and told him that he did not believe that Gordon would be able to accomplish the object of his mission, and that he no longer had any influence in the Sudan. He did not think that the Mahdi would attack Khartum but that he would try and starve it out and that "at the first sign of famine the population would riot and that the garrison would join the revolt". He estimated that there were about three months' stocks of provisions in Khartum.[4]

At Aswan Gordon received a message from Husain Pasha Khalifa, Mudir (Governor) of Berber, by the hand of one of his sons, who was to accompany the party to Berber. After reading it he cancelled his request to Baring for a reinforcement of five officers, and gave him his latest impressions regarding the Sudan. He told him that the Mahdi's army in Kordofan consisted of deserters from the Egyptian garrison at el-Obeid, some 6,000–8,000 Arab horsemen, and "some influential chiefs who are interested in the slave trade". He thought it unlikely that this army would advance out of Kordofan. The Mahdi, through his agents, had caused the revolt of the tribes round Sennaar. The "Hadendowa revolt" appeared to have been caused by the malfeasance of two Egyptian officials. "Altogether my impression is that the revolt in the Sudan, although perhaps serious, was and is only dangerous owing to the utterly effete Egyptian Government. . . ." He also told Baring that Husain Khalifa "hopes to open the Suakin–Berber route in a few days . . . I feel confident that you need not be alarmed either for me or for Colonel Stewart, or for the Suakin–Berber route, or for the Bahr-al-Ghazal or Equatoria provinces. The only province I feel any great anxiety for is Darfur."[5]

On Thursday, 31 January, after having discarded the Sultan of Darfur and his suite and written to Baring and Nubar warning them to take no notice of that potentate's complaints, Gordon and his party boarded the train which took them round the First Cataract to Philae for the next stage of their journey—by steamer from Philae to Korosko. They reached Korosko the following evening. Gordon spent most of the voyage elaborating the next instalment of his plans. He wrote a long letter to the King of the Belgians explaining his ideas for a settlement of the Sudan and proposing to H.M. that he should seek the British Government's agreement to his taking over Equatoria and Bahr-al-Ghazal and the garrisons there and making Gordon Governor. If this were agreed between H.M. and the British Government, he proposed, "as soon as the confederation of the Sudan Sultans is accomplished", "to go up to the Bahr-al-Ghazal and Equatoria and assume command there with a view to joining them to the Congo. . . . There would be no necessity for me to return to Europe. . . . The proposal cannot fail to be agreeable to those who look with apprehension on the revival of the slave trade and those opposed to giving up the Sudan."

Gordon sent this letter to Baring from Korosko for onward transmission, explaining that when he had been in Brussels Leopold had expressed his willingness to take over the two provinces if he could get them and that he would take over responsibility for the garrisons there. "You might mention this to the F.O. and send them a copy of the letter. It would settle the slave trade." Baring sent the original of Gordon's letter to Granville for him to send on to Leopold if he thought fit and recommended that Gordon "should not be allowed for the present to go anywhere south of Khartum".[6] Granville concurred in this recommendation and Gordon was informed accordingly by Baring, in a telegram which reached him at Berber. He also, with some reluctance, had Gordon's letter forwarded to Leopold, after a F.O. official had minuted that "this may be a great nuisance to our Congo treaty".[7] In the end nothing came of Gordon's proposal, which was incompatible with the delicate international negotiations being conducted by Leopold with Great Britain, France, Germany and Portugal for the recognition of the Congo Free State.

Also from Korosko Gordon sent a telegram to Baring asking that all messages sent by him should be published and requesting that Suakin and Massawa should be put under his direct control as soon as Husain Khalifa had opened the Suakin–Berber route. When that was done, he announced his intention of sending all the Bashibazouks (Turkish irregular troops) and Europeans at these places to Cairo.

It was in this somewhat euphoric mood that, on 2 February, Gordon took leave of Graham and set out with his little party on camel-back from Korosko on the 250-mile cross-desert journey to Abu Hamed. Before he left he had a long conversation with Graham. He told him about his letter to Leopold but expressed the fear that the British Government might object to his proposal. He also asked Graham to tell Baring that "he meant first to dismiss the Egyptian Divan [Council] and then the minor Egyptian officials, replacing them by natives. He would then form a Sudanese Army. In due course the time would come for sending back the Egyptian troops, when he would produce the Khedive's Firman of severance and give the troops the choice of going back to Egypt or staying in the Sudan, but no longer under Egyptian rule."[8]

Graham gives this description of Gordon's departure: "About eight o'clock he mounted his camel and said goodbye, but I walked beside him and he shortly after got down and walked with me. At last I left him, saying 'Goodbye and God bless you.' Then he mounted again and a handsome young Arab, Ahmed, son of the Sheik [*sic*] of Berber, rode beside him on a beautiful white camel. At the head of the caravan rode Ahmed's brother—both armed with the great cross-hilted swords and shields of rhinocerous-hide which Sudan warfare has made so familiar. These swords, together with a couple of very old double-barrelled pistols with flintlocks, made up the whole Arab armament. Gordon carried no arms, but Stewart had a revolver."[9]

The party took five days on the journey across the desert, reaching the Nile again at Abu Hamed on 7 February. Stewart wrote in his diary that "the road leads through a barren and waterless country and appears both to Gordon and myself as quite impassable for an army. . . . We both think it impossible that Egypt can be threatened by that road."

Between Abu Hamed and Berber, which was reached on 11 February, they were once more in inhabited and cultivated country, but, until they reached Berber, were not in telegraphic communication with Cairo or Khartum. Gordon, having had plenty of time for meditation during the journey across the desert, was full of new and ill-digested plans. From Abu Hamed he wrote a letter to Baring which took over a fortnight to reach Cairo and which, by the time it arrived, had already been overtaken both by events and by subsequent telegraphed recommendations. In this letter[10] Gordon expressed the view that "the country is far less disturbed than has been reported" and that "the prestige of the Cairo Government is not seriously shaken". He recommended that "the Government of Egypt should continue to maintain its position as suzerain Power . . . I would earnestly beg that evacuation and not abandonment be the programme and that the Firman be changed into one recognising moral control and suzerainty". The letter was accompanied by a note from Stewart in which he expressed disagreement with Gordon's recommendation "except on the assumption that H.M.G. would exercise effective control over Egypt". Gordon's recommendation, which bore no relation to reality, and which was inconsistent both with his previous views and his subsequent actions, was a good example of the extent to which he destroyed his reputation for good judgement by making recommendations on the spur of the moment without giving himself time for reflection and consideration. By the time he left Berber five days later he had reversed himself to the extent of publishing the Proclamation based on the Firman whose cancellation he had recommended from Abu Hamed.

At each village between Abu Hamed and Berber, Gordon announced a programme of "amnesty, remission of taxation by one-half, cancellation of arrears of taxes, and government of the Sudan by the Sudanese". But, Stewart commented, "nobody seemed to understand". On 9 February, the day after leaving Abu Hamed, Gordon wrote a letter to the Mahdi appointing him Governor of Kordofan, telling him that there was no necessity for war between them, and requesting him to release his European prisoners and resume telegraphic communication and trade between el-Obeid and Khartum. "The General's idea is to sow dissension among the Mahdi's followers and quiet the *fikis* and religious fanatics throughout the country. . . . The letter, with an order to issue a Proclamation to that effect at Berber, was sent to Husain Khalifa, who was instructed to wrap it in silk and send it to the Mahdi." The Mudir afterwards told Stewart that he thought the letter unwise, although he appears to have told Gordon the opposite.

On their arrival at Berber they found several telegrams awaiting them from Baring. The most momentous of these was one announcing the rout of Baker's force at el-Teb in an unsuccessful attempt to relieve Tokar. This put an end, for the time being, to any hope of opening the Suakin–Berber road from the Suakin end. A second telegram, referring to his letter to Leopold, forbad him to go south of Khartum without further orders. A third telegram peremptorily requested him to abandon any idea he might have of visiting the Mahdi. This arose from a communication which Baring had received from Clifford Lloyd, the British Adviser to the Egyptian Ministry of the Interior, who had received a message from Gordon through the intermediary of a Lieut. Rhodes, who had travelled with Gordon on the *Tanjore*, to the effect that, when he got to Sudan he might go and see the Mahdi and not be heard of for three months and that, if he did, nobody was to panic. Gordon made no mention of this possibility while in Cairo and Baring only heard about it on 6 February. He immediately telegraphed to Gordon asking for "a positive assurance that you will on no account put yourself into the power of the Mahdi", and explained that there "would be the strongest political objection to your making a visit to the Mahdi". Gordon telegraphed back giving the required assurance without comment and without protest.[11] It is probable that he had never seriously considered the idea. But it is another example of the way he was apt to destroy other people's confidence in him by his indiscretion, his impulsiveness and his habit of concealing his thoughts and intentions from those with whom he was working.

Gordon's activities at Berber were described by Stewart in his diary entries, which reached Baring from Khartum at the beginning of March. He and Stewart were not unduly dismayed by the news of Baker's defeat which, Stewart recorded, "does not materially alter our view of the state of affairs". On 12 February, the day after their arrival, Gordon, "having pondered deeply all night, came to the decision of opening the Pandora Box and proclaiming the divorce of the Sudan from Egypt".

With the assistance of the Mudir and Mohamed Tahir, the Judge of the Civil Court,[12] and after showing them the secret Firman (i.e. the one instructing Gordon to evacuate) a Proclamation was drawn up setting up a Provincial Government independent of Cairo but subject to Gordon as Governor-General and H.M.G.'s Commissioner. "So far as I am able to judge the people appeared to approve of it. . . . A deputation of notables came to inquire whether the Treaty of November 1877 by which all slaves would be freed in 1889[13] was in his present programme. Gordon, knowing the utter futility of saying 'Yes', replied 'No', and published a Proclamation to that effect. It is probable that this Proclamation interested and pleased the people more than anything else. . . . At 2 p.m. Husain Khalifa and the leading men of the province assembled in secret conclave and Gordon showed them the secret Firman. The document caused the most profound astonishment; we were told that it was a mistake. . . . The probable effect will be to lead all those who heard the Firman to conclude that the concessions made by Gordon were made with a view to getting the troops out of the country without danger and leaving the people to stew in their own juice. It may perhaps have been a mistake to show the Firman, but Gordon says that as the object of his mission is to get out of the country and leave them independent he could not have put a sharper spur into them. I would have preferred following Nubar's advice to delay any action until later. . . . Gordon feels that if only H.M.G. would agree to name a Governor-General there would be no difficulty about restoring order. . . . He feels quite confident that if H.M.G. refuse this small concession bloodshed and misery will result."

While in Berber Gordon appointed Giuseppe Cuzzi, an Italian merchant, as his representative. In the course of a conversation with him, in which Cuzzi expressed the view that some fighting would be inevitable, Gordon seems to have given him to understand that he would be supported by British troops if necessary.[14] He also sent a telegram to Khartum dismissing the Acting Governor-General, making Coetlogon a Pasha and appointing him Acting Governor, and appointing Ibrahim Haidar Pasha in place of Coetlogon as Commander of troops.

From Berber he sent a number of telegrams to Baring.[15] The most important matter to be dealt with was the situation created by Baker's defeat, about which Granville had sent several agitated telegrams to Baring, inquiring (*a*) whether Gordon should be recalled, (*b*) what Gordon's recommendations were about Tokar and Sinkat, and (*c*) whether the dispatch of a British force to Suakin would assist the task of evacuating the Sudan. Baring sent on these queries to Gordon at Berber. Gordon replied (*a*) "that it would reflect great discredit on our name to recall me"; (*b*) "that Tokar and Sinkat may be considered lost and you can do nothing for them except by proclaiming that chiefs of tribes should come to Khartum to the Council of Notables where the independence of the Sudan will be discussed"; and (*c*) that "as to sending forces to Suakin to assist withdrawal I would care more for rumours of such an intervention than for forces". On the general situation at Suakin Gordon sent Baring a number of somewhat incoherent telegrams in which he recommended (i) that no more Egyptian troops should be sent there, (ii) that a force of Sudanese troops should be raised locally, (iii) that a promise should be given that no further military operations would be undertaken unless the tribes refused to accept "terms which I am authorised to offer", and (iv) that consideration should be given to the raising of 3,000 Turkish troops in British pay with a view to creating "unofficially the fear of Turkish invasion". "That would settle the affair", since "a satisfactory solution may be expected if the Sudan people fear that unless they accept peace and independence from me they will face an invasion of the Sultan's troops". In another telegram advising Baring of his activities at Berber he warned him that "the question of getting out the garrisons and families is so interlaced with the preservation of well-to-do people as to be for the present inseparable", and that "any precipitate action" would "throw well-disposed people into the hands of the enemy".

Gordon was slowly coming to realise that a settlement of the country—meaning an effective coalition of "well-to-do" and "well-disposed" people in opposition to the Mahdi—was a necessary preliminary to, and not merely a desirable accompaniment of, evacuation. He was also beginning to realise that such a settlement would not be easy and might require the sanction of force. But he still hoped to accomplish it by the threat rather than by the use of force.

Baring transmitted Gordon's replies to London without comment except to express the hope that "in spite of what appears to be almost panic in London . . . H.M's Government will not think it advisable to make any change in the main lines of their policy". He also expressed his opposition to landing any British troops at Suakin, "except for the protection of the town" and stated that "there are many objections to conducting military operations in the interior".[16]

In spite of some annoyance he may have felt with Gordon over the *canard* about visiting the Mahdi, and over the letter to the King of the Belgians, the two men were in general agreement about the policy to be pursued, based on a common realisation that the problems of evacuation and a political settlement were inseparable.

On the evening of 12 February Gordon and Stewart left Berber for Khartum in a steamer which had been sent down for them. Before he left Gordon sent a telegram to Coetlogon "stopping all offensive movements until his arrival". After leaving Berber, Stewart noted in his diary: "Judging by what we have seen, it would really seem as if the proposed liberation of slaves in 1889 was one of the important causes of the present revolt. Another cause is undoubtedly the gross oppression of the Pashas and Bashibazouks. As a means of allaying any ill-effects which might arise as a result of having shown the Berber Notables the secret Firman . . . Gordon told them confidentially that they might, as soon as Egyptian troops were withdrawn, make an application to H.M.G. to be the Protecting Power in the Sudan."

On 17 February, a little downstream of Khartum, they met the dismissed Acting Governor-General and changed steamers with him. He told them that a British expedition was expected at Suakin and, when asked his opinion, expressed his opposition to the idea of Zubair's return.

On 18 February they arrived at Khartum, where they had been eagerly awaited. Frank Power, *The Times* correspondent, had written to his mother a few days before:[17] "I don't believe the fellows at Lucknow looked more anxiously for Colin Campbell than we look for Gordon". But he added: "As regards relief of the place, he can only carry out the retreat. . . . It was solely on my reports that England has recognised that the holding of Khartum is bosh. I believe that when Gordon comes he will support me in this."

The steamer arrived at the landing-stage at 9.30 in the morning. "An array of officials and officers in gorgeous uniforms and crowds of inhabitants received them. Shaking hands with a select few the Governor-General passed through lines of soldiers to the reception hall. After a short meeting with the officials Gordon proceeded to the courtyard where, before a gathering of the people, the Firman appointing him Governor-General was read. Gordon then made a speech."[18] According to Stewart, Gordon told the people: "I am glad to see you. It is four years since I was here, and the Sudan is miserable and I am miserable and I want your help to put it right. I have come here alone without troops and we must ask Allah to look after the Sudan if no one else can. I have granted you remission of half your taxes and will not interfere with your holding slaves." Power described the following scene. "The Government books recording from time immemorial the outstanding debts of the overtaxed people were publicly burnt in front of the Palace. The kourbashes, whips and other instruments used for administering the bastinado were all placed on the burning pyre. The evidence of debts and the emblems of oppression perished together."

In England, since the opening of Parliament on 5 February, the attention of Government, Parliament, Press and public had been concentrated on the Sudan. The enthusiasm with which Gordon's mission had been greeted was overshadowed by the news of Baker's defeat, which was received on the day after Parliament reassembled, and which produced reactions similar to those aroused by the news of Hicks' defeat a few weeks before. There were demands for the dispatch of a British force to Suakin. These demands were variously motivated—by an atavistic desire to avenge what was regarded as a defeat for British arms; by a chivalrous desire to relieve the garrisons of Tokar and Sinkat, whose gallant Egyptian commander, Taufiq Bey, had become something of a popular hero; by a realisation of the fact that Baker's defeat had diminished the chances for the success of Gordon's mission; by a desire on the part of many members of the Conservative Opposition, and others, to reverse the policy of evacuation.

On 8 February Wolseley submitted a memorandum to Hartington[19] pointing out that "the defeat of Baker Pasha on 4th inst. alters most materially the position of affairs in the Sudan. General Gordon, when he reaches Khartum, will find himself in a worse position than he anticipated when he left Cairo. . . . British troops are besieged in Suakin; they dare not go even a few miles outside their entrenchments."[20] "This will be proclaimed throughout the Sudan, and the people will see that the garrison of Khartum, commanded by British officers at one end of the line, is besieged, and Suakin, occupied by British troops, is besieged at the other end of it. We have proclaimed our intention of clearing out of the Sudan; it is not therefore to be expected that any chiefs will throw in their lot with us. They will consider what their position will be when all the Egyptian garrisons are destroyed and the country left to itself, and their line of conduct will be adopted with a view to the future . . . General Gordon will have to treat with them in the position of a suppliant. . . . To enable General Gordon to treat with the rebels on good terms you must show yourselves strong. . . . Unless 'something' is now done, and done at once, to manifest your power and strength in the most unmistakable manner, it is tolerably certain that Gordon will soon find himself shut up in Khartum, unable to do more than hold his own there as long as his provisions last." Wolseley, who had never believed in the evacuation policy, went on to tell Hartington that "the time has now come for a revision of the policy previously come to with reference to the Sudan . . . I would advise . . . that Gordon, in announcing to the inhabitants of the country his appointment as Governor-General, should announce his intention to retain possession of the country to the east of the White Nile, that in future it will not be ruled by Egyptian Pashas, that it will be ruled by Sudanese officials under British officers until a stable native government can be established". He went on to propose the dispatch of a British Brigade to Wadi Halfa and the reinforcement of Suakin with

British troops who would attack Osman Digna's forces in that area. "These operations would, I believe, so strengthen General Gordon's hands that he would be enabled to carry out whatever policy he deemed advisable at Khartum. Unless this is done I do not see what he can effect there. He will be besieged and, with troops such as those recently employed near Tokar, it is folly to imagine he would be able to cut his way out. The result I foresee is an irresistible demand on the part of our people to have him relieved, and to relieve Khartum under such circumstances would mean a costly war of considerable proportions." He advocated limited operations round Suakin (he regarded an advance to Berber as impracticable against opposition) as a means of enabling Gordon to "treat with neighbouring chiefs and so to become master of the position at Khartum", and as an alternative to the future necessity for the relief of Khartum with an army advancing "from Aswan in Egypt proper along the Nile valley—a very long and tedious operation".

This demand for "something" to be done was echoed both in Parliament and in the Press. Most of those voicing it, like Wolseley, regarded Baker's defeat as the occasion, rather than the real reason, for advocating a reversal of the evacuation policy. Lord Salisbury, speaking in the House of Lords on 5 February, contemptuously referred to the policy of evacuation as one of "scuttle", expressed the view that "it was not for the purpose of running away that Gordon accepted the mission he has undertaken", and stated that "England will not be permitted in the opinion of the world thus lightly to shift off on to others the responsibility for the policy she has permitted and encouraged Egypt to adopt." In the Commons an Amendment to the Address was moved criticising the Government's policy in the Sudan, but was defeated by 57 votes.

Also in the Commons, on 11 February, after several hostile questions, Chaplin, an Opposition member, moved the adjournment of the House on a motion asking "whether H.M.G. has taken or intends to take the most effective measures in their power for the relief of Sinkat and Tokar". In the course of his speech Chaplin quoted a British official in Cairo as saying that he was ashamed to own himself an Englishman, and said that, if Tokar and Sinkat were not relieved, it would be a "national humiliation, a national shame, and a national disgrace". Criticism was not confined to the Opposition benches. Forster, an ex-Minister and a Liberal, advocated an expedition to Suakin on the principal ground of his belief that such an expedition would deal a blow to the slave trade.

Most of the Press were also demanding the dispatch of troops to the Sudan. On 8 February a *Times* leader warned that "it would be hard to explain to the satisfaction of the nation why Gordon's mission was weighted at the outset by the declaration that England would not move a man or a gun to support him. To rely on the magnetic influence and chivalrous devotion of an individual is to ignore absolutely the relation between ends and means." Their first leader on 11 February expressed the same point even more urgently: "After Baker's defeat it would be idle to hold that even Gordon's extraordinary personal influence could produce a pacification of the country and secure the withdrawal of the garrisons", and that it was "imperatively necessary" to teach the rebels that "the Teb disaster was not a conclusive proof of the incapacity and feebleness of the Power in whose name Gordon has gone to Khartum".

The Cabinet, as usual, was divided and uncertain. At a meeting held on 6 February it was decided to instruct Admiral Hewett to assume command at Suakin, to defend the town itself, and to land a force of Marines there. Three days later they considered Wolseley's recommendation for reinforcements and offensive operations. Even Hartington, probably the most interventionist of the Ministers, was against further involvement in the Sudan, but he was already impressed both with the extent of the danger to Gordon and with the extent of the Cabinet's responsibility for Gordon's safety. On 6 February he wrote to Granville: "I know that the Cabinet would not agree to any effectual measure for the support of Gordon and I doubt whether an expedition to Suakin would really assist him in his mission, but it would be well to settle what sort of line we are going to take, both in and out of the House, in the event of Gordon coming to grief."[21] On 7 February Gladstone told Granville that he thought an expedition would "alter fundamentally the whole basis of our position as to the Sudan".[22] Eventually, on 11 February, a telegram, drafted by Gladstone,[23] was sent to Baring telling him that a "military authority" (meaning Wolseley) had suggested that, to assist the policy of withdrawal, a British force should be sent to Suakin sufficient to operate, if necessary, in the vicinity, and asking him to inquire from Gordon whether the dispatch of such a force would "injure or assist" his mission. As we have seen, Gordon replied that the rumour of the dispatch of such a force would be more efficacious than its actual presence, and Baring urged the Government not to "change any of the main points of their policy".

But pressure on the Cabinet was building up. On 12 February news of the destruction of the gallant garrison of Sinkat was received in London. That afternoon there were debates on the Sudan both in the Lords and Commons. In the Lords, Salisbury denounced the Government's "vacillating and inconsistent policy" and attacked them for having failed to relieve Sinkat. The Lord Chancellor, Selborne, replying for the Government, said that the great object of Gordon's mission was to extricate the garrisons by peaceful means and that it would not be consistent with his mission to "accompany it with warlike demonstrations". In the Commons, a debate on a Vote of Censure, moved by Sir Stafford Northcote, opened on 12 February and continued until 19 February. On the first day of this debate Gladstone was able to disarm the principal expected line of criticism by announcing that, after consultation with Gordon, who, "although he does not like military measures, is satisfied that an effort for the relief of Tokar would not interfere with his plans",[24] the Government had decided to send British troops to try and relieve Tokar, although this implied "no departure whatever from a policy of evacuation". This decision, which made nonsense of what Selborne had been telling the Lords a few hours before, was only reached after a good deal of heart-searching in the Cabinet. Gladstone was opposed to it;[25] Baring, as we have seen, was against it; Granville was unenthusiastic but, as he told Baring in a private letter[26], "You might as well try to stop a mule in a snaffle bridle as check the feeling here on the subject." Hartington, in spite of the opinion expressed to Granville on 6 February, had come round to Wolseley's view.

For the rest of the debate the Opposition divided their energies between (*a*) trying to trip the Government up by exposing the various anomalies and inconsistencies surrounding Gordon's mission, i.e. his anomalous position as a servant both of the Khedive and of H.M.G., and the fact that Turkey as the suzerain Power had not been consulted over the mission, and (*b*) attacking the policy of evacuation. The heaviest attack was mounted by Sir Michael Hicks Beach. After deriding the Government for expecting Gordon to carry out the objects of his mission "by his own personal influence aided by nothing whatever except an unlimited supply of money from an empty Egyptian Treasury", he proceeded to criticise the whole evacuation policy. "Gordon evidently anticipates that there will be a certain amount of fighting in the attempt to withdraw the garrisons." (Gordon's memorandum written on s.s. *Tanjore*, together with other official correspondence connected with his mission, had just been published in a Blue Book.) "Supposing the result of that fighting be unfavourable to Gordon? Are H.M.G. going to send an army to support him? Or are they going to leave him to shift for himself? H.M.G. must make up their minds and I hope they will tell him plainly that, having sent him, they will support him. . . . How far is Gordon to withdraw from the interior of the Sudan? . . . It is pretty well known that Gordon, before he went on this expedition, considered that Egyptian authority at Khartum should be maintained. I hope H.M.G. have left this question open to Gordon's decision. I believe that it would be a mistake to withdraw from Khartum."

Dilke, speaking for the Government, struck an optimistic note, saying that "we now have every reason to believe that General Gordon's mission will be an absolute and triumphant success", and emphasising that this mission had been undertaken, "not only at the wish of the Government but at his own wish and it can be accomplished only in his own way; his only chance of success is in an absolutely peaceful mission". He told the House that Gordon "has had all the support for which he has asked; he will have, I make no doubt, any support which he can need; we have implicitly followed the advice we have had from General Gordon".

On 19 February the debate was wound up by Hartington,

who told the House that "there are no British or European interests in the Sudan which would justify the employment of British forces or the expenditure of British resources to restore Egyptian authority there". With regard to Gordon's appointment, he said that "when we had given advice to the Khedive and insisted on its adoption, when a native Government had been formed which adopted that advice, and when they asked for the assistance of a British officer to conduct the operation of the evacuation of the Sudan, we were bound to render them that assistance, and we were no more justified in hesitating than Gordon himself hesitated. . . . Gordon never suggested to anyone before he left England that the relief of the garrisons of the eastern Sudan should be attempted by British forces." Referring to the force which it had been decided to dispatch to Suakin, he made clear the limited nature of its objectives and stressed that Gordon's mission was "an essentially peaceful one". In the division at the end of the debate the Government had a majority of 49.

During the course of the debate the Government's attitude with regard to Gordon's mission had been to some extent clarified. (1) The initiative for the Gordon mission had come from the Egyptian Government who had asked for a British officer to conduct the evacuation. (2) Although H.M.G. were prepared to try and assist in relieving or rescuing the Egyptian garrisons "as a simple service of humanity",[27] they "were not responsible for the rescue or relief of the garrisons either in the western or the southern or the eastern Sudan".[28] (3) Gordon's mission was "essentially a peaceful one" and the decision to send a British force to Suakin did not derogate from this since the Red Sea ports could not, for the purpose of the mission, be regarded as an integral part of the Sudan, since H.M.G. had undertaken to defend them, as they had undertaken to defend "Egypt proper". They could therefore be regarded as part of "Egypt proper", and armed intervention there did not imply armed intervention in the Sudan.[29]

All these positions were quite untenable. With regard to (1), it was not the Egyptian Government but Baring who had asked for a British officer to conduct the evacuation. With regard to (2), it was possible to maintain either that Gordon had been seconded to the Egyptian Government and his mission the responsibility of the Egyptian Government, or that he was responsible to H.M.G. and his appointment as Governor-General merely a matter of form. It was not logically possible to maintain both that he was responsible to H.M.G. and that H.M.G. were not responsible for the evacuation of the garrisons, which was the principal object of his mission. H.M.G. were trying to have it both ways—to retain control of Gordon's mission on the one hand and to evade responsibility for its consequences on the other. With regard to (3): Osman Digna's rebellion was an integral part of the Mahdist rebellion and armed intervention against Osman Digna was armed intervention against the Mahdi, thus vitiating what was intended to be the "essentially peaceful" nature of Gordon's mission and identifying both Gordon and H.M.G. with armed intervention against the Mahdi. Whether H.M.G. liked it or not, and whether they realised it or not, the dispatch of a British force to Suakin, not merely for the defence of the town but for offensive operations, undermined the peaceful character of Gordon's mission. As *The Times* put it on 25 February: "At Khartum General Gordon is offering peace and liberty in the name of England to a population akin to those which General Graham at Trinkitat, also in the name of England, must put to the sword." And this expedition was sent, not as a result of any request from Gordon or from Baring, but in deference to the advice of Wolseley and to the volume of Press and Parliamentary clamour.

As a result of the Cabinet decision, taken on 12 February, to send a British force to Suakin, General Stephenson, the G.O.C. in Egypt, was instructed to send three of his best battalions, with supporting arms, to Suakin under Major-General Graham with the object of relieving Tokar and of taking any measures necessary to defend the Red Sea ports. By 28 February Graham's force of some 4,000 men had disembarked at Trinkitat, the nearest port to Tokar, some thirty miles south of Suakin. Just before their disembarkation Tokar had surrendered. Baring was in favour of re-embarking Graham's force forthwith and concentrating on the defence of Suakin. But Graham himself and the British military authorities in

Cairo and London were, as Baring afterwards described them, "like greyhounds straining at the leash".[30] Gordon was not consulted. The War Office asked Graham for his opinion on the understanding that "no distant expedition will be sanctioned". Graham, supported by Stephenson, recommended an attack. Admiral Hewett was also in favour of an attack on the ground that "a decisive victory will re-establish order among the tribes". The War Office concurred on condition that, before attacking, the enemy should be given the chance of dispersing and sending their chiefs to "attend Gordon at Khartum for the settlement of the Sudan". On 29 February, this invitation having been ignored, General Graham and his force advanced to el-Teb, the scene of Baker's defeat, and drove the enemy back on Tokar with heavy loss. After having advanced as far as Tokar without more fighting, Graham's force returned to Trinkitat where they embarked for Suakin on 4 March. The question then arose as to whether any further offensive operations should be undertaken. There was in England on the one hand a demand that Graham's force should be used to open the Suakin–Berber road, and on the other hand a conviction that it had been a mistake to undertake any offensive operations at all. Admiral Hewett, on 2 March, recommended that a further attack should be made on Osman Digna's forces. Baring, supported by Stephenson, was against any further offensive operations "unless General Graham feels tolerably certain that he can bring on a decisive engagement near Suakin".[31] On 7 March the British Government decided that the tribal leaders should be called upon to offer their submission and, if they refused, that they should be attacked. A proclamation to that effect having been issued, and having been ignored, Graham advanced inland from Suakin on 13 March and engaged and defeated an enemy force of some 12,000 men at Tamai, a few miles from Suakin, in which some 2,000 of the enemy were killed against total British casualties of 221 killed and wounded. After his victory, Graham, in view of reports reaching him about Gordon's critical situation in Khartum, wished to advance on Berber and prepared plans accordingly. Admiral Hewett approved immediately and, later and after some hesitation, Baring, Stephenson and Wood concurred. But the Cabinet, supported by Wolseley, were adamant against any further operations. So, after burning Osman Digna's camp at Tamanieb, a little inland from Tamai, Graham's force returned to Suakin on 28 March and soon afterwards re-embarked for Egypt. Graham later expressed the opinion that, after his victory at Tamai on 13 March, "the road from Suakin to Berber was open for British or Indian troops and the opportunity for rescuing Gordon and for saving Berber and Khartum was actually within England's grasp".[32]

The effect of Graham's expedition on Gordon's mission will be considered in the next chapter. The Cabinet, in sending it, and in limiting it to offensive operations in the vicinity of Suakin, were acting in accordance with Wolseley's advice and in the belief, inspired by Wolseley, that the giving of a "bloody nose" to Osman Digna in the neighbourhood of Suakin would strengthen Gordon's position in Khartum, enable the Suakin–Berber route to be opened by negotiation and, above all, obviate the eventual necessity for sending an expedition for Gordon's relief. In all these expectations the Cabinet were disappointed. Seen in retrospect, the only logical choice was between non-aggression on the one hand, which would have kept alive such slender chance as might have existed for a peaceful settlement, and an expedition powerful enough to open the Suakin–Berber route and relieve Khartum on the other. Such an expedition might, at that date, while the Mahdi's main army was still in Kordofan, and while the country between Berber and Khartum was still relatively quiescent, have enabled the evacuation of Khartum to be successfully accomplished. But, at the time, anxious as they were to limit their commitments and at the same time fulfil their obligations to Gordon and to the Egyptian Government, the Cabinet could hardly be blamed for following the advice of their principal military expert, who insisted on the necessity for an expedition in order to fulfil these obligations, who believed in the efficacy of an expedition confined to offensive operations in the neighbourhood of Suakin, and who was fearful of the perils of an opposed advance from Suakin into the interior.

CHAPTER SIX

THE CONDUCT OF THE MISSION

When news of Gordon's slavery Proclamation at Berber reached London it created something of a furore. The slavery question was one which aroused strong and well-organised sentiment in Victorian England. There was some genuine humanitarianism behind it. There was also a good deal of hypocrisy. Like the modern sentiment in favour of racial integration, it was almost entirely confined to the upper middle class. But, although the masses, many of the aristocracy and, indeed, most of the middle class, were indifferent, it had no active hostility to contend with. Everyone, in theory, was against slavery provided that the term were not extended to include working conditions in most English factories and fields and to domestic service in middle-class homes. Less than a century before, slavery had been abolished in the British West Indian possessions. Much of the overseas activity of the Royal Navy, and much diplomatic activity, had, over the past fifty years, been devoted to attempts to suppress the still flourishing slave trade in the Ottoman dominions and elsewhere. Many supporters of the Liberal Party, who would otherwise have been opposed to intervention in the Sudan, were in favour of it on the ground that it was necessary in order to control the slave trade. Prominent among these supporters was W. E. Forster, an ex-Minister, who was one of the most influential and most vociferous members of the anti-slavery movement. Much of the admiration felt for Gordon in England derived from the campaign he had waged against the slave trade during his previous periods of service in the Sudan.

The anti-slavers did not always discriminate between the real horrors of the slave trade and the relative respectability of domestic slavery (analogous to the abuses of the Press Gang on the one hand and the existence of military conscription on the other), nor appreciate the very real difficulties attending the abolition of the latter. They enjoyed the support of the

Missionary Societies and that of various capitalist groups who were less altruistic than the missionaries in their desire to see the spread of European civilisation in the Dark Continent. Altogether, the anti-slavery movement was one which any British Government, and particularly a Liberal Government which regarded humanitarianism as part of its stock-in-trade, had to take seriously into account.

The first news about Gordon's slavery Proclamation appeared in the Press on 18 February and, on 21 February, in a message from its Cairo correspondent, *The Times* published the text of the Proclamation. There was some criticism, both in the editorials and in the correspondence columns, but the predominant attitude was a disposition to trust Gordon and assume that he knew best. On 19 February there were questions about the Proclamation both in the Lords and Commons, which Government spokesmen answered by referring to the wide discretion which Gordon had been given. On 25 February there was a more pointed question in the Commons asking why a representative of Her Majesty's Government appeared to have acted in breach of the 1877 Convention between the British and Egyptian Governments. In replying, Gladstone expressed approval for the sentiments of an interrupter who suggested that, "having regard to the exceptional character of Gordon's mission, it would be better to let him carry it out unmolested and in his own way", and asked the House to await the official text of the Proclamation. In the Lords on 29 February there was further criticism by Lords Salisbury and Carnarvon.

It is against this background that Gordon's renewed request for Zubair, made immediately after his arrival at Khartum, must be considered.

On 18 February, on the very evening of his arrival in Khartum, Gordon sent a long telegram to Baring.[1] Referring to his letter mailed from Abu Hamed (which Baring did not receive until later), he revised the view there expressed that a continuation of Egyptian suzerainty in the Sudan might be possible, but maintained that there must be some protecting Power to sustain the authority of any Sudanese government which might be set up. As Turkey was equally unsuitable with

Egypt, that Power must be Great Britain. He explained that it would only be nominal suzerainty, without the expenditure of money or troops, and drew an analogy with Afghanistan where the Amir was under British protection but where only moral support was given. He went on to recommend that H.M.G. should select a man, give him a commission and promise him moral support, but nothing more. "As for the man, H.M.G. should select one above all others, namely Zubair", as being the only man who would both have the capacity to rule the country and be generally acceptable. He went on to lay down suggested conditions for his appointment. He should be made K.C.M.G. and given presents. He should undertake not to go into Bahr-al-Ghazal or Equatoria "which I should evacuate", or to Darfur. He should undertake to remain at peace with Abyssinia, to pay the pensions granted by the Egyptian Government to ex-employees, and not to pursue anyone who had been engaged in suppressing his son Suleiman's revolt. He should undertake, in return for a small subsidy, to keep the Egyptian Government informed about the height of the Nile at Khartum (a very important matter for Egypt in connection with irrigation), and not to levy duties in excess of 4 per cent on imports and exports. He added to his telegram an opinion from Stewart to the effect that he agreed with Gordon's policy but was not sure about Zubair's suitability.

In the course of his journey to Khartum Gordon had discarded his idea about installing "petty Sultans" and had half come to realise that some alternative settlement of the country was an essential condition of a peaceful evacuation. At a time when the *Pall Mall Gazette* was still writing in euphoric terms about a Gordon dictatorship, Gordon himself, in spite of the enthusiastic welcome he had received all along the route, no longer had any illusions about the extent of his influence. And, while *The Times* was writing about the necessity of opening the Suakin–Berber route by force, Gordon was still intent on trying to secure a peaceful evacuation. Whatever indiscretions he may have uttered, and whatever the extent to which, wittingly or otherwise, he had encouraged the euphoria of the *Pall Mall Gazette* or the belligerence of *The Times*, there is no reason to doubt that his recommendation about Zubair represented a sincere attempt to carry out his instructions to the best of his ability. He had deprecated the dispatch of a British force to Suakin; he had made no request for the opening of the Suakin–Berber route by force; he had made no suggestion that the evacuation policy be modified or reversed. His recommendation was not only consistent with a determination to carry out a speedy and peaceful evacuation and leave some sort of settled government behind him; it was inconsistent with any other intention. Whether or not Zubair would have loyally attempted to carry out the role envisaged for him, and whether or not he would have succeeded, are matters of conjecture. But, on the assumption that some sort of settlement was a necessary condition of a peaceful evacuation, nobody had any other solution to suggest. The "petty Sultans" idea had been Gordon's and, now that Gordon had discarded it, nobody really believed in it. The possibility of negotiation with the Mahdi, whether or not Gordon had seriously considered it, had been vetoed by H.M.G. and was almost certainly quite impracticable.

Baring, forwarding Gordon's recommendation to London on the same day as he received it, expressed his modified approval. Foreseeing the objections which would be raised because of Zubair's slave-trading past (and which had been successfully raised a few weeks before when it was a question of sending Zubair to Suakin with Baker), he pointed out that Zubair's presence in Khartum would make no difference to the slavery question one way or the other except in so far as Zubair, whose residence in Cairo had contributed to his understanding of European prejudices and European power, was likely to be a preferable alternative, from this point of view, to the Mahdi. He thought, however, that Gordon and Zubair should not be in Khartum together and that Gordon should leave Khartum after having arranged for the withdrawal of the garrison and the Egyptian civilians and before Zubair arrived there. In making this recommendation Baring took no account of the probability, which Gordon had not mentioned, that Zubair's presence in Khartum was a necessary condition of a peaceful withdrawal. With regard to Gordon's suggested conditions for Zubair's employment, Baring scouted the idea of "moral support" as being a concept incomprehensible to Zubair, but saw no reason why Zubair should not be proclaimed ruler of the Sudan with British approval and, perhaps, receive a small and temporary subsidy from the Egyptian Government. In conclusion Baring told Granville that he had no idea whether Zubair would accept such a position if it were offered to him.

Baring's telegram arrived in the middle of the Press and Parliamentary agitation about Gordon's slavery Proclamation. This agitation was to have a great, and possibly decisive, effect on the Cabinet's attitude towards Gordon's and Baring's recommendation. But, apart from this, Gladstone thought that there were "conclusive objections" to Great Britain assuming a protectorate over the Sudan. He thought that it might be possible for the Khedive to "propose to Turkey the nomination of a proper person with the Sultan's authority and, in case of hesitation, arrange with the man provisionally and leave him to make good his ground".[2] In other words, Zubair might be appointed by the Khedive in the name of the Sultan in order to relieve H.M.G. of the odium and responsibility of appointing him themselves. This was quite a reasonable suggestion since, on the assumption that he would not receive military support, such authority as Zubair might be able to exercise in Khartum would be dependent on his own prestige and not on that of the appointing Power. But Granville and Dilke were frightened about Zubair's reputation in England and of the possibility of a Parliamentary defeat, brought about by a combination between the Opposition and the Liberal anti-slavers, if Zubair were appointed.[3] After a meeting of the Cabinet which discussed the matter, Granville telegraphed to Baring that "there are the gravest objections to the appointment of a successor to General Gordon by our authority. We do not as yet see the necessity for going beyond Gordon's Memorandum of 22nd ult. (i.e. the *Tanjore* memo.) by making a special provision for the government of the country. Public opinion here would not tolerate Zubair."[4] Baring relayed the contents of this telegram to Gordon, asking him whether he could suggest any other names "in view of the objections entertained in England against Zubair". His telegram reached Gordon on 26 February, after he had been in Khartum for eight days.

During his first few days in Khartum, Gordon, whatever

doubts he may privately have felt, started making arrangements for a peaceful withdrawal. He had already, from Berber, instructed that all offensive operations should cease. He ordered three gates in the ramparts to be opened in order to allow people to enter and pass out at will. He wrote to Shaikh al-Basir, the Mahdist leader in the Gezira, inviting him to Khartum for negotiations, offering a reduction of taxes, permission to own slaves and Sudanese self-government. He separated the Turkish and Egyptian from the Sudanese troops in the garrison and sent some of the former over the river to Omdurman preparatory to evacuating them. He sent Coetlogon and Ibrahim Pasha Haidar, the Egyptian military commander in Khartum, back to Cairo, giving the former a letter for publication in which he stated that Khartum was as safe as Kensington Gardens. He started sending sick and wounded back to Egypt via Berber and Korosko. On 27 February 207 Egyptian and 103 Turkish sick and wounded left Khartum by boat for Berber; on the following day 310 sick and wounded "and some women and children" were due to leave by the same route.[5]

To a great extent Gordon's arrival had improved popular morale in Khartum. Power, *The Times* correspondent, wrote: "He is dictator here. . . . It is wonderful that one man could have such influence on 200,000 people. Numbers of women flock here every day to ask him to touch their children to cure them; they call him the 'Father and Saviour of the Sudan'." But better-informed people were less impressed. Said Pasha, a member of the Council of Notables, and Faragh Bey, whom Gordon had placed in command of the Sudanese troops, both protested to Gordon against his intention of evacuating the Egyptian troops on the ground that they would be needed for defending the town. Saleh Bey, the Egyptian commander in the Gezira, told Gordon that the whole country south of Khartum was in a state of insurrection and that Gordon's Proclamations were not worth the paper they were written on. The fact that Gordon had come without troop reinforcements had discouraged loyal and wavering tribes and the Council of Notables feared that unless the garrison "showed its teeth" the whole countryside would go over to the rebels. Gordon, although he was being urged by Shaikh el-Obeid, a tribal leader on the Blue Nile who had gone over to the Mahdi, to pursue the possibility of a peaceful settlement, felt compelled by the advice he was receiving from his Notables to reverse his order for the cessation of offensive operations. Therefore, on 26 February, he issued a Proclamation stating that, since his advice to desist from rebellion had not been followed by "some of the people", he had been "compelled to have recourse to severe measures contrary to my own inclinations", and warned that "troops of the British Government are now on their way and in a few days will be at Khartum". On the same day he sent out two expeditions, one by land along the Blue Nile, and one, accompanied by Stewart, by steamer along the White Nile. He advised Baring of what he was doing in two brief telegrams. The first of these stated: "Having put out my programme of peace and allowed sufficient time to elapse I am now sending out forces to show our force." The second stated: "Expedition starts at once to attack rebels in vicinity of this." Baring relayed the substance of these telegrams and the text of Gordon's Proclamation to London,[6] where, as we shall see, they created an unfortunate impression. (In the event the land expedition was countermanded before it had started and was diverted to deal with a threatened attack on Halfaya, just north of Khartum. The White Nile expedition, after "showing the flag" and distributing copies of Gordon's Proclamation, returned to Khartum without firing a shot.)

On the evening of 26 February, Gordon heard from Baring that the Cabinet had rejected his request for Zubair. He immediately sat down to reply to Baring's query as to whether he could suggest anyone else. He told him:[7] "That settles the question. I cannot suggest any other." He went on: "Mahdi's agents active in all directions. No chance of Mahdi's advance personally from el-Obeid. You must remember that when evacuation is carried out Mahdi will come down here and by agents will not let Egypt be quiet. Of course my duty is evacuation and the best I can do for establishing a quiet government. The first I hope to accomplish. The second is a difficult task and concerns Egypt more than me. If Egypt is to be quiet Mahdi must be smashed up. Mahdi is most unpopular and with care and time could be smashed. Remember that once Khartum belongs to Mahdi the task will be far more difficult, yet you will for the sake of Egypt execute it. If you decide on smashing Mahdi then send up another £100,000 and send up 200 Indian troops to Wadi Halfa and send officer up to Dongola under pretence to look out quarters for troops. Leave Suakin and Massawa alone. I repeat that evacuation is possible but you will feel the effect in Egypt and will be forced to enter into a far more serious affair in order to guard Egypt. At present it would be comparatively easy to destroy Mahdi."

It was this telegram, together with the telegrams about "offensive operations" and the reference in the Proclamation to British troops being on the way, which seem to have convinced most members of the Cabinet that Gordon was ignoring his instructions. This conviction affected their attitude towards Baring's subsequent requests, first for Zubair, and then for the dispatch of a relief expedition. It also affected their confidence in all subsequent recommendations made by Gordon and, after regular communications with Khartum had been cut, caused them to believe that Gordon was deliberately refusing to answer the various questions which they addressed to him. Most important of all, it nourished their suspicion that Gordon was deliberately trying to force them to abandon their policy of evacuation and occupy the Sudan.

The attitude of most of the members of the Cabinet was probably expressed with accuracy in a speech made by Dilke in the Commons on 13 May: "Gordon was not only sent on a peaceful mission, but was sent at his own suggestion with instructions that were drawn out by Gordon himself. . . .[8] He spoke with absolute confidence . . . of being able by peaceful means and without the least thought of military support, to effect a peaceful arrangement which would lead to a withdrawal of the garrisons. We do not know the reasons which prevented that peaceful policy from being carried out. . . . He began by attempting his pacific mission and he sent away from Khartum women and children. . . . Then he suddenly changed his views as to the character of his mission and on 27 February told us that he was sending out troops to show his force, and later the same day said that an expedition would start immediately to attack the rebels in the vicinity and that he had put out a Proclamation in which he said that he was compelled to use severe measures. We have no information as to the cause of this sudden change. . . . From this date Gordon began to talk of 'smashing the Mahdi'."

Not for the first time, Gordon got himself into trouble by precipitantly expressing his immediate reactions without giving himself time for reflection. But this characteristic of his was well known and should have been allowed for. It was not allowed for, and the reaction of most members of the Cabinet to his telegrams was almost as ill-considered as Gordon's phraseology when he drafted them. This lack of consideration was almost certainly due (*a*) to a belief that Gordon had helped to inspire the Press campaign against the evacuation policy, and (*b*) to a suspicion that Gordon and Wolseley had entered into some sort of unholy alliance to defeat that policy.

On the face of them, and in the light of Gordon's actual conduct in Khartum, there was nothing in the telegrams to justify these suspicions. The reference in the Proclamation to British troops being on the way—stigmatised by Dilke as "this amazing lie"[9]—was an obvious reference to the imminent landing of Graham's force at Trinkitat. There was of course, at that time, no question of this force advancing into the interior, but the inhabitants of the Sudan were not to know this, and Gordon may have thought the threat justified as a *ruse de guerre*. Since the threat failed in its deterrent effect and was not made good, it turned out to be unwise to have uttered it. But that was not a ground for suspecting Gordon of ulterior motives. The telegrams about offensive operations were not accompanied by a statement of the reasons for these operations, or by a description of their limited objectives. But that was not a ground for assuming, without further inquiry, that Gordon had departed from the peaceful purposes of his mission. Nor do the telegrams seem to be sufficiently alarming to have "frightened the Cabinet out of their senses", as Dilke says they did.[10] The telegram about "smashing the Mahdi" seems to have alarmed the Cabinet even more than the others, particularly as it was accompanied by a telegram which Gordon had sent Baring the previous day (25 February) recommending, on the assumption that his Zubair recommendation would be accepted, that the Sudanese part of the Khartum garrison, consisting of some 3,000 troops, should be retained for the time being in Khartum to assist Zubair in keeping order. Dilke described these two telegrams as indicating Gordon's "policy of smashing up the Mahdi . . . and completely throwing over the evacuation policy".[11] But the recommendation to retain the Sudanese troops was a perfectly reasonable one on the assumption (still valid for Gordon on 25 February) that his recommendation about Zubair would be accepted; and his remarks about "smashing up the Mahdi", although not well phrased, should have been read in the context of Gordon's reaction to the rejection of his Zubair recommendation. He was saying in effect that "smashing up the Mahdi" was the only alternative to chaos if H.M.G. persisted in rejecting his recommendation about Zubair.

Baring, in a covering telegram, tried to make this point. He told Granville[12] that, although there were obvious inconsistencies in Gordon's various proposals, he entirely agreed with him that it would be a mistake, from the point of view of the security of Egypt, to evacuate the Sudan without arranging for some settled form of government, and that he and Nubar agreed that Zubair was the one man who might be able to provide this. He recommended that Zubair should be allowed to succeed Gordon with an annual subsidy of say £50,000, to be paid by the Egyptian Government, and conditional on his good behaviour. He considered it to be unimportant whether or not he was nominated on H.M.G.'s authority but, "whatever may be said to the contrary H.M.G must in reality be responsible for any arrangements which are now desired for the Sudan and I do not think it possible to shake off that responsibility". In view of the objections to Zubair which had been communicated to him by Granville, he concluded: "It is for H.M.G. to judge of the importance to be attached to public opinion in England, but I venture to think that any attempt to settle Egyptian questions by the light of English popular opinion is sure to be productive of harm and, in this as in other cases, it would be preferable to follow the advice of responsible authorities on the spot."

What neither Gordon nor Baring had made clear, and what neither of them perhaps as yet sufficiently realised, was that a refusal to send Zubair meant an abandonment not only of the settlement but also of the evacuation of the Sudan, since settlement had become a prior condition of evacuation. Rejection of Zubair faced the Cabinet with the alternative between a relief expedition and an order for *sauve qui peut.* The Cabinet were not prepared to consider the one and Gordon would have refused to obey the other. But these alternatives were not thus starkly presented to the Cabinet, who, selecting those portions of Gordon's and Baring's dispatches which suited them and rejecting the rest, proceeded to elaborate the fiction that there was nothing to stop Gordon from proceeding with the evacuation but that he was deliberately refraining from doing so in an attempt to blackmail the British Government into reconquering the Sudan.

If Gordon's messages of 25 and 26 February destroyed the Cabinet's confidence in him, the Cabinet's rejection of his Zubair recommendation destroyed his confidence in them. The tendency to persecution mania, never very far below the surface with Gordon, became more and more apparent until, at last, it gained entire possession of him. In this world of fantasy which Gordon began to inhabit, Baring was the principal persecutor. In fact, Baring supported Gordon's request for Zubair and later, in spite of his growing irritation with Gordon, urged the Cabinet to send a relief expedition. But Gordon, who had never overcome his personal antipathy to Baring, conceived at the time of the financial talks in 1878, chose to regard him as the chief villain in the tragedy which now started inexorably to encompass him. In Dilke's words[13] he came to regard Baring as responsible for "inciting the Government to drive him to his death".

During the days immediately following his "smash the Mahdi" message Gordon sent Baring a series of telegrams[14], which, if they had been consolidated into a single considered statement in reply to the Cabinet's rejection of Zubair, might have provided Baring with the ammunition he needed against the Cabinet and the Cabinet with the information which they needed to deal with Parliamentary and public opinion. Purged of their discursiveness and verbosity, these telegrams conveyed the message which had not yet been conveyed to the Cabinet, i.e. that a settlement of the Sudan was a precondition of evacuation. On 27 February Gordon told Baring that "evacuation of the Sudan, and I mean by evacuation the removal of all Egyptian employees, is impossible until the government exerts its authority. We can hold out here and force back the revolt, but the position will not ameliorate with time and our money must come to an end. You have to say whether the partial evacuation of the Sudan fulfils your desire. If it does not you must act by Indian Moslem troops from Wadi Halfa and do so at once." (It is to be noted that he has already started identifying Baring with the Cabinet.) And on 28 February: "There is just a chance of enticing the Mahdi's troops over with money. Shall I try it? Will you find the extra funds?" And on 29 February he told Baring that the choice before them was between (*a*) the Mahdi, (*b*) Zubair with £100,000, and (*c*) "200 British troops to Wadi Halfa and Adjutants to inspect Dongola, and the opening of the Suakin–Berber road with Indian Moslem troops." He thought that (*c*) would cause "an immediate collapse of the rebellion". On 1 March he told Baring that news of Baker's defeat was generally known in Khartum. He defended his decision to resume offensive operations by saying that, if he had not done so, "many loyal tribes would in desperation join the Mahdi". On the same day he telegraphed that he maintained firmly the policy of eventual evacuation but "it is impossible to get Cairo employees out of Khartum unless the Government helps. . . . You have refused Zubair . . . but it was the only chance. I will do my best to carry out instructions but I feel convinced that I shall be caught in Khartum." (These and some subsequent telegrams were, with the Cabinet's permission, not relayed to London as and when they arrived but mailed to London in weekly batches. Baring in effect, took over, but soon abandoned, the task of acting as interpreter between Gordon and the Cabinet. His first task was to try and persuade the Cabinet to agree to Zubair's appointment.)

On 1 March Granville sent Baring a temporising reply to his telegram of 28 February about Zubair, stating that "H.M.G.

desire further information as to the urgency of any immediate appointment of a successor to General Gordon who, they trust, will remain for some time longer at Khartum . . . H.M.G. will carefully weigh your opinions as to the proper person for the post. . . . If such an appointment is made it might be advantageous that it should receive the confirmation of the Sultan."[15] This seemed to Baring to indicate that the Cabinet's refusal need not be regarded as absolute and he told Gordon that the question of Zubair could be regarded as "still under discussion and not finally settled".[16]

On 4 March Baring received a long telegram from Stewart,[17] in whom he had much more confidence than he had in Gordon and whom he had asked to communicate with him independently of Gordon. In this telegram Stewart, who had previously been dubious about Zubair, told Baring that he now agreed with Gordon as "it is impossible for us to leave this country without leaving some sort of established government, and Zubair is the only man who can ensure that. . . . No other course is open except British annexation or anarchy. . . . None are more anxious to leave this country than Gordon and myself and none more heartily approve the Government policy of evacuation. Unless, however, Zubair is sent here I see little probability of this policy being carried out. . . . Every day we remain . . . causes us to incur responsibilities towards the people which it is impossible for us to overlook." He also, referring to Graham's force at Suakin, recommended that "when the Berber–Suakin road is clear, a small force of British or Indian cavalry should be sent to Berber and a small force of British cavalry to Wadi Halfa". These measures, Stewart told Baring, "would greatly assist negotiations with rebels and hasten evacuation". It is clear from this that, whatever Gordon thought, Stewart regarded these measures as essential additions, and not possible alternatives, to sending Zubair.

This telegram from Stewart convinced Baring that "if anything was to be done in the way of establishing an anti-Mahdist government at Khartum there was no time to be lost".[18] He therefore told Granville that he was "still of opinion that Zubair Pasha should be allowed to succeed General Gordon", that "delay would be injurious" and that he now thought that Zubair should go to Khartum at once if he were willing to do so. He also told Granville that he disagreed with Stewart's recommendation to send British troops to Berber.[19] Later he recorded that "so long as any prospect existed of sending Zubair to Khartum and thus settling the Sudan question quietly by diplomacy I was not prepared to take the responsibility of recommending that a British force should be sent into the interior of the Sudan".[20]

On 5 March Granville replied to this telegram in terms which, Baring recorded, gave him a "feeling akin to despair". He was told that "H.M.G. see no reason at present to change their impressions about Zubair" and that "unless these impressions could be removed H.M.G. could not take upon themselves the responsibility of sending Zubair to Khartum". He inquired how Baring reconciled his recommendation with "the prevention or discouragement of slave hunting and the slave trade, with the policy of evacuation and with the security of Egypt". He also asked to be informed "as to the progress which has been made in extricating the garrisons and the length of time likely to elapse before the whole or greater part may be withdrawn. As H.M.G. require details as to each garrison, your report should be a full one and may be sent by mail."[21] In this last sentence Granville clearly indicated the Cabinet's refusal to regard the question as urgent and their desire not to be bothered with it any more for the time being.

Baring, whose advocacy in the matter can perhaps be criticised as persistent rather than forceful, repeated Granville's telegram to Gordon, told him that he could "regard the Zubair question as still under consideration", and asked him for "a careful and well-argued answer" to the points raised by Granville, with particular reference (*a*) to the possible appointment of Husain Khalifa, the Mudir of Berber, as an alternative to Zubair, and (*b*) to the possibility that Zubair "might make common cause with the Mahdi . . . and prove a source of danger rather than of assistance to Egypt".[22] On 8 March Gordon replied in what was, for him, a well-reasoned telegram.[23] He told Baring that "Husain Khalifa has only power at Dongola and Berber" and that "there is not the least danger of Zubair making common cause with the Mahdi" as he "would be far more powerful than the Mahdi and he would soon make short work of him". He emphasised that the "sending of Zubair means the extrication of the Cairo employees from Khartum and the garrisons from Sennaar and Kassala" and that "I can see no possible way to do so except through him" as "it is quite impossible to get the roads open to Kassala and Sennaar or to send down the white [i.e. the Egyptian and Turkish] troops unless Zubair comes up." "If you do not send Zubair you have no chance of getting the garrisons away."

"If you do not send Zubair you have no chance of getting the garrisons away." That was the real point at issue and Gordon had, at last, made it clear. Baring repeated Gordon's telegram to London on 9 March with a covering telegram[24] which did not, however, drive this point home with sufficient force. Instead, he concentrated on arguing (*a*) that sending Zubair was consistent with the policy of evacuation, (*b*) that encouragement of the slave trade, whether Zubair were sent or not, was among "the inevitable consequences of the policy of abandonment", and (*c*) that, as regards the security of Egypt, the risk of sending Zubair was a small one compared with "the certain disadvantages of withdrawing without making any provision for the future government of a country which would thus be sure to fall under the power of the Mahdi". The real point was that a refusal to send Zubair would not merely involve those "certain disadvantages" but would also make it impossible to implement the Cabinet's policy of a peaceful evacuation. Baring did, however, "urge upon H.M.G. the necessity of settling this question without delay", tell them that Gordon "thinks there is a considerable danger of his being hemmed-in and blockaded by the rebels", and warn them that Gordon "exercises little or no influence outside Khartum" and that "his influence (there) is sure to decline as time goes on."

Up to this time there had been no public knowledge in London of the proposal to send Zubair to Khartum. It was therefore possible for the Cabinet to consider the question without being harassed by the waves of emotion and denunciation which public mention of Zubair was certain to arouse. But, in Khartum, as long as the telegraph line to Cairo remained open, Gordon was, once more, in a position to communicate his views to the Press through the medium of Frank Power, *The Times* correspondent, who was living with Gordon in the Palace, who had conceived something like a hero-worship for Gordon (he was a young man of 25), and to whom Gordon appears to have taken a fancy. Gordon was not a discreet man and, since he was not on particularly intimate terms with Stewart, it was not unnatural that he should have made a confidant of the only other Englishman in Khartum. Power, on his side, would no doubt have respected Gordon's confidences. But it was not long before Gordon was using Power, as he had used Stead, as a means of addressing the British public direct over the heads of the Cabinet.

The Times of 5 March carried a message from Khartum dated 3 March which stated: "It is now admitted that Zubair Pasha is the only man connected with the Sudan who is endowed with the ability and firmness to head any government here. It is out of the question that Gordon should leave Khartum without having first formed a government . . . Zubair . . . is more fit than any other man to replace the Egyptian government. . . . He would come here under certain stated conditions. Gordon has foreseen this ever since he left Cairo. Slave hunting will be stopped in the Congo and he believes that in a year . . . there will be a rising of slave dealers against the Mahdi." In the same day *The Times* carried a leader expressing doubts about Zubair but reiterating its well-worn thesis that Khartum was of the highest importance to Egypt and ought to be retained for Egypt. On the next day a message from Alexandria in *The Times* supported the idea of Zubair as "a Sudanese of undoubted energy and ability holding Khartum and keeping open the routes to Korosko and Suakin via Berber", but emphasised that he must be under British and not Egyptian control. On 7 March *The Times* had another leader again objecting to Zubair and stating that the alternative was "the adoption by Gordon of measures to establish British influence directly at Khartum and on the Red Sea".

On 10 March *The Times* published an interview with Gordon telegraphed by Power on 7 March. In this interview Gordon was reported as stating that "there is a certainty that the Mahdi will succeed in raising the tribes between Khartum and

Berber. This is owing to fears caused by the policy of abandoning the Sudan. We cannot blame them when there is no sign of establishing a permanent government here. If Graham's victory were followed up by sending two Squadrons to Berber they could keep open communication between here and Berber. Zubair should be sent to succeed me and Egyptian regiments should go to Dongola and 100 British troops to Wadi Halfa. If this were done I could relieve Sennaar. Then I would take out the Cairo employees and Zubair would put his own men in. I would evacuate Bahr-al-Ghazal and hand over the troops to Zubair who, before the end of the year, would fend off the Mahdi. Zubair should be given a subsidy dependent on my safety. If H.M.G. do not act promptly Graham's victory will go for naught." He went on to emphasise that communication between Khartum and Berber would be cut in a matter of days if not of hours and concluded: "I am dead against any British expedition to reconquer the Sudan. It is unnecessary if H.M.G. do what I recommend."

Baring comments[25] that the publication of this interview "practically destroyed all hopes of utilising Zubair Pasha's services". He also quotes from a letter received from Stewart dated 8 March telling him what had happened: "The telegram shown you by Bell this morning [i.e. the telegram from Power containing the interview which Power sent to Moberly Bell, *The Times* correspondent in Cairo and which Bell showed to Baring before sending to London] has no doubt surprised you. Gordon also sent you a telegram giving in his resignation if his views were not carried out. Yesterday evening he got very irritated with me because I did not at once accede to his request to send you a telegram about Zubair and the propriety of sending him up with a British force to Berber. I said you had already told us the chief difficulty was not at Cairo but in London. I did not refuse to write the telegram, I merely asked for a little time to think. Gordon get very impatient and finally left the table. Seeing that he was annoyed I got up and wrote the telegram as he desired. On returning I found him with *The Times* correspondent. The result was the telegram which you have been shown. We had a discussion on the subject but it was of no avail. He then telegraphed his resignation to you but I fortunately succeeded in getting this put into cipher. The affair is annoying but I think the Ministry at home ought to let him have his wish and give him Zubair."

It is possible that, but for Gordon's indiscretion, the Ministry would have done so, although, by then, it would probably have been too late. But Gladstone, whose views on the Sudan were more realistic and clear-sighted than those of his Foreign Minister, was away ill, and Granville, as usual, was terrified of public opinion. On 6 March, the day after the first public reference to Gordon's request for Zubair had appeared in *The Times*, there was a question about it in the Commons. On 10 March, in a Commons debate on the Army Supplementary Estimates, there was a volume of protest against Zubair, who was described as "the greatest slave dealer in history". The formidable Forster stated: "If Gordon has given this advice I am not prepared blindly to follow him", and demanded that "if the Government are considering this, they will not commit the House and the country without giving us the opportunity of expressing our opinion. . . . Do not let the Government suppose that they will get rid of responsibility by replacing Gordon with Zubair." Almost all Members who spoke on the subject, including many, like Ashmead-Bartlett, who were normally almost fanatical supporters of Gordon, were united in their feelings about Zubair. Hartington, replying for the Government, admitted that the objections to sending Zubair were obvious, but "it would not be just to Gordon to set aside summarily any suggestions he should make until H.M.G. have before them all the reasons which induced him to make them". He indicated that the Government had expressed to Gordon their surprise at and their objections to his recommendation and concluded: "We are most anxious that Gordon should complete his task and return from his critical and dangerous position, but it would be far better that Gordon should remain a longer time and complete the work himself than that he should have the assistance of and leave the succession to an objectionable agent."

The following day—11 March—a Cabinet meeting was held which discussed the Zubair question. Gladstone was still away ill. Dilke described the meeting[26]. "On 11 March we further considered pressing demands from Gordon and Baring for Zubair. Mr Gladstone had taken to his bed but was known to be strongly in favour of sending Zubair. The Cabinet were unanimous the other way, and Hartington was sent to see Mr Gladstone, we waiting till he returned. When he came back he laconically stated what had passed as follows: 'He thinks it very likely we cannot make the House swallow Zubair but he thinks he could.'" Dilke went on to state that the Cabinet decided that Zubair could not be sent. In another account[27] it is stated that "viewed as an abstract question three of the Commons members inclined to favour it, but on the practical question the Commons members were unanimous that no Government from either side of the House could venture to sanction Zubair".

After the Cabinet meeting Granville telegraphed Baring that the Cabinet "do not consider that the arguments against the employment of Zubair Pasha have been satisfactorily answered. They are prepared to agree to any other Mohammedan assistance as well as to the supply of any reasonable sum of money. . . ." He also told Baring that "H.M.G. are not prepared to send troops to Berber", and added: "They understand . . . that the withdrawal of the garrisons will take a considerable time and that the chief difficulty arises from the uncertainty felt by the inhabitants of the Sudan with regard to the future government of the country. While attaching great importance to an early evacuation, H.M.G. have no desire to force General Gordon's hand prematurely and they propose therefore to extend his appointment for any reasonable period . . . to enable him to carry out the objects of his mission."[28]

In deference to the views of the Prime Minister, and of the Queen who, for once, agreed with Gladstone, the Cabinet again considered the Zubair question at meetings held on 13, 14 and 16 March, but, according to Dilke, "Mr Gladstone at last unwillingly gave up Zubair as impossible".[29]

It is quite clear that the decision was taken, not on its merits, but in the light of its expected effect on Parliamentary and public opinion. Gladstone later recorded[30]: "Had my views about Zubair prevailed, it would not have removed our difficulties, as Forster would certainly have moved, and with the Tories and Irish have carried, a condemnatory address." Northbrook, in a letter to Baring dated 12 March[31], wrote: "It is clear enough, our H. of C. people say, that Zubair's appointment will not be tolerated here. Gordon's slave trade Proclamation[32] was swallowed with a very wry face here." And Granville, in a letter to Baring dated 14 March[33], told him that the unanimous opinion of the Commoners in the Cabinet was that no Liberal or Conservative Government could appoint Zubair.

Meanwhile Gordon, on 9/10 March, expecting that the telegraph line between Khartum and Berber would be cut at any moment, had sent a stream of telegrams to Baring.[34] In the first he told him: "I have the written authority of the King of the Belgians to take over the provinces of Equatoria and Bahr-al-Ghazal", and indicated that Stewart would be retreating with the Khartum garrison to Berber, but that their onward movement from there would be "most difficult unless the Berber–Suakin road is opened". In the second telegram, sent half an hour later, he stated that "there is no possibility of the people rallying round us. If you mean to make the proposed diversion to Berber of British troops and to accept my proposal *re* Zubair, it is worth while to hold on to Khartum. If you decide on neither of these steps I can see no point in holding Khartum, for it is impossible for me to help the other garrisons and I shall only be sacrificing troops and employees here. Your instructions had better be that I should evacuate Khartum with all the employees and troops and move the seat of government to Berber. This would mean sacrificing all outlying places except Dongola and Berber. You must give a prompt reply to this as even the retreat to Berber may not be within my power in a few days, and even if carried out at once will be of extraordinary difficulty. I should have to leave large stores and nine steamers here. . . . I may utterly fail in getting the Cairo employees to Berber. If I attempt it I could only be responsible for the attempt to do so. Once the Mahdi is in Khartum operations against him will be very arduous and will not save Sennaar and Kassala." Ten minutes later he telegraphed: "If the immediate evacuation of Khartum is determined in spite of outlying towns, propose to send down all Cairo employees and white troops with Stewart to Berber where he would await further orders. I would also ask H.M.G. to accept resignation of my commission and take all steamers and stores up to Equatoria and Bahr-al-Ghazal and consider these provinces as under the King of the Belgians. You would be able to retire all Cairo employees and white troops with Stewart from Berber to Dongola and thence to Halfa. If you decide on the immediate evacuation of Khartum this is my idea. If you object tell me."

On the morning of the following day—10 March—he resumed: "Through delay in sending up Zubair, sending him now is inseparable from sending British troops to Berber. Zubair's value naturally diminishes as tribes take up sides with Mahdi. Should I send Stewart and Power to Berber? They can be of no use here if you decide on the immediate evacuation of Khartum." And an hour or two later: "Should telegraph line be cut I have told Husain Khalifa to send scouts out and himself meet . . . the forces which might be advancing from Suakin. I shall detail three steamers which can pass the cataracts to remain at Berber. If any force comes from Suakin, Husain Khalifa is ordered to send off the black troops at Berber to Khartum and I will send down the white troops. . . . If I could have given any hopes to the people as to their future government things might have been better. It is evident that no one will throw in his fortunes with a departing government."

Faced with this spate of telegrams, Baring telegraphed Gordon to "hold on at Khartum until I can communicate further with H.M.G." and told him that he should "on no account go to Bahr-al-Ghazal and Equatoria".[35] Baring later[36] expressed regret for having sent these instructions and expressed the view that "it would have been better for me, instead of telling General Gordon to hold on to Khartum, to have taken on myself the responsibility of directing him to retire at once on Berber if he thought fit to do so". The point was, however, academic, since the telegraph line between Berber and Khartum was cut sometime on 10 March and never restored. Gordon never received Baring's instructions.

At the same time, Baring, considering that the wording of Granville's telegram of 11 March still left a loophole for negotiation, continued his efforts, asking Granville, if the

Cabinet eventually decided to send Zubair, to keep the matter secret.[37] Granville, replying on 13 March, reiterated that the Government's mind was made up and told him, with reference to Gordon's telegrams of 9/10 March, which he had just received, that the Government agreed to Gordon staying in Khartum if he thought that "the prospect of his early departure diminishes the chance of his accomplishing his task", but that otherwise "he should evacuate Khartum and save that garrison by conducting it himself to Berber without delay. . . . He should act according to his judgement as to the best course to pursue with regard to the steam vessels and stores."[38] Baring, in reply,[39] told Granville that there was no object in merely prolonging Gordon's stay in Khartum since "the difficulty in establishing a settled government will increase rather than diminish with time". On the other hand, "the alternative . . . of evacuating Khartum at once and retiring on Berber . . . will be most difficult to execute. It involves the certainty of sacrificing the garrisons of Sennaar, Bahr-al-Ghazal and Gondokoro . . . I do not think that the retreat could be carried out without great personal risk to Gordon and Stewart. . . . The two questions of withdrawing the garrisons and of arranging for the future government of the country cannot be separated. . . . The real question is not whether or not the appointment of Zubair is objectionable but whether any other practicable and less objectionable alternative can be suggested. I can suggest none."

Granville replied on 16 March in a telegram which almost defies comment: "While the objections of H.M.G. to Zubair are unaltered, the prospect of good results attending his appointment seem to be diminished. The instructions to General Gordon to remain in the Sudan only apply to that period of time which is necessary for relieving the garrisons throughout the country and for affording the prospect of a settled government. If General Gordon agrees with you that the difficulty of establishing a settled government will increase rather than diminish with time, there can be no advantage in his remaining and he should, as soon as practicable, take steps for the evacuation of Khartum. . . . On evacuating Khartum he should exercise his discretion as to what is to be done with the steamers and stores there."[40] As Baring commented later, "It was evidently useless to continue the correspondence." He telegraphed Gordon: "You must now regard the idea of sending Zubair as finally abandoned and . . . act as well as you can up to the instructions contained in Lord Granville's telegrams."[41] Gordon never received either Baring's telegram or Granville's instructions.

The cutting of the telegraph line between Khartum and Berber signalised the fact that the tribes inhabiting the Nile valley between Khartum and Berber had, after months of wavering, come down on the side of the Mahdi. Not only Khartum but Berber was now in a state of siege. The possibility of Gordon being able to set up an alternative government to that of the Mahdi no longer existed. It was now a question of whether it would be possible to reopen, not only the Berber–Suakin but also, the Berber–Khartum route, so as to enable Khartum to be evacuated at all. River communication by armed steamers, of which nine were available, was possible between Khartum and Berber, but it was impossible to evacuate all who wished to leave Khartum by this means and would in any case have merely transferred the problem of evacuation from Khartum to Berber. Most of the steamers could not negotiate the rapids downstream of Berber, the Berber–Suakin road was closed, and the Berber–Korosko route, besides being impracticable for any large body of troops or refugees, was also closed between Berber and Abu Hamed.

Berber was the key. A temporary British occupation of Berber had now become a condition of the evacuation of Khartum. Graham's force of 4,000 troops was still in the vicinity of Suakin and, on 13 March, had defeated Osman Digna at Tamai. The force had been sent to the eastern Sudan as a result of Wolseley's recommendation for limited operations in the neighbourhood of Suakin. He had thought, erroneously, that such limited operations would relieve Gordon's position in Khartum. Graham's two victories at el-Teb and Tamai did not have this effect. The tribes had risen between Khartum and Berber and the Suakin–Berber route was still closed. Any relief for Khartum would involve Graham's force fighting its way across the desert to Berber. Graham himself, and Admiral Hewett, after the battle of Tamai, and in the light of the position in Khartum, were in favour of this. They were supported by Baring who, on 16 March, telegraphed Granville[42] that "it has now become of the utmost importance not only to open the Berber–Suakin route but to come to terms with the tribes between Berber and Khartum. If we fail in the latter point the question will very likely arise of sending an expeditionary force to Khartum to bring away Gordon." In London, Wolseley, who was already thinking in terms of sending an expeditionary force up the Nile valley, was opposed to an advance on Berber from Suakin. Granville told Baring[43] that Graham was being authorised to advance as far as Sinkat "but we cannot authorise the advance of any troops in the direction of Berber until we are informed of the military conditions and are satisfied that it is necessary for Gordon's safety and confined to that purpose. . . . Our present information is that it would not be safe to send a small body of cavalry as proposed and that it would be impossible to send a large force." On 21 March he asked Baring to investigate the possibility of negotiations with Osman Digna with a view to getting the Suakin–Berber road opened.[44] Baring consulted Graham who told him that "it would be useless to get into communication with Osman Digna". He then recommended to Granville that Graham "should be allowed to attack Osman Digna as he proposed".[45] Various telegrams from London followed in which a further limited advance by Graham was authorised and suggestions, emanating from Wolseley, made for "a portion of the Egyptian Army to garrison Wadi Halfa in order to lend moral support to General Gordon", and the dispatch to Berber of some British officers "with some knowledge of Arabic and experience in dealing with natives . . . there to await instructions from General Gordon". Baring, after consultation with Generals Stephenson and Wood, rejected the proposal to send Egyptian troops to Wadi Halfa as a "half measure which would be of little use". Attempts were made to send two British officers—Major Kitchener and Major Rundle—to Berber, but it was considered unsafe to allow them to proceed further south than Aswan. Instead, Baring concentrated on trying to get the Cabinet to agree to send all or part of Graham's force to

Berber. On 24 March he telegraphed Granville[46] that "the question now is how to get General Gordon and Colonel Stewart away from Khartum", bearing in mind that "they will not willingly come back without bringing with them the garrison of Khartum and the Khartum officials". He went on to say that there were only two solutions: "the first is to trust General Gordon's being able to maintain himself at Khartum until the autumn when . . . it will be less difficult to conduct operations on the Suakin–Berber road than at present. . . . The only other plan is to send a proportion of General Graham's army to Berber with instructions to open up communication with Khartum. . . . We all consider that, however difficult the operations from Suakin may be, they are more practicable than any operations from Korosko and along the Nile." On the same day he wrote a private letter to Granville[47] saying he was quite sure that Gordon would not be able to obey the instructions which he had been sent and, after telling Granville "I blame myself for ever having consented to his going", stated: "I do not think we can leave him stranded if from a military point of view it is at all possible to help him."

On 25 March Granville replied to the telegram that, in view of "the extraordinary risk from a military point of view, H.M.G. do not think it justifiable to send a British expedition to Berber". He asked Baring to convey this to Gordon "in order that he may adopt measures in accordance therewith. H.M.G. desire to leave full discretion to General Gordon to remain in Khartum if he thinks it necessary or to retire by southern or any other route which may be found available."[48] On the following day he sent Baring another telegram in which he informed him that the Government had no intention of sending British troops to Berber and that they had told Graham that his operations, which "must be limited to the pacification of the districts round Suakin", should be brought to a speedy conclusion.

On receipt of this telegram Baring sent a message to Gordon, via Cuzzi in Berber, who sent it on to Gordon by messenger, telling him that "there is no intention on the part of H.M.G." to send a force to Berber. This message reached Gordon on 9 April. Two days before—on 7 April—he had received similar information from Cuzzi who, not having possession of the cipher, had received a telegram *en clair* from Baring to the same effect.[49]

Baring also, on 26 March, replied to Granville in what Dilke described as "a very unpleasant telegram",[50] and Granville as "a heavy cannon-ball".[51] He has recorded that the tone of Granville's last telegrams grated on him. He was receiving a series of desperate messages from Cuzzi at Berber telling him that the situation was critical. He was irritated at the complete lack of any sense of urgency displayed by Granville and by the insouciance with which he had given Gordon discretion to act upon two impracticable alternatives after having turned down every recommendation which he had made. In his telegram[52] he asked the Cabinet "to place themselves in the position of Gordon and Stewart. They have been sent on a most difficult and dangerous mission by the English Government. Their proposal to send Zubair . . . was rejected. The consequences they foresaw have ensued. Coetlogon assures me that as long as the rebels hold both banks of the river above the sixth cataract, it will be quite impossible for boats to pass.[53] He does not believe that Gordon can cut his way through by land. He ridicules the idea of retreating with the garrison to the Equator, and we may be sure that Gordon and Stewart will not come away alone. . . . If it be decided to make no attempt to afford present help, then I would urge that Gordon be told to try and maintain his position during the summer and that then, if he is still beleagured, an expedition will be sent as early as possible in the autumn to relieve him. . . . The mere announcement of the intention of the Government would go a long way to ensure his safety. . . . Having sent Gordon to Khartum it appears to me that it is our bounden duty, both as a matter of humanity and policy, not to abandon him."

In reply, Granville told Baring privately, on 29 March, that "we could not agree to pledge ourselves to a promise to Gordon to send a military expedition to him in the autumn",[54] and officially, on 28 March,[55] that "we cannot accede to the proposals in your telegram and . . . do not see how we can alter our instructions of the 25th", in which Granville, disregarding the physical facts of the situation, instructed Baring to tell

Gordon that the Cabinet were not prepared to add to these instructions "until we hear what is General Gordon's actual condition and prospect as to security and his plans of proceeding and desires under present circumstances".

On the same day as this telegram was sent—28 March—a long mailed dispatch, apparently drafted by Harcourt,[56] was sent to Baring in Granville's name explaining the Government's reasons for not sending Zubair and for not sending an expedition. This dispatch[57] which, in spite of Dilke's information about its authorship, bears in places the unmistakable stigmata of Lord Granville, for the most part expanded the arguments against Zubair and the Berber expedition which had already been expressed by cable. But, in its opening passage, it contained a remarkable perversion of the Cabinet's original intentions in sending Gordon to Khartum. Referring to the instructions which Baring had given Gordon in Cairo, on which the Cabinet had made no adverse comment at the time, the dispatch stated: "H.M.G., bearing in mind the exigencies of the occasion, concurred in these instructions, which virtually altered General Gordon's mission from one of advice to that of executing, or at least directing, the evacuation, not only of Khartum, but of the whole Sudan." As Baring remarked,[58] and as the documents and the course of this narrative make clear, this statement "is wholly devoid of foundation". Granville, over whose signature this dispatch was written, knew perfectly well that Gordon's mission, as explained to him by Granville himself, had been one of "directing the evacuation", and one can only assume that he, and some other members of the Cabinet, now that Gordon's mission had gone awry, were trying to shift the responsibility from themselves on to Baring.

In their refusal to send a military expedition to Berber, the Cabinet had been fortified by the advice of Wolseley, who was already in favour of a full-scale expedition by way of the Nile valley, and by the original opinions expressed by Baring and his military advisers in Cairo, who, in February, had been opposed to sending any troops to Suakin at all except for the purpose of defending the town itself. Their decision was a military one with which Stewart, in a letter written to Baring on 11 March, had expressed his private agreement, telling him that "I really fail to see how you can, at this season of the year, send an expedition from Suakin to Berber."[59] The Cabinet's refusal, expressed in Granville's telegram of 28 March, to commit themselves to a relief expedition in the autumn, was a different matter. It was a political decision, taken against the advice of Wolseley and in face of the nascent opposition of about half the Cabinet. This half, Dilke recorded on 2 April,[60] consisted of Hartington, Northbrook, Selborne, Derby, Chamberlain and Dilke himself. The other half, who were against an expedition, consisted of Gladstone, Granville, Harcourt, Kimberley and Dodson.[61]

Of those in favour of an expedition, Hartington, in a letter to the Queen on 16 March, replying to a protest from H.M. against the Cabinet refusal to send an expedition to Berber, gave her to understand that an expedition would be sent in the autumn "if it should eventually be necessary to relieve him by force".[62] Selborne, the Lord Chancellor, gave the Cabinet to understand that he would resign if an expedition were not sent in the autumn.[63] Dilke records that he had made up his mind that "we must send an expedition" and thought "that if sent at high Nile it would be in time".[64]

Of those against an expedition, only Gladstone and Granville had been at all directly concerned with sending Gordon on his mission. Gladstone had given a reluctant agreement, apparently on the understanding that it was to be a reporting mission only. Subsequently, he had unsuccessfully opposed the dispatch of Graham's force to Suakin on the ground that this committed the Government to armed intervention in the Sudan, and had unsuccessfully advocated sending Zubair to Khartum on the ground that this might enable the Government to relinquish their responsibility for the Sudan. In both of these matters he sought unsuccessfully to pursue a consistent policy in face of public opinion. Granville, moved, according to his own account, by public opinion, had been the Minister principally responsible for sending Gordon on his mission in the knowledge that it was an executive and not a reporting one. He had, by inadvertence or design, omitted to make it clear in Gordon's instructions, which he drafted, that any reinforcement by British troops was out of the question. Moved again by public opinion, and without any consideration of the merits of the questions concerned, he had successfully and successively advocated the dispatch of Graham's force to Suakin and opposed the sending of Zubair to Khartum. Immediately after having sent Gordon on his mission, he had expressed to Hartington his regret at having done so. On 6 March he had publicly, in the House of Lords, expressed his doubts about Gordon. ("There was never an act of greater confidence shown by any Government to an individual than the mission of General Gordon. That confidence may turn out to be misplaced.") And he, together with Gladstone, had been responsible, in face of opposition from nearly half the Cabinet, for the very definite wording of the telegram to Baring of 28 March, which was intended to slam the door on any possibility of a relief expedition later in the year.

In the minds of many members of the Cabinet there was a suspicion, hardening into a conviction, that they were being deliberately manœuvred by Gordon and his friends away from the policy of evacuation and towards a policy of reconquest. The *Pall Mall Gazette* interview, the subsequent opinions attributed to Gordon by the Press, Gordon's request to Baring for the publication of all his messages, the reference to the imminent arrival of British troops in his Proclamation of 26 February, his "smash the Mahdi" telegram, his interview with Power about Zubair on 7 March, and a subsequent message from Power which appeared in *The Times* on 1 April referring to the expected arrival of British troops (see next chapter), all seemed to point to a double game being played by Gordon in which, on the one hand, he professed to be obeying the orders of the Government and, on the other hand, appeared to be carrying out a policy in contradiction to those orders. Certainly, Gordon's indiscretions to the Press, the more calculated activities of some of his friends, the impulsiveness of his telegrams, and the wide gap between his confident assertions while in London and the extent of his achievements after reaching the Sudan, all lent some colour to this conviction in the minds of those Ministers, like Gladstone and Harcourt, who were resolutely opposed to any British intervention in the Sudan and who had been unenthusiastic about Gordon's mission at the outset. But in this conviction there was an element of paranoia not dissimilar to that in Gordon's own conviction that Baring and the Cabinet were leagued together in a conspiracy to drive him to his death. Neither conviction had any basis in fact. Up to 10 March, after which there was no more hope for the success of his mission, Gordon's actions and recommendations, although not always wise or well-considered, had been entirely consistent with his instructions and with the objects of his mission as stated to him by the four members of the Cabinet and by Baring. He might reasonably have been criticised for over-optimism, for misleading the Government about the seriousness of the rebellion, and for drawing hasty conclusions from insufficient and unreliable information. He might reasonably have been criticised for an error of judgement in divulging the contents of the evacuation Firman at Berber (although it seems unlikely that this made any difference), and for various other errors of judgement. He showed a certain lack of frankness, both with the Cabinet and with Baring, over his dealings with the King of the Belgians. He was certainly indiscreet in his relations with the Press. His interview with Power over Zubair on 7 March was stupid, in that it produced, and might have been expected to produce, a result opposite to that which he had intended. But there is nothing reprehensible for a man in Gordon's position seeking to reinforce his recommendations in this way. It was not a case of advocating through the Press a policy opposed to that which he had been instructed to pursue. It was a case of trying (and failing) to use the Press to support a recommendation which was in accordance with his instructions and which he was trying to induce his Government to accept. Neither in this, nor in any other of his actions or communications, until 10 March, is there any evidence or indication of disobedience to his instructions. After 10 March his attitude was less impeccable. But this can be attributed to a not altogether unjustified belief that the predicament in which he found himself had been brought about by the Government's rejection of his recommendations, and was being exacerbated by their suspicion of his motives.

CHAPTER SEVEN

THE FAILURE OF THE MISSION

GORDON'S MISSION HAD failed. Whether it had failed as a result of errors of judgement by Gordon, or errors of commission by H.M.G., or because it had no possibility of success, or because of the force of unforeseeable circumstances, is a matter of opinion. But indubitably, by the middle of March, when Khartum was invested and Berber threatened, the two objects of the mission—the peaceful evacuation of the garrisons and the Egyptian inhabitants, and the setting-up of a buffer-State between Egypt and the Mahdi, had become impossible of achievement. It remained for the Cabinet to decide whether Gordon and those whom he had gone to rescue should be left to their fate or whether an expeditionary force should be sent to accomplish by force of arms what Gordon had failed to accomplish by force of personality.

It suited the members of the Cabinet to conceal from Parliament, from the public, and even, possibly, from themselves, the fact of this failure, while they argued as to whether, and if so, when, by what route, in what strength, and for what objects, they should send a relief expedition. Those members of the Cabinet, like Gladstone and Granville, who were against sending an expedition were those who had found themselves reluctantly committed to a British occupation of Egypt and who now suspected that they were being inveigled by Gordon himself, by the Tory Opposition and Tory Press, by the military, by some of their Cabinet colleagues, and even by Baring, their agent in Egypt, into a British occupation of the Sudan and into a war with people whom Gladstone was to describe as "rightly struggling to be free". But they were unwilling publicly, or even privately, to adopt the logical and tenable position, adumbrated by Hartington in the Commons on 19 February, that H.M.G. had no responsibility for the Egyptian garrisons, and by Granville in the Lords on 27 February, that it would be unreasonable for any Government to send an expeditionary force to rescue a man who had volunteered for a forlorn hope. Instead, they propagated, and perhaps came to believe, the fiction that Gordon was in no real danger, that he could save himself and his companions if he chose, and that they had to await his replies to various questions they had addressed to him before they could decide on any course of action. In propagating this fiction, they were able to make use of various optimistic remarks which they unscrupulously selected from such of Gordon's messages as were still reaching them.

On the other side of the Cabinet were those, like Hartington and Selborne, who were pressing for a relief expedition. They were variously actuated by a feeling of personal responsibility towards Gordon and Stewart, by a feeling that British honour was involved, by a conviction that the defence of Egypt demanded it, by the increasing insistence of Wolseley and the War Office, and by a belief that it was desirable for Great Britain to stake a claim in the Sudan. They started pressing within the Cabinet for a relief expedition from the time of the receipt of Baring's "heavy cannon-ball" on 26 March. But they wanted to avoid a split in the Cabinet which would have led to a change of Government; they had other Government business to do, some of which was more important than Gordon's predicament in Khartum; some of them shared the mistrust of Gordon felt by those who were opposed to a relief expedition. They were not prepared to precipitate the Government's resignation by stretching their disagreement with what was still a majority of the Cabinet to the extent of resigning themselves. And so they confined themselves to urging the case for a relief expedition by the slow process of persuasion within the Cabinet.

Gladstone, the Prime Minister, still, at 75, the most powerful personality of them all, both in the Cabinet and on the floor of the Commons, became more obstinate as the year wore on in his determination not to agree to a relief expedition, using all the devices of rhetoric, of casuistry, and of procrastination, to fight a delaying action both against the Opposition in the Commons and against an increasing body of his colleagues in the Cabinet.

The battle in the Cabinet was fought out between Gladstone and Hartington, with Granville, the confidant of both, acting as an occasional go-between. The others hardly counted. The Marquis of Hartington, scion of a great Whig family, Secretary of State for War, and Leader of the House of Commons, was, in popular estimation and in fact, second only to Gladstone in the hierarchy of the Liberal Party, which he had led for a time in Opposition during Gladstone's temporary retirement. His resignation would inevitably have led to the resignation of the Government. But Hartington, a politician through-and-through, although less agile and less unscrupulous than Gladstone, had no desire to precipitate this and to let the Tories in. What he wanted was what every politically-minded Cabinet Minister wants—to convert the Cabinet to his way of thinking without either resigning himself or (which in Hartington's case would have come to the same thing) forcing the Government to resign. And so, in the matter of the relief expedition, he aimed at getting what he wanted without breaking up the Government. This involved a simultaneous process of private persuasion and public equivocation. In the end he got what he wanted. But he got it too late to save Gordon, too late to establish British influence in the Sudan (if that was what he wanted), and too late to save the Government's credit in the eyes of the public or the House of Commons.

On 1 April a message from Power dated 23 March from Khartum was published in *The Times* which stated: "We are daily expecting British troops. We cannot bring ourselves to believe that we are abandoned by the British Government." A leader in *The Times* the same day echoed Power's words, stating: "We absolutely refuse to believe that the Government mean to abandon Gordon." Hartington, questioned about this in the Commons, stated that there had been no request from Gordon for a relief expedition. (This was true only in the very narrowest sense.) In a leader on 2 April *The Times* ridiculed Hartington's casuistry in telling the House that Gordon had not asked officially for a relief expedition and commented that the Government seemed to be dependent on *The Times* for information about Gordon. On 3 April Gladstone, who had recovered from his illness, and Hartington, made statements about Gordon in the Commons. Gladstone, elaborating on the fiction about Gordon's instructions which had embellished Granville's mailed dispatch to Baring on 28 March, told the Commons that Gordon had been sent by H.M.G. to ascertain the best means of executing the evacuation of the Sudan and that he had received from the Egyptian Government the executive power to do so. In other words, Gordon's mission was a reporting one as far as H.M.G. were concerned and an executive one as far as the Egyptian Government were concerned. With regard to the executive part of his mission, Gladstone stated that "H.M.G. feel great interest and responsibility". But the inference was clear. Gladstone went on to say that he "did not believe that any modification was needed to Gordon's instructions", and that "we have not received any full report from General Gordon about the best means of withdrawing from the interior of the Sudan. . . . The principle we should act upon in all matters relating to him is never to interfere except in a case of clear necessity . . . Gordon needs no constraint and needs no orders to remain in the Sudan. . . . He is authorised to use his own discretion and to withdraw from the Sudan if he thinks proper. . . . Neither is he under any inability to leave the Sudan at the moment of his choice. . . . We gather quite definitely that Gordon believes himself to be safe at Khartum." Hartington gave the House a long explanation about Zubair, saying that Gordon's recommendation appeared to be founded on "the conviction that, in order to secure quiet in Egypt, . . . it was necessary that the Mahdi should be crushed and that Zubair was the only man capable of this. It appeared to H.M.G. that Gordon had overrated the danger. . . . We also thought that he had underrated the danger of installing Zubair in Khartum [and] given undue weight to the assumed necessity for the immediate evacuation of Khartum." He explained that, when the Zubair proposal had been rejected, Gordon had been asked to "remain in Khartum as long as he might think necessary and as long as he should think it possible to carry out the original objects of his mission. . . . As yet we do not know what Gordon proposes to do and whether his plans are modified by H.M.G.'s refusal of Zubair." He went on to say that "General Gordon has never suggested the employment of troops for the relief of Khartum. He left this country with the distinct understanding . . . that the mission he was going to undertake was one he was prepared to undertake with such resources as he might find on the spot and he distinctly understood that it was not a part of the policy of the Government to risk having to send an expedition". The possibility of sending part of Graham's forces to Berber had been considered but "after full consideration the Government has declined at present to send to Berber a small force at very great risk with no advantage to Gordon or anybody else. The Government have accepted responsibility for Gordon's actions in so far as they have sanctioned them, and for his safety . . . but it is impossible to state what measures may have to be taken to discharge that responsibility." Gordon believed when he undertook his mission that it "would be possible for him, without any material assistance from the British or Egyptian Governments, to withdraw the garrisons and establish some form of native government. . . . The time has not yet come when it can be said that Gordon has failed, and certainly nothing has happened to induce H.M.G. to engage in any military operations. . . . Gordon has discretion to remain in Khartum or to withdraw."

The Commons were not satisfied with these ingenious but casuistic statements and a debate was held that evening on a motion for the adjournment of the House. Sir Stafford Northcote told the Government that he had heard from Gordon's friends that any statement sent by Power could be regarded as authoritative, and asked them what they proposed to do about a relief expedition. Gladstone, in reply, protested against the implication that Gordon's mission had failed and said that the Government proposed to wait and see what plans Gordon had and "what substitute he may have for the Zubair proposal".

On 4 April, in the Lords, Lord Hardwick criticised the Government for not sending a force to Berber and told them that "in the whole history of this country no Plenipotentiary ever sent to carry out a mission has been so ill-treated as Gordon. Every suggestion he has made has been refused." He went on to say that it was "evident that Gordon felt that he would be supported in case of emergency" and asked the Government whether they proposed to wait for "another terrible disaster before they sent troops to Khartum". Lord Salisbury said that no plans appeared to have been made for a relief expedition and described Gordon's position as "forlorn". Granville, in reply, repeated what Hartington had already told the Commons that "neither in Gordon's instructions given in London or in Cairo was there the slightest indication that he would be backed up by a British army".

There were further critical questions in the Commons on 8 April, after which Parliament adjourned for the Easter recess.

Up to this time there had been no news from Khartum since the telegraph had been cut on 10 March except for the message from Power in *The Times*, which had been sent by messenger to Berber and telegraphed from there. But a batch of Gordon's telegrams, sent off by the same route between 11 March and 1 April, reached Baring via Berber on 9 April. Baring telegraphed them to London and, when they arrived, the Cabinet had a fair idea of the state of affairs in Khartum up to 1 April. (The fact that *The Times* message arrived quicker than, and conveyed a different and more pessimistic picture of the position from, the official telegrams, increased the mistrust of Gordon already felt by some members of the Cabinet.)

Fighting had broken out on 13 March when one of Gordon's steamers, reconnoitring downstream, was fired on when passing Halfaya, a few miles north of Khartum. It became apparent that the small garrison at Halfaya was surrounded by Dervishes and Gordon sent an expedition to their relief. This was successfully accomplished by the dispatch of three steamers but, two days later, a land attack against the enemy was ignominiously defeated, apparently as a result of treachery by the two Egyptian officers who were leading it. These officers were, by Gordon's orders, tried by court martial, convicted and shot. On 22 March messengers arrived from the Mahdi, who was still in Kordofan, rejecting Gordon's offer of peace and the governorship of Kordofan, which Gordon had sent him from Berber, and calling upon Gordon to surrender and embrace

Islam. "By so doing you will save yourself and all those under you. Otherwise you shall perish with them and your sins and theirs shall be on your head." Gordon replied that he would have no more communication with him. Henceforth, so far as Gordon was concerned, his peaceful mission was at an end. Next day he sent steamers north to Halfaya and south up the Blue Nile to fire on enemy positions and prevent them from closing too tightly on Khartum. But, by the end of the month, Khartum was under enemy fire from the south.

In his messages Gordon made no direct request for a relief expedition. In one, sent on 31 March, he told Baring: "The town is all right . . . and for the next two months we are as safe here as at Cairo." In the same message he referred to "the truly trumpery nature of the revolt which 500 determined men could put down". In another message he suggested that "if you could get by good payment 3,000 Turkish infantry and 1,000 Turkish cavalry the affair, including the crushing of the Mahdi, would be accomplished in four months".

On 11 April, a day after the Cabinet had received Gordon's official messages, there appeared in *The Times* a report of an interview with Gordon on 21 March in which Gordon was reported as saying: "God's ways are not men's ways, but as a whole the course of events tends to a good end since (1) if Egyptian troops had not gone to Tokar Moncrieff would not have been killed and Baker would not have been sent. (2) If I had gone to Suakin Baker's attempt would not have taken place. (3) If Baker had not been defeated a British force would not have interfered. (4) If Baker had not been defeated the rebels would not have risen here. (5) Our defeat at Halfaya persuaded H.M.G. to retain Graham's troops."[1]

From this it was quite apparent that Gordon had expected Graham's force would be sent to his relief. He was only undeceived about this when he received Baring's messages via Cuzzi on 7 and 9 April when, as we shall see, he reacted strongly. But this *Times* interview made nonsense of any further pretence by the Cabinet that Gordon was not expecting a relief expedition, although they may well have been exasperated at his indirect way of conveying that information. Some members of the Cabinet were also becoming exasperated as a result of their belief that he was receiving their messages and refusing to answer them. They appear to have assumed that, since they were receiving his messages (or some of them), he must be receiving theirs. They did not consider the likelihood, which was also the fact, that it was much easier to send messages out of a beleagured town than into one, since in the one case the messenger was escaping to freedom and in the other case risking captivity. In fact, most of the Government's messages to Gordon after 10 March never reached him at all, and those that did only after several weeks' or months' delay.

On 11 April, the day on which *The Times* interview had been published, Hartington told Gladstone that "we can scarcely say any longer that he does not want the expedition".[2] He also told him: "Lord Wolseley has at my request prepared (confidentially) a rough sketch of an expedition which he thinks practicable by the Nile. The movement could not take place before the Nile rises in a month or six weeks, but preparations would have to be made almost immediately." He added that Sir Charles Wilson, who was also at the War Office, "thinks that Wolseley has underrated the difficulties and delay of the Nile route and thinks that the Suakin–Berber route . . . should be used". He proposed to Gladstone that they should "ask Baring to consult Stephenson and Wood on the practicability and scope of an expedition to relieve Gordon", and suggested that "the mere announcement that preparations were being made would help to relieve Gordon's position". Gladstone replied on 13 April[3] deprecating the idea of an expeditionary force as being "the most vital and radical change that could be made in our policy", and suggested that, instead, "we ought to set about sending a set of carefully prepared questions to Gordon about his future condition and plans", adding that "he takes very little notice indeed of any general questions that we put to him". Hartington, sending a copy of Gladstone's letter to Granville on 15 April, ridiculed the suggestion about "carefully prepared questions" and told him that "it is clear enough that, whether he (Gordon) has a right to do so or not, he expects help . . . and it is also clear that he will not be able to leave Khartum without some such help".[4]

Meanwhile, on 13 April, Hartington had received a long

memorandum from Wolseley about Gordon.[5] In it Wolseley wrote that Gordon's position "is that of an officer commanding a besieged garrison", and that, "putting aside the possibility of his dying or being killed within the next six months, one of three things would happen. Either Khartum would be taken by assault or by treachery or have to surrender through lack of food or ammunition, or it would be relieved by a British force, or the siege would be raised by a change of Sudanese feeling towards General Gordon." He did not think it possible that Gordon would be able to fight his way out of Khartum "owing to the miserable stuff of which the garrison is composed". He presumed that "the Government is not prepared to allow General Gordon and his garrison to fall into the hands of the cruel and barbarous enemy now besieging Khartum, if he can hold out until the march of an English force to relieve him becomes climatically possible". He calculated that Gordon had enough food and ammunition to last until the autumn and thought that he ought to be able to do so. He urged that "the Government should at once determine upon the line of action or inaction it means to pursue", and that Gordon should be immediately informed of the decision arrived at. "My own opinion is that a telegram should be sent to Berber without delay addressed to Gordon in clear c/o the Governor of that place saying that, as soon as the climate admitted of British troops moving, an expeditionary force would be sent to them. No further information to be given in clear, but a message to Gordon in cipher should accompany this telegram telling him that he might calculate on being relieved before 15 November. . . . The British people will force you to do this whether you like it or not, and therefore you had better make all the arrangements accordingly. . . . At the same time I think that every endeavour should be made to avoid the necessity of having to send this British force to Khartum." He then went on to discuss the possibility of raising the siege through "some change in Sudanese feeling towards General Gordon". "If we even now made it public with authority that a settled government under Gordon, and after him some other English officer, were to be established east of the White Nile with Khartum as its capital . . . many strong men might even now join his standard." Wolseley enclosed a draft telegram which he suggested should be sent to Gordon asking him about this possibility, and went on to suggest that, if the British Government did not want to accept this responsibility, the King of the Belgians might be prepared to do so, and offered to go to Brussels to discuss the matter with him.

Hartington, on 16 April, sent Wolseley's memorandum to Granville with a covering note.[6] "I do not know on what he founds his inference that the Government intends to relieve Gordon. I may have indicated my own opinion that it will have to be done, but I have not the slightest idea what the Government at present proposes to do. But it is nearly time for us to make up our minds what we will do. . . . We are now waiting in hopes that Gordon will send us a message to say that he does not want British troops and that in some other way he is going to effect the evacuation of the Sudan without them. This is rather a broken reed to lean on . . . I do not agree with Northbrook that it would be of any use to send Gordon the most positive orders to come away, leaving the main part of the garrison behind him. I do not think that he would obey and I believe that public opinion in England would support him in disobeying. . . . The first thing we have to do is to decide whether we intend to leave Gordon to his fate, because, if we do not, the sooner we begin preparations the better. Then, if we are compelled after all to send an expedition, I think we shall have to reconsider our decision to abandon the eastern Sudan. I doubt whether we were right at first in accepting Baring's opinion that it was impossible for Egypt to hold it. Events seem to show that it would have been easier to hold it than to get out of it. . . . It would not be necessary to establish Egyptian government there, but to replace it by some sort of independent government under our protection."

On 21 April Hartington circulated to the Cabinet two memoranda by Wolseley containing detailed schemes for expeditions (*a*) by the Suakin–Berber route, and (*b*) by the Nile route, with Wolseley expressing a decided preference for the Nile route, with reasons to support his view. The Cabinet met to consider these memoranda on 23 April. They had other documents before them as well:

(1) A telegram from Baring dated 14 April[7] urging that H.M.G. were responsible for Gordon's safety and recommending that, if a relief expedition were to be sent by the Nile route, "no time should be lost in making preparations, so as to be ready to move directly the water rises". It might be that Gordon would be able to extricate himself, in which case the preparations would be unnecessary, but "unless they are undertaken now, it may be that, when the necessity for moving arises, so long a delay will ensue as to frustrate the objects of the expedition". Prophetic words.

(2) A telegram from Gordon, undated, but sent from Khartum on about 9 April, after he had received Baring's intimations that British troops would not be sent to Berber. It had reached Cairo on 16 April and been relayed from there.[8] "As far as I can understand, the situation is this: you state your intention of not sending any relief force up here or to Berber and you refused me Zubair. I consider myself free to act according to circumstances. I shall hold on here as long as I can and, if I can suppress the rebellion, I shall do so. If I cannot, I shall retire to the Equator and leave you with the indelible disgrace of abandoning the garrisons of Sennaar, Kassala, Berber and Dongola, with the certainty that you will eventually be forced to smash the Mahdi under great difficulties if you would retain peace in Egypt."

(3) A message from Power dated 7 April and published in *The Times* on 17 April, also referring to the decision not to send troops to Berber. After describing the situation in Khartum as being "very critical", the message went on: "Because I am confident that General Gordon is abandoned by the Government and that without Zubair Pasha he can never beat the rebels, I fear that he will be driven to retreat by Central Africa. For to-day arrived an unciphered telegram sent from Sir Evelyn Baring to Berber saying that no English troops will be sent to that place, in a word clearly indicating that General Gordon and the others who have been faithful to the Government are thrown over."

(4) A number of other messages from Gordon, sent during the first ten days of April. The most important of these was one dated 8 April[9] in which he told Baring that he had telegraphed

to Sir Samuel Baker to make an appeal to British and American millionaires "to give me £300,000 to engage 3,000 Turkish troops from Sultan and send them here". "I do not see the force of being caught here to walk about the streets for years as a dervish with sandalled feet. It would be the climax of meanness, after I had borrowed money from the people here, had called upon them to sell their grain at a low price &c., to go and abandon them . . . and I feel sure that, whatever you may feel diplomatically, I have your support—and that of any man professing himself a gentleman—in private."

This was strong stuff and may have done much further to antagonise the "anti-Gordon" members of the Cabinet. The meeting, which lasted for four hours, was apparently a heated one.[10] In the end, Gladstone got his way, and it was agreed to adopt his suggestion for "sending a set of carefully prepared questions to Gordon about his future condition and plans". After the meeting, a telegram, drafted by Gladstone, was sent to Cairo in the following terms: "Gordon should be informed at once, in cipher by several messengers at some intervals between each, through Dongola as well as Berber . . . that he should keep us informed to the best of his ability, not only as to immediate, but as to any prospective danger at Khartum; that . . . he advise us as to the force necessary in order to secure his removal, its amount, character, route of access to Khartum, and time of operation; that we do not propose to supply him with Turkish or any other force for the purpose of undertaking military expeditions, such being beyond the scope of the commission he holds and at variance with the pacific policy which was the purpose of his mission; that if, with this knowledge, he continues at Khartum, he should state to us the cause and intention with which he so continues." This message[11] was sent to Mr Egerton, who had temporarily replaced Baring as British Agent in Cairo. Baring had left for London on 17 April to attend an International Conference on Egyptian finances, which were in a very critical state, which had grave international repercussions and which were, at that time, absorbing more of the Government's attention than the affairs of the Sudan.

The message was eventually received by Gordon at the end

of July. It was quite clearly a delaying tactic on the part of Gladstone and other members of the Cabinet who were attempting to head off the growing demand in the Cabinet for a relief expedition. Hartington was most unhappy about it and told Granville the next day: "I don't think I can agree in the course which is now being taken."[12] However, he took refuge in a quibble between the words "removal", to which he objected, and "relief" which he would have preferred, and, after consulting Gladstone, who raised no objection, sent a long telegram to Stephenson asking whether there would be any appreciable difference in the size of the force necessary for Gordon's "relief" as distinct from his "removal".[13] Stephenson replied on 5 May[14] that exactly the same force would be required for either purpose, and that in any case it was improbable that Gordon "would ever contemplate coming away from Khartum accompanied by his suite only and leaving the garrison to their resources". This seems to have satisfied Hartington's conscience for the time being, until it was again stirred by a memorandum from Wolseley on 9 May. In this memorandum[15] Wolseley explained that he had advised against the dispatch of a small force from Suakin to Berber "unless it was to be part of a large and serious attempt to relieve Khartum". Having explained that a decision to make such an attempt had not been made at that time, he told Hartington that "Khartum can only be relieved after long preparations for moving a force there" and urged that "we should at once begin to make these preparations".

Meanwhile, Parliament had assembled again on 21 April after the Easter recess. Members did not yet know about the "indelible disgrace" telegram (which was published in a Blue Book early in May). But they had seen *The Times* message, about which Gladstone was questioned in the Commons. In reply he drew his famous distinction between Gordon being "hemmed in" and "surrounded", reiterated that the Government had had no request from Gordon for troops, and expressed the view that "Gordon's plans have nothing to do with his safety in Khartum", thereby implying that his indirect request for troops had some ulterior purpose. There were several days of increasingly hostile questions in the Commons, in which

Opposition spokesmen demanded a relief expedition and Government spokesmen reiterated that Gordon was in no danger, that he had not asked for troops, etc., and refused to commit themselves to any undertaking about a relief expedition. Then, a Censure Motion was put down in the following terms: "That this House regrets that the course pursued by H.M.G. has not tended to promote the success of Gordon's mission and that even such steps as are necessary to secure his personal safety are still delayed." The debate on this motion was fixed to take place on 12 May.

There had been no news from Khartum since Gordon's "indelible disgrace" telegram. Cuzzi had told Cairo that it was impossible to send to Gordon the message conveyed in Granville's telegram of 23 April as Khartum was closely invested.[16] This was later confirmed by the Mudir of Dongola who told Cairo that his messenger had returned with the message undelivered. (It eventually reached Gordon via Massawa towards the end of July.) Husain Khalifa, the Mudir of Berber, was sending despairing messages to Cairo saying that he would have to surrender to the Mahdi if he were not relieved. Cuzzi was sending messages to the same effect. An Egyptian battalion was sent from Aswan to Wadi Halfa.

In England no one outside the Cabinet (or inside it, for that matter) could gather, from the equivocal utterances of the Government spokesmen in Parliament, whether or not Gordon was going to be relieved. Behind the scenes, there was a certain amount of rather futile activity. Gladstone, intent as ever on washing his hands of the Sudan, was in favour of Gordon's proposal for encouraging Turkish assistance and for allowing Gordon to make his own arrangements to that effect.[17] But, even if the Cabinet had agreed, the idea was quite impracticable. Hardly more practicable were two other schemes which were being canvassed at about the same time. One was for the recruitment of a voluntary force of a thousand "sportsmen" to fight their way from Suakin to Khartum to rescue Gordon.[18] Another proposal was put forward by Wilfred Blunt, who wrote to Gladstone offering to go to Kordofan as H.M.G.'s representative to negotiate with the Mahdi for the release of Gordon and the garrison.[19] Nothing came of the volunteer proposal and

Blunt's offer was turned down by the Cabinet. There was also apparently a plan for sending a big game hunter, "Curly" Knox, to Khartum with a letter to Gordon from the Government, ordering him to leave Khartum with Knox.[20]

Agitation for a relief force, actuated partly by an humanitarian anxiety for Gordon's safety and partly by an imperialist desire to establish British influence in the Sudan, continued in the Tory Press. A letter in *The Times* on 24 April pointed out that "over £4 million worth of Sudan merchandise is sold annually in the Cairo bazaars while the amount of British goods sold in Khartum is even greater. It seems a pity that the International African Association should fail to realise that it is via Suakin and Khartum that they should open up Africa to commerce and civilisation. . . . Khartum and the Eastern Sudan must be retained . . . in the interest of British trade and industry." On 22 and 24 April there were leaders in *The Times* urging the sending of a relief force and, on 29 April, a leader, apparently referring to the "Curly" Knox proposal, attacked the Government for "turning their attention to a scheme for sending, by some Englishman of position and authority, a message suggesting that [Gordon] desert his post and save himself, if he is able, by flight, leaving the garrison behind to be massacred or given over to the Mahdi". On the same day *The Times* published a letter from Sir Samuel Baker advocating the dispatch of a force of "500 negroes, 10,000 Indians and 5,000 British" to march on Berber simultaneously via the Nile valley and Suakin. "No confidence will ever be established until we remove the disastrous policy of the abandonment of the Sudan." On 2 May there was a *Times* leader dealing with the two Blue Books on the Sudan,[21] which had just been published, giving most of the official correspondence which had passed up to the end of March, and referring to the fact, revealed in this correspondence, that Generals Stephenson and Wood had been in favour of sending an expedition to Berber. Next day there was another *Times* leader referring to the Censure Motion which had just been put down as being the "temperate expression of a deep and universal feeling. . . . The great mass of Gordon's countrymen are persuaded that there is a sacred duty to relieve him from his peril . . . which is not affected by whether Gordon has acted with prudence and whether all his suggestions should be endorsed." Another leader on 5 April, quoting from the Blue Books, pointed out that Gordon "was forbidden to go to the Mahdi, he was ordered not to go south of Khartum, . . . he was refused leave to set up Zubair as an independent ruler, and lastly he was told that his request for an advance of a small force of British troops from Suakin to Berber . . . could not be entertained".

On 5 May a further batch of correspondence, containing most of the Gordon correspondence during April, and including, *inter alia*, the text of the "indelible disgrace" telegram and the Government's reply, was published in two Blue Books.[22]

In spite of all the adverse Press comment, members and supporters of the Government seem to have thought that public interest in Gordon, which had been maintained at fever heat since January, was beginning to die down and that they would be able to avoid the necessity for a relief expedition. On 29 April Morley told Wilfred Blunt that "the Government were willing to bite their tongues out" for having sent Gordon, and that "they were very angry with him, for he had done everything he said he wouldn't do and done nothing that they told him to do", but that although, "if Gordon's death had happened two months ago it would have turned out the Ministry, now people are tired of him", and that "though there would be a row, it would blow over".[23] And so the Cabinet appear to have approached the Censure debate, which opened on 12 May, with some confidence.

Sir Michael Hicks Beach, opening for the Opposition, and making full use of the correspondence published in the Blue Books, attacked the Government for having rejected virtually all Gordon's recommendations, defended Gordon from the various insinuations made against him by the Government, and stigmatised as "disgraceful" the suggestion that Gordon had disobeyed his orders and thereby forfeited his claim to support. Gladstone replied. He accused the Opposition of wanting to reconquer the Sudan, and said that "we are determined not to reconquer the Sudan nor to place this country in conflict with people struggling for their freedom". He reiterated that Gordon's mission had been understood by all concerned to be a peaceful one, and ridiculed the idea that Gordon's expectation of "support and consideration" (expressed in his *Tanjore* memorandum to Baring) committed the Government to military intervention. "The situation in the Sudan with regard to Egypt was hopeless. Egypt had no means of extricating the garrisons or of pacifying the country. It appeared that Gordon's mission might give a chance of escape to those who would otherwise had no chance at all." Regarding Zubair, Gladstone indicated that he had been in favour of sending him but reminded the Opposition that they had opposed it. He drew attention to the fact that there were other beleagured garrisons in the Sudan besides Khartum and inquired whether the Opposition advocated sending expeditions to relieve them all. "Gordon has never at any time asked for British soldiers. He has never stated that he was prevented from leaving Khartum. . . . He has never represented that he was in any danger from without." Gladstone concluded by saying that the real difference between Government and Opposition was that the Opposition wanted to reconquer the Sudan and regarded Gordon's mission as the beginning of a means to that end, whereas the Government were determined not to reconquer the Sudan and had sent out Gordon on a peaceful mission to try and assist the Egyptian Government to evacuate the Sudan.

After Gladstone had sat down it was still not apparent whether or not the Government were prepared to send a relief expedition in any circumstances.

Forster, whose attitude and influence had been largely responsible for the rejection of the Zubair proposal, announced that he could not support the Government and attacked Gladstone for his obstinate refusal to recognise that Gordon was in peril. He said that Gordon's appointment as Governor-General was, in the circumstances, "incompatible with a purely peaceful mission", and told the Government that "if no other means than peaceful persuasion were to be used, he ought to have been warned of this before he left".

Forster was followed by Hartington, who told the House that "H.M.G. are under no moral obligation to use the resources of the Empire for the relief of the garrisons". He insisted that H.M.G., "who did not send the garrisons into their position of danger", had no responsibility for extricating them, that H.M.G. did not intend to reconquer the Sudan, either for themselves or for Egypt, and that it was "no part of their duty to risk English treasure and life to enable the Egyptian garrisons to march out with flying colours". But, he added, "some effort should be made to mitigate the sufferings of their retreat", and explained that this was the basic object of Gordon's mission. He said that Gordon, in his talk with members of the Cabinet before his departure, had told them that "in his opinion the danger of massacres of the garrisons was greatly exaggerated, that the power of the Mahdi was greatly exaggerated, and that probably no opposition would be offered to the peaceful withdrawal of the Egyptian officials and such portions of the garrisons as might wish to leave." Gordon had further expressed the opinion that "probably most of the Egyptian inhabitants would not wish to leave, that the greater part of the troops would probably join the Mahdi . . . and that the withdrawal of the rest could be effected without great difficulty or risk of massacre." He explained that, though evacuation was the primary object of his mission, Gordon "thought it might be in his power to secure the establishment of a government to replace the Egyptian Government", but "evacuation, even if it should lead to the establishment of the Mahdi in Khartum", was the primary object. "It is possible that he overrated the possibilities as to the success of his mission; he may have overestimated his own strength, not merely in removing the garrisons but in the reconstruction of the government and, in what he thought was a necessary prelude, the smashing of the power of the Mahdi." Defending the Government's refusal to send troops to Berber, he said that "Gordon's proposal to send troops to Berber was never made in isolation but only in conjunction with the Zubair proposal".[24] The moral effect of such an expedition "would not be what Gordon contemplated", and he asked what Members would have thought of a situation in which, in addition to Gordon being shut up in Khartum, "we also had 200 cavalry shut up in Berber". He then proceeded to the core of the subject—which Gladstone had evaded—the possibility of the dispatch of a relief expedition. "Such an expedition should not be sent to 'smash the Mahdi' or to give a good government to the Sudan, or to enable the garrisons to march out with the honours of war . . . but only if it is necessary to secure the safety of Gordon and of those for whose safety he has made himself responsible. . . ." "We should be satisfied that the original view of the possibility of evacuation is now impracticable." He stressed that Gordon would not "be called upon to do anything derogatory to his honour or character. Those who have trusted themselves to his service, those who have fought for him, those who have increased the peril in which they stood before by entering his service" should be taken into consideration. "But if escape is possible for Gordon it is possible also for them. But the Government are not responsible for the safe withdrawal of the garrisons. . . . For the relief of the garrisons Gordon is not bound in honour, but he is bound not to desert those who have co-operated with him and taken arms under him." He went on: "The Government are thinking now and have long been thinking what measures they should take for the relief of Gordon", and concluded that no measures would be attempted "until their practicability has been clearly demonstrated. . . . If so I believe that the country will be prepared to grudge no sacrifice to secure the life and honour of General Gordon."

At the end of the debate, the Motion of Censure was defeated, the Government having a majority of 28. It is probable that many Liberals, unimpressed with and even irritated by Gladstone's evasions, were persuaded to support the Government by Hartington's speech. Most Members, on both sides of the House, regarded his concluding remarks as a contingent undertaking by the Government to send a relief expedition.

On 17 May, after the debate, a telegram was sent to Egerton[25] for transmission to Gordon by such means as might be available: "As the original plan for the evacuation of the Sudan has been dropped, and as aggressive operations cannot be undertaken with the countenance of H.M.G., General Gordon is enjoined to consider and either report upon or, if feasible, to adopt at the first proper moment, measures for his own removal and for that of the Egyptians at Khartum who have suffered for him or who have served him faithfully, including their wives and children, by whatever route he may consider best, having special regard to his own safety and that of other British subjects." The message went on to say that Gordon was authorised to spend or to promise "money rewards" at his discretion to facilitate these measures. This message reached Gordon sometime during August.

It had now been publicly admitted that the original objects of Gordon's mission were no longer possible of execution, and it seemed that the Government had accepted responsibility for endeavouring to secure the safety, not only of Gordon and Stewart, but also of those who, in Hartington's words, had "co-operated with Gordon or taken arms under him". This was a larger undertaking than it seemed at first sight, and might well have been taken, and would probably have been taken by Gordon, to include virtually anyone in Khartum, or even in the whole of the Sudan, who wished to leave and who had not actually gone over to the enemy. There was also a general impression, derived from Hartington's speech, that the Government had committed themselves to the preparation of a relief expedition. *The Times*, on 15 May, described the result of the Censure debate as a moral defeat for the Government, and wrote: "The relief of Gordon and the extrication of the garrison will have to be undertaken at the earliest possible moment. It is now generally understood that Khartum is the most important point to be held if Lower Egypt is to be secured." And, on 21 May, another *Times* leader stated that "Little doubt is now entertained in military circles that the Government has come to a determination to employ a British force in the autumn for the relief of Gordon at Khartum if he has not made good his retreat before then."

The Government in fact had come to no such determination. "Military circles" were certainly pressing them to do so, but these "military circles" were not agreed as to whether the appropriate route for a relief force was via the Nile valley or via Suakin–Berber. A great controversy arose behind the scenes, with Wolseley supporting the Nile, and nearly everybody else, including Stephenson in Cairo, and Sir Charles Wilson and Sir Andrew Clarke at the War Office, the Suakin–Berber, route.

Apart from any military considerations, the Suakin–Berber route was attractive to those who regarded a relief expedition primarily as a means, not for rescuing Gordon but, for opening up the Sudan to British trade and influence. It would involve the construction of a railway between Suakin and Berber and thus provide a secure route to the interior of the Sudan independent of Egypt by which British trade could "follow the flag" into the interior of Africa via the Upper Nile valley. The construction and necessary maintenance of such a railway would tend to commit the Government to something in the nature of a permanent occupation in a way that a river-borne expedition up the Nile would not do. Even Wolseley, who was in favour of the Nile route, but who seems genuinely to have wished to avoid the necessity for a major expedition, thought that a start on the construction of a railway from Suakin might, as an earnest of the British intention not to abandon the Sudan, enable the Suakin–Berber road to be opened by negotiation. In a memorandum to Hartington dated 18 May[26] he wrote: "If the Cabinet decide upon announcing that immediate preparations will be made for the eventual dispatch of an expedition to Khartum, and if you were to follow up that announcement by beginning the construction of a railroad to Berber, it would be a good move to send me to Suakin as soon as the railroad is to be begun. The announcement that I was to start without delay to Suakin would make everyone feel you were thoroughly in earnest. . . . If the business be well-managed all serious fighting might be avoided. Once you begin your railroad, negotiations ought to be possible with the Arab tribes, and through their aid we ought to be able to open out the road to Berber in a short time after the first ten miles are laid. With the road to Berber opened, a small force could be pushed on there very soon, and with British troops there and the assured fact that more were waiting to be sent forward, it is . . . quite possible that Khartum would be relieved of its besiegers before the railroad was half finished."

The question of a railway, eagerly seized upon, one imagines, by those members of the Cabinet anxious to delay the necessity for any immediate decision about a relief expedition, was debated back and forth for some time. It was discussed in Cabinet on 27 May[27] but it was decided that "orders were not yet to be given". Next day, Gladstone, writing to Northbrook, expressed the view that "clear as is the case for the railway from Suakin as against the large expedition by the Nile, in every other view it is attended with the most formidable difficulties of a moral and political kind". He feared that "the turning of the first sod of a Sudan railway" would mean "the substitution of an Egyptian domination there by an English domination . . . more unnatural, more costly, more destructive and altogether without foundation in public right. It would be an immense advantage that the expedition (should one be needed) should be one occupying little time and leaving no trace behind it."[28] Gladstone also wrote to Dilke on 31 May that "Suakin and Berber has utterly beaten the Nile route for a larger expedition", but expressed his preference for two small expeditions, one up the Nile, and one across the desert from Korosko, which had been suggested in a paper by Admiral Sir Cooper Key, at the Admiralty, in the event of any expedition being necessary at all. But this did not commend itself to Hartington who, in this matter, relied on Wolseley's advice.

On 10 June the Cabinet again discussed the proposed railway and agreed to "make some preparations for putting the port of Suakin into a condition to receive the heavy stores required either for a railway or for an expedition".[29]

Meanwhile, Hartington, on 15 May, after the Censure debate, had circulated a note to the Cabinet proposing the setting-up of a committee consisting of himself, Northbrook and "any other member of the Cabinet who may wish to join", together with Wolseley and other military and naval experts. "We should decide in the first instance on the route to be adopted and, of course subject to the approval of the Cabinet, on any immediate measures to be taken."[30] Gladstone, more than ever determined to fight a delaying action, replied on 16 May, suggesting that the first thing would be "for the War Office to go to work and frame its estimates, taking care . . . to frame them . . . so as to bring out the full charge. Also, ought there not to be a medical report on the degree of risk to life which will have to be encountered?"[31]

In the end, owing partly to the "red herring" of the railway, no committee was set up and, on 21 June, after more than a month's delay, the Cabinet, in Dilke's words, "decided to wait ten days before settling anything and to see whether we heard from Gordon in reply to the silly questions which had been asked".[32]

Nothing had been heard from Khartum for over two months. There had been no telegraphic communication with Berber since about the middle of May and, on 27 June, news arrived in London that Berber had been taken by Mahdist forces on 26 May. The Mudir, Husain Khalifa and Cuzzi, Gordon's agent, had been made prisoners. This seemed to dispose of any remote possibility that Gordon might be able to evacuate by his own efforts.

On 1 July Hartington wrote to Gladstone[33] asking for "a short Cabinet to consider the question of military preparations for the Sudan before the Conference [i.e. the International Conference on Egyptian finances] and the Franchise Bill[34] again absorb the whole attention of the Cabinet". He complained that he did not "know the mind or intention of the Government in respect of the relief of General Gordon", and that he might "at any moment be placed in a most painful position from the want of some clear indication of what the policy of the Government is". After referring to the authority he had received from the Cabinet for making some preparations at Suakin, he pointed out that "towards the construction or preparations for the railway or for the organisation of the force to protect it, or for the organisation of an expedition, nothing has been done. We may receive any day news from Khartum which may show the necessity of an expedition for Gordon's release; the time is approaching when military operations would be possible as regards climate; but I may have to tell the Cabinet that, for want of preparations, nothing can be done." Gladstone circulated this letter to the Cabinet with the remark that "the laying of any rails for a permanent way would be a great and serious measure, especially if, as I incline to think, the chances of an expedition thus far are not increasing". Once more the railway had proved a useful red herring.

On 15 July Hartington wrote to Granville[35] complaining of the Cabinet's refusal to come to any decision about a relief expedition and told him: "I cannot be responsible for military policy in Egypt under such conditions." With his letter he enclosed a memorandum of a meeting he had had with Northbrook, Baring and Wolseley. In this memorandum it was pointed out that no messages had been received from Gordon for over three months and that "there is little hope that news can now be received direct from him. It is to be feared that this silence points to a close investment of Khartum", and that "the possibility, even if he were likely to avail himself of it, of peacefully withdrawing from Khartum is not open to General Gordon, and the Cabinet must decide whether he is to be left to his fate or rescued by force". It was pointed out that "the delay in deciding any action on the Berber–Suakin route" had rendered the construction of the railway academic from the point of view of Gordon's relief, owing to the capture of Berber and the concentration of Osman Digna's forces near Suakin. Furthermore, "a movement by Suakin and Berber will do little to protect or tranquillise Upper Egypt. On the other hand, a movement by the Nile to Khartum, or to whatever point might be necessary to secure the retreat of Gordon, would, incidentally, completely protect Upper Egypt. Notwithstanding all the difficulties of the river route, Lord Wolseley is confident that a force of 6,000 or 7,000 men collected at Wadi Halfa on 1 October could reach Khartum in three months. . . . But the first and indispensable condition of forming an opinion on any of the military questions is a decision whether Gordon is to be rescued or abandoned."

The following day, 16 July, there was a Cabinet meeting at which, according to Dilke, "Hartington . . . gave up the Berber–Suakin route and pressed for a decision as to an immediate expedition by the Nile. He was supported by the Lord Chancellor [Selborne], Northbrook, Carlingford and Dodson. Mr. Gladstone, Harcourt and Childers opposed."[36] Dilke also recorded that he and Chamberlain "opposed a large expedition by the Nile and supported a small expedition under the control of the Navy".[37]

Gladstone, Harcourt and Childers, with Granville, as usual, waiting to see which way the cat jumped, were quite determined that there should be no expedition. Their objection was based on the conviction that most of those who were advocating one were really advocating the reconquest of the Sudan and that the question of Gordon's relief was being used by the Opposition, by the Tory Press, by the War Office, by some members of the Cabinet, and by Gordon himself, as a stick with which to coerce the Cabinet into reversing the policy of evacuation. In the circumstances they probably considered that the death or captivity of Gordon and Stewart, and a possible massacre in Khartum, were lesser evils than sending a relief force, and they may genuinely have thought that Gordon's own conduct had relieved them of any responsibility for doing so. But it was politically impossible, after Hartington's speech in the Censure debate, and even after some rather equivocal public pledges made by Gladstone himself, to take this line either publicly in Parliament or privately in Cabinet. So they continued, against all the evidence, to cling to the fiction that Gordon was in no danger and that he could save himself and his companions if he wanted to. In short, a good case for not sending an expedition became more and more discredited by the march of events, and had finally to be abandoned, because of the assumed political necessity for resting this case on untenable premises.

These premises became even more untenable when, on 20 July, a message arrived in London from Egerton[38] to say that the Mudir of Dongola had received a message from Gordon dated 23 June to the effect that Khartum was holding out and asking for news of the expected relief expedition. This message was discussed at a Cabinet meeting on 22 July when, according to Dilke,[39] Gladstone wanted to investigate the possibility of sending Zubair to Khartum in order to avoid sending a British expedition. Nothing was done about this but, on 24 July, a telegram was sent to Egerton for Gordon.[40] After referring to previous messages it stated: "H.M.G. continue to be anxious to learn from himself his views and position so that, if danger has arisen or is likely to arise . . . they may be in a position to take measures accordingly." This message reached Gordon on 25 November, after he had sent his cipher downstream with Stewart. He was therefore unable to read it, recording in his Journal that "I am sure we are deprived of a treat."

Gladstone's revival of the Zubair proposal was probably the result of a conversation the previous day with Gordon's brother,

Sir Henry, who had told him: (1) Expedition or no expedition, Gordon would not leave Khartum without leaving some sort of government behind him; (2) Gordon considered himself bound, not so much to the garrison as to the civil population of Khartum; (3) the Nile was impossible for an expedition and Suakin–Berber was the only possible route; (4) Gordon could go south to the Equator any time he pleased; (5) an expedition to Khartum would not be what Gordon wanted and would only have to stay there; and (6) the only solution was to send Zubair. Sir Henry had expressed much the same opinions as had been expressed by an anonymous "friend" of Gordon's in the *Contemporary Review* the previous month. It is not clear how Sir Henry, or the anonymous "friend", were in a position to form their opinions about conditions in the Sudan or about Gordon's state of mind. But Sir Henry's opinions were certainly welcome to Gladstone, who lost no time in sending them on to Granville for propagation to the rest of the Cabinet.[41]

On 25 July the Sudan was discussed again at a Cabinet meeting. Dilke recorded that "the issue was narrowed down to that of sending some sort of British force to or towards Dongola; this was supported by Hartington, the Chancellor, Derby, Northbrook, Carlingford, Dodson, Chamberlain and me, while on the other side were only Mr Gladstone, Harcourt and Kimberley. Lord Granville said nothing. By the stoutness of their resistance the three for the moment prevailed over the nine."[42]

But, at long last, there was a clear majority in the Cabinet in favour of a relief expedition, and Hartington felt able to act. On 29 July he circulated a memorandum to the Cabinet[43] stating that he wished "before Parliament is prorogued and it becomes absolutely impossible to do anything for the relief of Gordon, to bring the subject once more under the consideration of the Cabinet". He referred to Wolseley's memorandum giving reasons in favour of the Nile rather than the Suakin–Berber route and proceeded to give details of a plan prepared by Wolseley for the dispatch of a Brigade to Dongola by way of the Nile. He wrote that Wolseley's plan had been "examined . . . by three officers who accompanied Lord Wolseley on the Red River expedition" and that "these officers have reported . . . that a Brigade can easily be conveyed in small boats from Cairo to Dongola in the time stated by Lord Wolseley (to be in Dongola by about 1 November) and further that, should it be necessary to send a still larger force by water to Khartum, that operation will present no insuperable difficulty. They say that, if it be found necessary to take a fighting force to Khartum before the end of the year, or at the end of January, the Nile will, in their opinion, be found the easiest, the safest, and immensely the cheapest line of advance to adopt." After giving details of costs, etc., he concluded: "I have not entered into the question whether it is or is not probable that General Gordon can leave Khartum without assistance. As we know absolutely nothing, any opinion on this subject can only be guesswork. But I do not see how it is possible to redeem the pledges which we have given, if the necessity should be proved to exist, without some such preparations and measures as those which I now suggest."

On the same day Lord Selborne, who was the only Cabinet Minister apart from Hartington who had been consistently in favour of making preparations for an expedition, also circulated a memorandum[44] in which he powerfully defended Gordon's conduct throughout his mission and expressed his aversion to "acting towards a public servant . . . who has accepted at our instance a mission of extraordinary difficulty as if we have no real sense of the responsibilities we have publicly acknowledged and as if something (of which I can see no evidence at all) had happened to absolve us from those responsibilities".

On 31 July Hartington, writing to Granville, and referring to his and to Selborne's memoranda, told him: "I, with you and Northbrook, are more responsible than any other members of the Cabinet for sending out Gordon, but I consider that I had the largest share of the responsibility. I gave the assurances in the debate on the Vote of Censure which certainly had some effect on the decision. I must attach my own meaning to those assurances and no explanation by anyone else can absolve me from what I consider to be their obligation. I think this is a different sort of question from the numerous ones on which I have differed from the Cabinet. It is a question of personal honour and good faith and I don't see how I can yield on it."[45] In reply, Granville agreed that declarations made in Parliament by Hartington, by Gladstone and by himself "commit us to a certain degree but not as far as I gather you believe".[46] Granville was never able to believe that anything he said, wrote or did ever committed him to anything.

Hartington's letter, which was circulated to the Cabinet, was intended to be, and was regarded as, a threat of resignation. Gladstone minuted his "strong conviction that to send an expedition either to Dongola or Khartum at the present time would be to act in the teeth of evidence as to Gordon which, however imperfect, is far from being trivial, and would be a grave and dangerous error".[47] But he recognised the nature of Hartington's threat which, as he told Granville,[48] "created a very formidable state of things". He went on: "I do not think the evidence as to Gordon's position requires or justifies in itself military preparations for the contingency of a military expedition. There are, however, preparations of various kinds which might be made and which are matters simply of cost and do not include necessary consequences in point of policy." In Gladstonese, this was, if not a surrender, at all events a withdrawal to new positions. On 5 August, just before Parliament adjourned for the summer recess, Gladstone himself asked for and obtained from the Commons a grant of £300,000 "to enable H.M.G. to undertake operations for the relief of General Gordon should they become necessary, and to make certain preparations in respect thereof".

CHAPTER EIGHT

THE RELIEF EXPEDITION

THE WAR OFFICE immediately set about making preparations for an expedition on the lines already laid down by Wolseley, which envisaged sending a brigade of British troops, with supporting arms, up the Nile to Dongola, with the prospect of advancing from there to Khartum should this prove necessary. General Earle, Stephenson's second-in-command in Egypt, was to command the expedition, with General Buller, who was sent out from the War Office, as his Chief of Staff. General Stephenson, as G.O.C. in Egypt, was to be in supreme command. Difficulties soon arose as a result of Stephenson, supported by the naval officers who had for some time been surveying the marine problems presented by the Nile route, disagreeing with Wolseley's plan, based on his experience in command of the Red River expedition in Canada in 1870, for using specially-made boats sent out from England, and Canadian boatmen recruited in Canada, for negotiating the cataracts and rapids between Wadi Halfa and Dongola. Stephenson and the naval experts preferred to rely on native boats and local boatmen. (Stephenson, apart from disagreeing with Wolseley's Nile plans in detail, was still in favour of the Suakin–Berber as against the Nile route). The War Office insisted on adherence to Wolseley's plan on the ground that although "Stephenson and the people in Egypt . . . can get to Dongola by their plan . . . it is doubtful whether they can get back again even from Dongola this winter and . . . if we should be forced to go to Khartum, it is certain that they could not get there and back again during the winter."[1] Hartington, because of the "risk of failure in unwilling hands", and because "it is not fair either to Wolseley who has proposed, or to me who has adopted, or to Stephenson who has to execute, the operation, that it should be entrusted to men who do not believe in it rather than those who do",[2] eventually decided that Wolseley should go to Egypt to take over the supreme command of the expedition from Stephenson.

On 15 August Hartington told Dilke that he had already spent £750,000 out of the £300,000 sanctioned for the expedition.[3] But Gladstone was still fighting a rearguard action against sending an expedition at all, and insisting that all which had been sanctioned was money for preparations for an expedition in case one was needed. On 18 August, before Stephenson's supercession by Wolseley had been decided on, Hartington told Gladstone that Stephenson "will shortly be in a position to direct the advance of a small force . . . from Wadi Halfa to Dongola or Debbeh", and asked him whether he saw "any political reasons for delaying this step" which he regarded as "extremely desirable".[4] Next day Gladstone replied that "a movement of British troops to Dongola . . . would be a step of great political importance and clearly could not be decided on without reference to members of the Cabinet. . . . If the time has come when a decision must be taken whether we go to Dongola or not, then I think the Cabinet should know what force you propose to send there and, most of all, for what purpose it is to go." "May we reasonably believe that Gordon, if he thinks fit, can make his way to Dongola? This I can believe probable. But will he do it?" He went on to suggest an idea adumbrated by Northbrook that Mustafa Pasha Yawir, the Mudir of Dongola, who had impressed the Cabinet by his apparent loyalty to Cairo and ability to keep order in his province, should be asked to "play the part of Zubair and take over Khartum, so putting an end to this most perplexing and distressing affair". He thought that such a plan would be "better forwarded by money, and perhaps material, than by a British force" which he feared might involve "the very serious danger of stirring a religious war", and asked Hartington to discuss the matter with Northbrook, who was shortly due to go to Egypt for conversations in connection with the financial situation. (The International Conference on Egyptian finances had recently broken up without coming to any agreement.) Gladstone concluded his letter: "Would it be quite fair to the Cabinet, or to certain members of it, to ask them to take a step in advance, without a plan, that they might know what they were about and be assured that they were not about to become, unawares, the slaves of Gordon's (probably) rebellious ideas?"[5]

On 22 August Hartington told Gladstone about the difficulties between Wolseley and Stephenson and proposed that Wolseley should go out to Egypt and take over the supreme command.[6] He also told Northbrook and Granville. Granville, in reply,[7] objected on the ground that this would make an expedition inevitable and told Hartington that he could "hardly conceive Gladstone consenting". But Gladstone did consent, and Wolseley, travelling with Northbrook and Baring, immediately left for Egypt.[8]

On 26 August Hartington wrote to Gladstone in reply to his letter of 19 August and told him: (*a*) that he agreed that "all possible use should be made of the Mudir of Dongola" who, "by an extraordinary piece of good fortune appears to be loyal and to a certain extent powerful", but that "there is no reason to suppose he has any influence in Khartum", and (*b*) that "we need not be afraid of raising a religious war by sending troops to Dongola", since the Mudir of Dongola himself, Gladstone's new *deus ex machina*, had asked for them. He went on to say that nobody in the Cabinet "except Harcourt who objects to everything including the vote of credit", would object to sending troops to Dongola, but "if . . . I have to wait . . . to collect the opinions of Ministers, subject perhaps, in the case of difference, to the delay of summoning a Cabinet" (members of the Cabinet were at this time scattered all over England and Scotland), "I despair of acquitting myself of the responsibility which will be placed on me by my colleagues and by Parliament". He went on to say that the preparations which had already been made were "of such a character as will make it almost absurd not to send an expedition when they are complete".[9]

By this time the question of an expedition had passed effectively out of the Cabinet's hands and into those of Wolseley. Henceforth, such delays as there were, were due to military and not to political reasons. Wolseley, with Northbrook and Baring, arrived in Cairo on 9 September. As is the way of military commanders, he immediately asked the War Office for more troops. As this demand was supported by Northbrook, the War Office agreed and told Gladstone afterwards.[10]

Wolseley had received no written instructions before leaving London. Officially, no expedition had yet been agreed to by the

Cabinet. But Hartington had told him verbally (*a*) that he was not to undertake any expedition except in case of absolute necessity, and (*b*) that he was not to send more than a small force beyond Wadi Halfa and not to send any force at all beyond Dongola without instructions from H.M.G. He also told him that the object of the expedition, if it should take place, would be "to enable General Gordon and Colonel Stewart, with the Egyptian garrison at Khartum, to leave that place if it should appear that they cannot do so by any other means".[11]

This was not what Hartington himself would have liked, but what he believed to be the policy of the Government. His own opinion, as he told Granville,[12] was "that if it is necessary to go to Khartum, and if that operation is successfully accomplished, it will be found desirable and necessary to keep Khartum, Berber and Dongola in one form or another. I have for some time thought that our decision to abandon these places was a mistake."

Later, after consultations between Wolseley, Northbrook and Baring in Cairo, draft instructions were sent to London for approval[13] and, after approval, issued on 8 October to Wolseley, who, by that time, was in Wadi Halfa. In these instructions Wolseley was told: "The primary object of the expedition . . . is to bring away General Gordon and Colonel Stewart from Khartum. When that object has been secured, no further offensive operations of any kind are to be undertaken. Although you are not precluded from advancing as far as Khartum, should you consider such a step essential to ensure the safe retreat of General Gordon and Colonel Stewart, you should bear in mind that H.M.G. is desirous to limit the sphere of your military operations as much as possible. They rely on you, therefore, not to advance any further southwards than is absolutely necessary to attain the primary object of the expedition." The instructions also authorised Wolseley to "use your best endeavours to ensure the safe retreat of the Egyptian troops who constitute the Khartum garrison, and of such of the civilian employees of Khartum, together with their families, as may wish to return to Egypt". "The policy which H.M.G. desires to pursue is to establish a government at Khartum . . . which would be wholly independent of Egypt", although the Egyptian Government would be prepared to pay a "reasonable subsidy" to "any chief sufficiently powerful to keep order along the Nile valley from Wadi Halfa to Khartum". No attempt was to be made to rescue any of the garrisons south of Khartum.

The Cabinet also decided that Wolseley should assume supreme command in the Sudan and that Gordon should come under his orders. On 20 September Granville telegraphed Baring[14] requesting Wolseley to take "the earliest opportunity of informing Gordon that H.M.G. expect that he will obey Wolseley's orders". He also requested Baring to send a message to Gordon to the same effect, and suggested that the Khedive did the same, adding, characteristically, that "perhaps this should be deferred to avoid publicity".

In the event, the Khedive, moved by Baring, sent Gordon a message in Arabic to this effect on 21 September—the only intimation on the subject which Gordon ever received. This message, after congratulating Gordon on his courage, etc., went on to tell him that "British troops will shortly be at Dongola", that "Colonel Chermside, Governor of Suakin [a British officer in the Egyptian Army] is in charge of negotiations with the tribes about Kassala, and Major Kitchener [another British officer in the Egyptian Army who, for some weeks, had been at Dongola] is in charge of negotiations at Dongola and hopes shortly to communicate with you. Under these circumstances, it is necessary so far to revise the Firman granted to you and to limit your powers as Governor-General to Khartum, Sennaar and the immediate neighbourhood of Berber. You are not without further instructions to send steamers or any expedition up the White Nile for the relief of Bahr-al-Ghazal or Equatoria garrisons. You are to make every endeavour to bring the Sennaar garrison back to Khartum. You will receive H.M.G.'s instructions through Baring and Wolseley."[15]

This message reached Gordon on 25 November. As the result of a translator's error, deliberate or otherwise, Gordon does not appear to have understood its purport. It is apparent from his Journal that he regarded it as a decision by H.M.G. to reverse their policy of evacuation and to appoint British officers to govern various parts of the Sudan. He also gathered the impression that Wolseley and Baring were coming up to Khartum together to "settle the question of the Sudan" and derived some pleasure from the thought of Baring "bumping along on camelback".

The Cabinet's decision to demote Gordon was largely the result of an access of anger due to a message which had just been received from him. Up to 17 September, only three messages had been received from Gordon over the previous four months. The first, through the Mudir of Dongola, saying that Khartum was still holding out and asking for news of the relief expedition, had been sent from Khartum on 23 June and received in London on 20 July. The second, sent from Khartum on 13 July, and received at Dongola on 25 July, was sent to London on 29 July.[16] It stated that "Khartum and Sennaar are still holding out; we have 3,000 soldiers in Khartum and the Nile has risen." It also asked for details about "the expedition coming from Cairo". Major Kitchener, who arrived in Dongola on 3 August, was able to question the messenger, who told him that Gordon, Stewart and Power were all well, that no messages from outside had reached Khartum for some time, that there was still plenty of provisions, that the enemy had retreated from their first positions but were keeping up the siege. He estimated that the besieging forces amounted to about 16,000 men.[17] The third communication consisted of a batch of five messages received at Dongola towards the end of August, but these had all been sent from Khartum during April and contained nothing new.[18]

Then, on 18 September, a message sent by Gordon from Khartum on 23 August and received in Cairo via Dongola, was received in London.[19] This message, which was addressed to the Khedive, Nubar and Baring, read: "*Re* evacuation of the Sudan: (1) English troops must be sent to the Sudan. (2) Zubair Pasha must also be appointed with assistance and a salary of £8,000 p.a. (3) If the Sultan would send 200,000 of his troops[20] the Sudan could be handed over to him. (4) If no part of this scheme is carried out, and if the rebels attack the people of the Sudan and kill them, you will be responsible for their lives and salaries. (5) The expenses and pay of the soldiers in the Sudan amount to £1,500 per day. (6) The troops in Dongola, Khartum, Bahr-al-Ghazal, Equatoria, Kassala and Sennaar are more than 30,000. (7) You have now become responsible to these troops for the sum of £300,000. (8) I hope shortly to take Berber. I have already sent Stewart Pasha, the English Consul [Power] and the French Consul [Herbin] with regular troops and Bashibazouks for that purpose.[21] (9) I have already written to you that I should send Egyptian troops to take Berber[22] and to occupy it, and that these troops would be under your protection, but fearing that your reinforcements would not be sent, and fearing that you might pay no intention to the troops I shall send, and naturally fearing that a panic might occur among the troops, I thought it more advisable that, after taking the town, they should remain in it for 15 days and burn it and then return to Khartum. Stewart Pasha will proceed to Dongola. Then I will send to the Equator to withdraw the people who are there. After that it will be impossible for Mohamed Ahmed [i.e. the Mahdi] to come here and, please God, he will meet his death at the hands of the Sudanese. If the Sultan's troops come they should come via Dongola and via Kassala. You should give them £300,000. Mohamed Ali Pasha[23] is the only person I can rely on here to replace me."

This message was received in London on 18 September. It had been "leaked" to the Press in Cairo and more or less accurate summaries appeared in the English Press on the same day. It was almost immediately followed by the texts of two messages sent by Gordon to the Khedive which arrived in Cairo on 18 September. These messages were undated but appeared to have been sent by Gordon a little before the message which had arrived the previous day.[24] The first message read: "On my arrival in Khartum I found it impossible to withdraw the soldiers and employees to Egypt on account of the insurrection of the Arabs and the communications being interrupted. I therefore asked that I might be helped with some reinforcements. Hitherto they have not arrived and there occurred the events which have taken place at Berber. I had previously asked for attention to be paid to that town. I will consider in what manner it can be recovered from the rebels and in what manner troops can be stationed there for a period of two months just before high Nile. After that time, if troops do not come, the same will occur again as occurred before and the troops will be destroyed. Is it right that I should have been sent to Khartum with only seven followers, after the destruction of Hicks' army, and that no attention should have been paid to me since communications were cut? . . . I hope you will send a telegram showing clearly the present situation . . . and that it will be in Arabic so that the inhabitants may read it. The telegrams that come in English cipher do not say what their intentions are. They only ask for information from us and the result is a useless loss of time. Thus, through having so often promised to the people of Khartum that assistance would come, we are now become in their eyes like liars. . . . If the intention is to charge me to hold the Sudan only with the Sudanese troops, I will do all that I can do, although without money. It is, however, impossible to resist with them the thousands of men with the false Mahdi. It would be best to negotiate with the Porte for the dispatch of Imperial troops belonging to the Sultan. They should be given £200,000 for expenses. Here I am in Khartum as a hostage and a guardian . . . I hope that, as long as I remain here when the Sultan's troops arrive, the people of the Sudan will be unable (unwilling?) to resist them and will not fire a single rifle and that peace and quiet will return. It is impossible to leave Khartum unless a regular government is established on the part of one of the Powers. I will look after the soldiers of Equatoria, Bahr-al-Ghazal and Darfur although it may cost me my life. Perhaps H.M.G. will be displeased at the advice I have given. The people of the Sudan are also displeased with me on account of my fighting against them and on account of their not attaining their object in following the Mahdi. I shall send Stewart and Power with the soldiers to open communication with Dongola and to carry out necessary measures in connection with the Sudan." The second message informed the Khedive that it had been impossible for him to publish the evacuation Firman as, if he had, the people "would think there is no government but that of the Mahdi". "If it is still intended to abandon the Sudan and to withdraw the soldiers and employees and if the news had become known to the Mahdi, he would have left Kordofan and come to Khartum with a large army and have captured it. When it was at last known that the Sudan would not be abandoned and that troops were coming to Khartum, the Mahdi did not move from his position and he remains there until now. I hope that on the arrival of troops at Khartum it will be possible at once to stop all the movements in the Gezira [i.e. the area south of Khartum between the two Niles) and restore safety as before. . . . The Nile route is now the most important object. The prosperity of Egypt can only follow the restoration of peace in the Sudan. Seeing that the rebels have already captured Berber, I intend to send the necessary troops to retake it and re-establish communication with Dongola and Egypt."[25]

These messages confirmed Gladstone and Granville, and some other members of the Cabinet, in their conviction that Gordon had never had any intention of carrying out the evacuation policy, and that he had succeeded in "conning" the Government into sending a relief expedition for the purpose of implementing a policy which he was trying to impose on them and to which they were resolutely opposed. Gladstone told Granville that Gordon's message of 23 August to the Khedive, Nubar and Baring "beats everything I have ever seen. I called him at the outset inspired and mad, but the madness is now uppermost."[26] Even Hartington, writing to Granville on 24 September,[27] told him that he was "utterly unable to understand" Gordon's messages. But he declared himself unable to accept Gladstone's view, shared by Granville, that they proved that Gordon was disobeying his instructions. "We have no proof that he could have done anything different from what he has done and is doing, or that he has wilfully disobeyed or disregarded our instructions. We knew that the dispatch of the Egyptian employees, invalids, etc., from Khartum was followed by the rising of the country between Khartum and Berber and by the attack on and fall of Berber. It is not probable that, since these events, he could have left Khartum without sacrificing the lives of himself and of those who followed him, and also of those whom he left behind. He had no alternative but to hold on to Khartum and to keep the insurgents at bay. We have no knowledge that even now he could make any movement of retreat without bringing down the tribes upon him and on the garrison. I think therefore that our troops must go on to Dongola at least. . . . If we are not in a position to say to him (as I do not think we are now), 'You must come away from Khartum with the garrison and inhabitants who want to come with you', I see no use in giving him further vague and general instructions. Neither do I think we can limit his action strictly to Khartum, disregarding the fate of the other garrisons in the Sudan. If it should thereafter appear that, by allowing Gordon to remain somewhat longer at Khartum and to follow up his successes, the whole of the Sudan might have been pacified or the garrisons peacefully withdrawn, and that this result has been prevented by our precipitate action, what excuse shall we have?"

Gladstone and Granville remained under the impression, derived from his messages, that Gordon, in the words of a Liberal newspaper[28], was "careering up and down the Nile, crying for the blood of the Mahdi, burning towns and slaying rebels to his heart's content". This was a grotesque misreading of the situation. Behind the erratic phrasing of Gordon's messages, there was a note of desperation. He did not know which, if any, of his messages had been received in Cairo and, since some of the messages from London which he had received indicated that help would be sent to him if he indicated that it was needed, he may reasonably have assumed that a relief expedition was on the way. In the light of his previous desire to liberate the Sudan from oppression, his request for Turkish troops was certainly illogical. But five months of being besieged and bombarded by the people he had come to liberate, spent in close companionship with the people he had come to liberate them from, had not unnaturally changed his point of view. Many members of the Cabinet were particularly outraged by Gordon's statement of his intention to burn Berber. In deference to their view, Baring instructed Kitchener to contact Stewart (who, Gordon had wrongly stated, had left Khartum for Berber by 23 August) and tell him that Berber was not to be burnt. The Khedive also, in his message to Gordon of 21 September, ordered him not to burn Berber. Since Berber was nothing but a collection of mud huts, H.M.G.'s anger and apprehension were somewhat excessive.

On 20 September two more messages from Gordon were received in Cairo via Dongola.[29] They were undated but appear to have been sent from Khartum about the end of July, some three weeks before the message about burning Berber which had caused so much alarm. In the first message, addressed to the Khedive, Nubar and Baring, Gordon acknowledged receipt of H.M.G.'s telegram of 23 April, which had reached him via Massawa, "asking me whether Khartum was in danger and as to the best route by which troops could be sent to me. I have already sent you my opinion by telegraph and I now inform you that to-day my soldiers have killed Ibrahim, the son of el-Obeid, and slain his followers north of Khartum. I also hope to overthrow the rebels west of Khartum and then there will be no more rebels left in the vicinity. I heard that the Mahdi was coming but he has not yet come. Khartum and Sennaar are all right. We have provisions for five months." The second message, addressed to the Khedive, told him that he was sending three Egyptian colonels with Egyptian troops to Berber and "from there they will proceed to Cairo". Another party of Egyptian troops would be sent to Berber and would remain there "until the reinforcements about which I have written to Cairo arrive there". He also told them that he was trying to withdraw the Egyptian garrison from Sennaar and that, when it arrived in Khartum, he would also send it to Berber, "because I do not want harm to happen to any of the Egyptian officers or soldiers. . . . The Sudanese troops are, however, accustomed to fighting in the Sudan." He went on to tell the Khedive that he wished for negotiations with the Sublime Porte "so that the necessary assistance may quickly be sent so as to . . . extinguish the flame of the false Mutamahdi[30] before it becomes difficult".

On 21 September a message was received in Cairo addressed to the Khedive from twenty-four Egyptian Army officers and eighteen civilian officials in Khartum. It was dated 18 August and was in the form of a petition asking for a speedy relief from the privations from which they were suffering.[31]

On 22 September Baring received a telegram from Kitchener in Dongola telling him (erroneously as it turned out) that Gordon's projected expedition to Berber had not left Khartum as Gordon was awaiting the return of a steamer from Sennaar.

"I have no fear that I can communicate with Stewart before he burns Berber." He also told Baring that he was trying to get news to Gordon about the relief expedition.[32]

On the same day, the French Consul-General in Cairo received an (apparently undated) message from Herbin, the French Consul in Khartum, telling him that he and Stewart were on the point of starting for Dongola, that they hoped to be in Berber by 15 September, that Khartum was once more in communication with Sennaar, and that the enemy round Khartum had retreated.[33] This message from Herbin was probably sent on or about 8 September—since he and Stewart actually left Khartum on 8 September—and was thus the latest news received from Khartum.

On 25 September Baring received news from Suakin that five letters from Gordon, addressed to himself, had just been received at Massawa. Of these, three were dated in April and the other other two on 30 and 31 July respectively. In the letter dated 30 July[34] Gordon referred to the queries addressed to him in Granville's telegram of 23 April, which he had only just received via Massawa. (As we have seen he sent another reply to these queries via Dongola which had reached Cairo on 20 September.) He told Baring, in reply to H.M.G.'s query about the "cause and intention" of his staying in Khartum, that "I stay in Khartum because the Arabs have shut us up and will not let us out." With regard to the implied criticism about the "pacific policy which was the purpose of his mission" he protested that "hostilities are far from being sought for, but we have no option, for retreat is impossible unless we abandon civil employees and their families, which the general feeling of the troops is against". He stated that he had issued paper money to the amount of £26,000 and that he had borrowed £50,000 from the merchants. He told Baring that "the troops and people are full of heart" but that he could not say the same of the Europeans. In reply to H.M.G.'s query about routes, he stated: "I have told you that the one from Wadi Halfa along the right bank of the Nile to Berber is the best and, had not Berber fallen, would have been a picnic. The other route is from Senheit to Kassala and to Abu Haraz on the Blue Nile, which would be safe to Kassala."He concluded: "I will not leave Khartum until suitably replaced. . . . Before abandoning the Sudan I must remove the Egyptian population; even if the road was open the people would not let me leave unless a government was established. My stay is indefinite unless you send Zubair with an annual subsidy or let the Sultan have the Sudan back."

The letter of 31 July[35] was, Baring commented to Granville,[36] "more rational than anything he has written since he arrived in Khartum". Neatly written on both sides of a small sheet of notepaper in Gordon's own precise, very legible, handwriting, it read: "We continue to drive the Arabs up the Blue Nile and hope to open the road to Sennaar in 8 days or less and to recapture a small steamer lost by Saleh Bey. We then hope to send an expedition to surprise and capture Berber. It is a *sine qua non* that you send me Zubair, otherwise my stay here is indefinite, and you should send £50,000 to Dongola to be forwarded to Berber if we take it. River begins to fall in say 4 months and by that time you must either let the Sultan take over the Sudan or send Zubair with a yearly subsidy. DV we will go down to Berber and take it with Egyptian troops, so that they will be on their way home, and I shall send Stewart who, although he does everything I could possibly wish him to do, and is a good honest fellow, yet his heart is not in the matter and he does not like the people as I do. We hope DV to capture the two steamers which we lost at Berber when it fell. . . . The Equator and Bahr-al-Ghazal provinces can DV be relieved later and the troops brought here. As to Darfur, it must be thought of afterwards, for we do not know if it still holds out. As for Kordofan, I hope and believe the Mahdi has his hands full. I would evacuate Sennaar if it was possible, but I do not think it is, and also the moral effect of our evacuation would be fatal to our future success, while we have not the food to feed the refugees who would come here. If we open the road to Sennaar from here we could cut the Arab movement in two by the Blue Nile. I repeat that I have no wish to retain the country; my sole desire is to restore the prestige of the Government in order to get out the garrisons and to put some ephemeral government in power in order to get out."

The picture of the situation in Khartum at the end of July

as given by Gordon in these two letters, was supplemented by a series of messages from Power, which arrived at Massawa with Gordon's two letters, and which were published in *The Times* on 30 September. Power wrote: "We have been now five months closely besieged and can at best hold out but two months longer. The soldiers and people live in hopes of English relief, as since last May there are daily reports of English troops advancing from Dongola and Kassala. The Arabs have strong forts with cannon along the river and they push the siege as vigorously as ever. General Gordon has protected all the steamers with bullet-proof plates of soft wood and iron, and on the six armoured barges has put up castles twenty feet high giving a double line of fire. We have no fears of a rising in the town as, before the siege, 8,000 to 10,000 men left and joined the rebels. The troops, to be loyal, must be paid and General Gordon is badly off for money, none of that which left Cairo for his use having reached Khartum. He has issued £50,000 worth of paper money. Food is distributed daily to the poor." Power then recounted various episodes in the siege since March, of which the following were the most noteworthy:

"March 23. Hasan and Said Pashas were put to death for treachery in the battle of 16 March in which we lost 350 killed and wounded.

"April 16–20. Attacks by the rebels on the Palace from the villages opposite. Fearful loss of life to the Arabs from the mines put down by Gordon.

"April 27. We heard of the surrender of Saleh Bey at Messalamia to the rebels with 50 shiploads of food, 70 boxes of cartridges, 2,020 rifles and a steamer.

"May 6. Heavy attack from the Arabs at the Blue Nile end of the works; great loss of life from the mines we had placed at Buri.

"May 7. Great attack from a village opposite; nine mines were exploded there and we afterwards heard that they killed 115 rebels. The Arabs kept up a fire all day. Col. Stewart, with two splendidly-directed shots from a Krupp 20-pounder, drove them out of their principal position.

"May 25. Col. Stewart, while working on a mitrailleuse at the Palace, was wounded by rebel fire but is now quite well.

"May 26. During the expedition up the White Nile Saati Bey put a shell into an Arab magazine. There was a great explosion, sixty shells going off.

"During May and June steamer expeditions were made daily under Saati Bey. Our loss was slight and much cattle were captured.

"June 25. Mr Cuzzi, who is with the rebels, came to our lines and told us of the fall of Berber.

"June 30. Saati Bey captured 40 ardebs of corn from the rebels and killed 200 of them.

"July 10. Saati Bey, having burnt Kalakala and three villages, attacked Gatarneb but, with three of his officers, was killed.

"July 29. We beat the rebels out of Buri on the Blue Nile, capturing munitions and 80 rifles. The steamers advanced to Eilafun clearing 13 rebel forts and breaking 2 cannon. Since the siege began our loss has been under 700 killed."

In what proved to be his last message, dated 31 July, Power referred to the "dispatch which arrived the day before yesterday" (the contents of Granville's telegram of 23 April), as a result of which, "all hope of relief by our Government is at an end, so, when our provisions, which we have at a stretch for two months, are eaten, we must fall, nor is there any chance, with the soldiers we have and the great crowd of women and children, etc., of our being able to cut our way through the Arabs. We have not steamers for all, and it is only from the steamers that we can meet the rebels."

By the end of September, therefore, the Cabinet, and Wolseley, and the British public, had a fair idea of the position in Khartum at the end of July, although Power was much more pessimistic than Gordon over the amount of provisions left. Gordon had estimated five months and Power only two. There can be no doubt that Gordon knew of the contents of Power's messages and had connived at, and possibly instigated, their pessimism as a means of using the pressure of public opinion in England to expedite the dispatch of the relief force. There was nothing illegitimate or unreasonable about this, however much it might have annoyed the Government. It appeared probable that Khartum could hold out until about the end of

December and that, so long as the Nile remained high enough, which was until about the end of November, communication by river would be possible between Khartum and Berber and Khartum and Sennaar. (This meant that it might be possible to augment the stock of provisions in Khartum by bringing grain in from Sennaar, which was in the centre of a grain-growing area.) It was certain that there was no possibility of the garrison of Khartum, and still less the Egyptian inhabitants, being able to extricate themselves without Zubair, or a British or Turkish relief expedition. At the end of July Gordon, speaking with his official voice, seems to have thought that sending Zubair alone might be sufficient, although, speaking with his unofficial voice through Power, he obviously did not. From his messages sent during August, which had been received earlier, it is apparent that, as well as Zubair, he considered that a British or a Turkish relief force would be necessary. Since he was referring to the possibility of taking Berber, it did not appear that the military situation had deteriorated between his letter to Baring of 31 July and his message of 23 August. But Gordon's patience and temper certainly had. They may have been tried beyond endurance by the contents of Granville's telegram of 17 May, which had reached him sometime during August. This may explain the difference in tone between his letters to Baring at the end of July and his message of 23 August.

By the end of September, when the British Government were in possession of all this information, the relief expedition was in being and about to begin its advance into the Sudan. But there was never any expectation that it would be able to be in Khartum before the end of the year, by which time, according to Gordon's latest estimate, his provisions would have been exhausted. Wolseley, soon after his arrival in Egypt, wrote to his wife about "shaking hands with Gordon near Khartum about 31st January next".[37] At the end of August, Egerton, just before leaving Cairo, had written, "The boat expedition will take up too much time; if it hadn't been for the infernal plan of those Red River men, we would in a day or two have had a Brigade at Dongola—for everything was ready for it, stores up the river and men handy."[38]

Wolseley was a safe and sound, rather than a dashing, commander, a meticulous administrator and a fighter of carefully-prepared, set-piece battles which he felt sure of winning. He was a General who liked to have a secure line of communications behind him and a carefully-reconnoitred line of advance in front. He was not the man to lead a race against time into the interior of Africa. He was retarded by his insistence on having specially-made boats from England and specially-trained boatmen from Canada instead of relying on local facilities. He was also delayed by the incompetence of his Chief-of-Staff, who failed to arrange for sufficient coal for steamers taking supplies up the Nile to Wadi Halfa.[39] But the most serious delay arose from the tardiness of the Cabinet in authorising preparations for the expedition. From about the end of September the Nile started to fall and it became progressively more difficult to haul the boats over the cataracts and rapids up-stream of Wadi Halfa. For this, the politicians and not the soldiers were responsible. Paper plans worked out by the War Office were ready to put into immediate operation as soon as the necessary credit had been voted by Parliament at the beginning of August. But, by then, it was too late to take full advantage of the season of high Nile for conveying men and stores rapidly to Dongola.

After his arrival in Cairo in September, Northbrook, in effect, became the Cabinet Minister principally responsible for events in the Sudan. On 8 October, in the light of the various messages which had been received from Gordon, and after telegraphic consultations with his Cabinet colleagues, he wrote a long letter to Gordon[40] from a Nile steamer on which he was making a tour of Upper Egypt. Gordon never received this letter, which was captured by the Mahdi's forces en route, but it serves to show the mind of the Cabinet at the time. After telling Gordon about his own mission to Egypt, Northbrook proceeded: "It is not within my mission to propose any changes in the decision at which the Government arrived before you left England, i.e. that Egypt should give up the government of the Sudan and that H.M.G. should not undertake any responsibility which would involve any further interference in its affairs. The expedition under Wolseley . . . is not sent for the purpose of defeating the Mahdi but only of enabling you and the Egyptian garrison of Khartum, with the civilian employees, within reasonable limits, to return to Egypt. I hope, owing to the favourable turn which affairs have taken, that the expedition will not have to go to Khartum." (Such indications as there were of a "favourable turn" do not seem to have amounted to more than the facts Gordon had held out for so long and that the Mudir of Dongola had remained loyal.)

After a little "soft soap", and the intimation that the Queen had expressed a wish to award him the G.C.B., Northbrook referred to the "paramount importance" of "making some speedy arrangement by which the Eastern Sudan may be settled in such a manner as to re-open trade and possess some government even if . . . only ephemeral". (Cf. this with Northbrook's subsequent remark about Gordon's "hankering after the 'ignis fatuus'" of arranging for a settled government.)[41] On the subject of Zubair, Northbrook defended the Cabinet's decision in March on the ground, *inter alia*, that "at that time the power of the Mahdi was supposed to be greater than it turned out to be". (There was no ground for this assertion except for the fact that Gordon had not yet been overwhelmed by the Mahdi. In any case, Northbrook, writing to Baring at the time, had given public opinion as the only reason for the Cabinet's rejection of Zubair.) He then went on: "Some of the considerations which affected our decision and public opinion at the time have somewhat changed. Your life will be safe from Zubair; the power of the Mahdi is diminishing, the idea of an army marching on Egypt from the Sudan is a bugbear. . . ." On the other hand, Northbrook pointed out, Zubair was still suspected of communicating with the Mahdi and, on the whole, his employment was still regarded as undesirable, although "I do not say that [it] is entirely out of the question." He told Gordon that he must "set aside altogether" the idea of Turkish troops. "The Sultan is quite hopeless for action of any sort. . . . He has no money and we would not lend him any for the purpose. H.M.G. would rather leave the Sudan alone than help the Turks to conquer it." With regard to the possibility of a successor government, Northbrook expressed the view that "the Mudir of Dongola seems to be a possible man". (The Mudir of Dongola was Northbrook's particular "ignis fatuus".) "The plan we should like to see carried out is that some Ruler should be placed at Khartum who might also hold Berber and Dongola—or separate Rulers for each district—and that he or they should receive a moderate subsidy from Egypt on condition of keeping peace, opening trade and abolishing the slave trade." (This of course is precisely what Gordon had proposed eight and a half months previously when asking for Zubair.)

It is apparent from this letter that the Cabinet, or some members of it, were still clinging to the illusion that the relief force would not have to advance beyond Dongola, that the Mahdi and his armies would somehow melt away, that Gordon and the Khartum garrison and the civilian employees, "within reasonable limits", might, by some feat of legerdemain, be able to get away from Khartum, and that the Mudir of Dongola, or someone else acceptable to Mr Forster, might be installed in Khartum and "abolish the slave trade".

It is amusing to record that Northbrook, on his return to England from his financial mission to Egypt, was treated by his Cabinet colleagues in much the same way as he, together with most of them, had been treating Gordon for months. That is to say, his recommendations were rejected and he was accused of having exceeded his instructions. In complaining about this, he was to refer to "the sacrifice I had made in undertaking the mission at Mr Gladstone's earnest request . . . when the Government was in a difficulty".[42] There are sacrifices and sacrifices.

Meanwhile, the expedition was pursuing its somewhat leisurely advance. By the end of October its advanced columns had reached Dongola, but the main body was still negotiating the Second Cataract, just upstream of Wadi Halfa. On 2 November Wolseley wrote in his diary that there was no chance of having his force "in the neighbourhood of el-Debbeh", on the Nile about 100 miles upstream of Dongola, "in fighting trim" and ready for an advance up-river to Khartum, before Christmas, whereas he had hoped to be in Berber by then. If he persevered with his original plan of advancing with his whole force up the Nile, round the great Abu Hamed loop, this would mean that he could not be in Khartum before the middle of February.[43] Since this would be too late, he then determined, when he had got his force assembled in the neighbourhood of el-Debbeh, to take 1,500 of his "finest men" across the desert from el-Debbeh to Metemme, about 100 miles downstream of Khartum and half-way between Khartum and Berber, by-passing the Abu Hamed loop and leaving Berber in his rear. From there he calculated that he would be able to "push on to Khartum without halting" and arrive there about the beginning of February.[44] As we shall see, this plan was amended at the end of December, when his whole force was assembled "in fighting trim" at Korti, in the neighbourhood of el-Debbeh, because of information believed to have come from Gordon, warning Wolseley not to leave Berber in his rear. As a result he decided that the desert column would not "push on to Khartum without halting" but, having captured Metemme, assist the river column to capture Berber before making a joint advance on Khartum.[45]

The delay in assembling his force at el-Debbeh was attributed by Wolseley to troubles over steamers and coal on the Aswan–Halfa reach.[46] In fact, there was a complete stoppage of steamer movement between Aswan and Wadi Halfa from 28 October to 10 November.[47] Others attributed the delay to Wolseley's insistence on imported boats and boatmen in preference to local resources.[48] Whatever the cause, this delay, preceded by the Cabinet's procrastination, and followed by Wolseley's reaction to Gordon's supposed message, was fatal to Gordon.

CHAPTER NINE

THE AGONY OF THE MISSIONARY

ON HIS ARRIVAL in the Sudan Gordon seems quite genuinely to have done his best to carry out the evacuation policy in accordance with his instructions. At Berber he announced that policy to the notables in the expectation that the resultant enthusiasm would enable a local administration to be set up independently of, and capable of defending itself against, the Mahdi. But he seems to have had his doubts even before leaving Berber. He was coming to realise that the Mahdist rebellion was, in part, a social revolution. The "conservatives"—the men of property and the Shaikhs of tribes—would probably have liked to oppose it, and, in spite of their dislike of Egyptian and Turkish rule, would have given at all events passive support to any outside force—whether British or Turkish or Egyptian—which seemed likely to be able to master it. What they wanted was, not a declaration of independence, which would expose them to the depredations of the Dervishes, but an assurance of armed support which would save them from these depredations. But, if no such armed support were to be forthcoming, they had not the resources to stand by themselves against the rebellion, and had no intention of compromising themselves with the rebels by a futile resistance. Far better to make a virtue of necessity, to throw in their lot with the rebels before it was too late, and save what could be saved from the wreck. But, if troops were coming from outside—from England or Egypt or Turkey—to crush the rebellion, they would be throwing everything away by joining the rebels. So long as the prospect was uncertain it was necessary to temporise, as far as possible neither helping nor antagonising one side or the other.

Gordon soon realised that he had no chance whatever of being able to rally any significant body of resistance to the Mahdi without the prospect of troops from outside. He also may have realised, although he did not make it clear at the time, that the creation of some, even temporary, body of resistance to the Mahdi was a necessary condition of evacuating the garrisons and Egyptian civilians. He thought it possible that Zubair might have enough influence to do what he could not do, and his urgent request to Baring for Zubair's services, made immediately on his arrival at Khartum, is an indication of his anxiety to avoid asking for troops and, perhaps, an indication of his knowledge that the British Government would be very reluctant to send them.

Before he had been in Khartum many days, he realised that Zubair, even if he were sent, would not come in time to prevent the rebellion from spreading beyond the point of no return, unless the tribes in the Gezira and between Khartum and Berber could be kept from joining the Mahdi by the existence of a "credible deterrent" in the shape of a British, or other, force which, whatever its actual movements, looked as if it had the intention of advancing to Berber and the Nile valley. But, after communications between Khartum and Berber had been cut on 10 March, indicating that most of the tribal leaders in that area had declared for the Mahdi, a "credible deterrent" was no longer sufficient. If the situation were to be restored, Zubair or no Zubair, the actual presence of troops at Berber would be necessary. The intimation from Baring, which reached him on 9 April, that no British troops would be sent to Berber seems to have convinced him that there was no further chance of fulfilling his mission peacefully on the lines originally planned. From henceforth his task was a military and not a political one, his primary object not evacuation but defence. This change had been brought about not by any change in Gordon's mind but by the movement of events. The resources of diplomacy were at an end since there was no one with whom to negotiate. The Mahdi had contemptuously rejected his overtures. The chiefs of tribes had ignored his invitation to come to Khartum. The town itself was invested. There was no further possibility of evacuation. They had not the strength to fight their way out. It was a question either of surrendering or of defending the town until, somehow or other, it was relieved. His political mission having failed (largely, as he saw it, because the British Government had rejected his recommendations), Gordon's subsequent efforts were devoted, on the one hand to the defence of Khartum, and on the other hand to trying to arrange for its relief from outside.

His primary duty, as he saw, it, after the enforced change in the character of his mission, was, not to the British Government which had sent him, nor to the Khedive who had appointed him Governor-General, but to the garrison and inhabitants of Khartum who were under his orders and under his protection, and towards whom, as time went on, and in spite of the cowardice of many of the soldiers, the greed of many of the merchants, and the venality of many of the officials, he felt an increasing sense of comradeship derived from common hardships, perils and disappointments. Gordon probably agreed with Gladstone that the Sudanese were a people rightly struggling to be free. But, beleaguered in Khartum with the oppressors, borrowing their money, requisitioning their grain, giving them their orders, dependent on their loyalty, and living with these oppressors under the lengthening shadow of starvation, slavery and massacre by the liberators who surrounded them, Gordon's sympathies naturally shifted away from the liberators and towards the oppressors, away from his enemies and towards his comrades. It would have been extraordinary if this had not been so. One cannot command a besieged garrison under the conviction that one is fighting on the wrong side, and the fact that one's own Government's sympathies are suspected to be with the besiegers is more likely to induce disloyalty to one's Government than to one's comrades.

In the light of these considerations, and of his justified doubts as to the British Government's willingness to send a relief expedition, Gordon's attempts to obtain Turkish troops are readily comprehensible. In his first request of the kind, during March, received by Baring on 9 April, Gordon asked him to "put your pride in your pocket and get by good pay 3,000 Turkish infantry and 1,000 Turkish cavalry". On 8 April he sent a message to Sir Samuel Baker asking him to try and raise funds to enable 3,000 Turkish troops to be recruited. He wrote direct to the Sultan on 16 April asking him to send 3,000 troops and to the European Consuls in Cairo, and to the Pope, asking them to obtain financial support for such an expedition.[1] These messages never reached their destinations. He continued his requests for a Turkish force until September, when he received news that a British expedition was on its way. In so doing, he irritated the Cabinet who still regarded him, not as the commander of a beleaguered garrison but as their own political emissary who had been sent upon and who, in their eyes, was still engaged upon, a peaceful mission which did not envisage the dispatch of Turkish, or of any other, troops to the Sudan.

While the Cabinet were arguing as to the pros and cons of a relief expedition, Gordon had the responsibility of trying to defend Khartum until a relief force should arrive. In his previous great military exploit—in China—he had commanded an attacking force and had several times taken part in the siege and capture of towns. Now he was himself besieged and in a defensive role. Although he had not for the past twenty years done much soldiering, he was quite equal to it, and his defence of Khartum, although ultimately unsuccessful, was, apart from its aura of romance, not the least of his achievements.

The town of Khartum, which had been built by the Egyptians as the capital of the Sudan after Mohamed Ali's occupation of the country in 1820, is situated at the junction of the Blue and White Niles. The defended area was in the shape of a triangle, with its apex, facing north, at the point of junction of the two rivers; the eastern side was bounded by the Blue, and the western side by the White, Nile, and the base, facing south, was formed by a line of fortifications stretching between the two rivers. On the west bank of the White Nile, opposite Khartum, was the fort of Omdurman. In the middle of the Blue Nile, opposite Khartum and stretching northward, was the island of Tuti. The line of fortifications across the base of the triangle consisted of a ditch and a parapet on which cannon were mounted. Gordon strengthened this line of defence by laying mines and erecting barbed wire entanglements on the further side of the ditch. The fortifications, extending from river bank to river bank, were about four miles long at low Nile. On the Blue Nile side the river ran between steep banks and the flood water did not encroach on the fortifications. But, on the White Nile side, the land ran down to the river in a gentle slope and, at high Nile, about 1,500 yards of the fortifications were under water. When the river receded, which it started to do from October, it was necessary to repair the fortifications which had been damaged by the flood water. At the Blue Nile end of the defensive line there was a fort, Fort Buri. The town itself, and the Palace, which had been converted into a fortress, lay along the bank of the Blue Nile. Another fort, Mogren, lay within the perimeter near the apex at the junction of the two rivers. The perimeter enclosed by the two rivers and the fortifications covered an area of about twelve square miles, forming a rough isosceles triangle with the two riverine sides about five miles long, and the landward base about four miles long. Outside the perimeter there was one fort—North Fort—on the east bank of the Blue Nile, opposite Fort Buri, one at Omdurman on the west bank of the White Nile opposite Khartum, and one at Halfaya, on the east bank of the Nile about nine miles downstream of Khartum.

Apart from this passive defence, Gordon had at his disposal ten steamers, and some barges, which he armed and armoured. These steamers were his principal offensive weapons during the siege, being used to maintain communications with Sennaar, to make foraging raids in the Gezira for grain and cattle, to attack enemy positions up and down the river, and, later in the siege, to attack enemy positions in the immediate vicinity of Khartum. Gordon wrote to the Captain of *Euryalus*, at Massawa, on 24 August: "We are pretty well matched with the Mahdi. He has cavalry and we have steamers."

These steamers were wood-fired paddle boats, of about the size and appearance of the old "penny steamers" on the Thames. The larger ones were between 140 and 150 feet in length with engines of from 40 to 60 h.p.; the smaller ones were between 60 and 70 feet in length with engines of from 20 to 30 h.p. They had not been built as warships but, fitted by Gordon with "bullet-proof plates of soft wood and iron" and gun turrets "twenty feet high giving a double line of fire", they did very well. Their principal usefulness was during the early days of the siege for raiding parties up and down river. Later, when the Dervishes were closing in on Khartum, and when the Mahdi had brought up artillery from Kordofan, they were vulnerable to this artillery at close quarters. Gordon then used five of the seven he had left (four had either been captured or sunk or wrecked and one more had been assembled at Khartum dockyard) to try and make contact with the advancing relief force.[2]

The siege of Khartum can be divided into two parts. During the first part, which lasted from the middle of March to the middle of September, while the Mahdi's main army was still in Kordofan, the besieging troops consisted mostly of local tribesmen under their tribal leaders. Their numbers must have fluctuated but, towards the end of July, were reported to be in the neighbourhood of 16,000. Our knowledge of this first period is limited, since Stewart's diary was lost, and is confined to such messages of Gordon's and Power's as got through.

During this first period the enemy had little or no artillery and the town was neither closely invested nor bombarded. Those inhabitants who wished were allowed to leave the town and many did so. By September it was estimated that there were 34,000 people left in Khartum.[3] Conversely, a much smaller number entered the town, mostly Sudanese soldiers of the Egyptian Army who had surrendered at el-Obeid, been conscribed into the Mahdi's army and who had subsequently deserted. There was a fairly frequent interchange of emissaries between besiegers and besieged. At the end of June Cuzzi, who had been Gordon's representative in Berber, came to tell Gordon of the fall of that town and brought with him a message from the Mahdi calling upon him to surrender. He came again on a similar mission in September. Gordon refused to see him on either occasion, believing, probably unjustly, that he had been responsible for betraying Berber to the enemy.

The tactics of the besiegers during this period were: (*a*) to keep the river route between Khartum and Berber cut by occupying the strong-point of Halfaya, nine miles downstream of Khartum and commanding a narrow stretch of the river; and (*b*) to deny to the defenders of Khartum the food supplies of the Gezira, along the Blue Nile between Khartum and Sennaar. In mid-March, in one of the earliest engagements of the siege, Gordon was compelled to evacuate a small detachment of the Khartum garrison stationed at Halfaya. An immediately following attempt to recapture this strong-point failed (this was the action which led to the two Egyptian commanders being shot for treachery) and Halfaya remained in enemy hands until it was recaptured by a steamer expedition towards the end of August, thus reopening the river route to the north, which remained in continual use by the defenders until near the end of the siege. But, by that time, Berber had been captured by the enemy and its recapture was a necessary preliminary to any relief of Khartum. As we have seen, Gordon, encouraged by his victory at Halfaya, meditated recapturing it himself. He was prevented from attempting to do so by a disaster which overtook the defenders on the Blue Nile in September.

On the Blue Nile front, the defenders, by using steamers on a succession of armed raids, had been successful in keeping the enemy at a distance, in maintaining communication with Sennaar, and in bringing in a fairly regular supply of provisions. There had been some reverses. On 27 April the town of Messalamia, on the Blue Nile, about half-way between Khartum and Sennaar, where there was a small Egyptian garrison commanded by an Egyptian officer, Saleh Bey, surrendered with "50 shiploads of food, 2,000 rifles, and a small steamer", *Mohamed Ali.* On 10 July, Saati Bey, one of Gordon's officers, on a raiding party up the Blue Nile, was defeated by an enemy band and killed with three of his officers and a large number of men. As a result the enemy advanced up the west bank of the Blue Nile to Buri on the outskirts of Khartum. But, on 29 July, they were driven out of Buri and a raiding party, with two steamers, made a successful foray for some twenty-five miles up the Blue Nile, as far as Eilafun, "clearing 13 rebel forts and breaking two cannon".

Up to that time, the defenders' loss in killed amounted to under 700 men, most of whom had been killed in the March defeat near Halfaya.

Towards the end of August, Mohamed Ali Pasha, whom Gordon regarded as his best commander, led another raid up the Blue Nile and inflicted two severe defeats on Abu Girgeh, commanding the Mahdist forces in the Gezira, first at Geraf, just outside Khartum, and then at Abu Haraz, about half-way between Khartum and Sennaar, on the east bank of the river.

As a result of these victories, Mohamed Ali brought back to Khartum large supplies of arms, ammunition and grain.

At the beginning of September Mohamed Ali went on another, bigger, raid up the Blue Nile with the object of striking a blow at Shaikh el-Obeid, the principal tribal chief in the area, who had recently declared for the Mahdi and who was reported to be collecting a large force at Eilafun. After capturing Eilafun and a large store of provisions, Mohamed Ali advanced inland with most of his force in pursuit of Shaikh el-Obeid. On 5 September, when he was about twenty miles from the river, his force was ambushed by the enemy. Mohamed Ali himself, and a large part of his force of 1,000 men, were killed. This was the most serious loss which had been suffered during the siege. Gordon had lost, not only his best commander, but about a third of his best troops.

This grave depletion caused Gordon to abandon his plans for the capture of Berber, which caused so much perturbation in the Cabinet when they came to hear of them. Instead he decided to take advantage of his recent recapture of Halfaya by sending Stewart downriver to Dongola, from where he could make his way to Egypt, to report on the state of affairs at Khartum and expedite arrangements for sending a relief expedition. Stewart and his companions left Khartum on 9 September, the same day on which Wolseley arrived in Egypt. Major Kitchener had been in Dongola province since the beginning of August and had sent several messages to Gordon about arrangements for the relief expedition, none of which Gordon had received by the time Stewart left.

Stewart left on *Abbas*, one of Gordon's smaller steamers. He was accompanied by Herbin, the French Consul, and by Frank Power. He took with him his diary giving a day-by-day account of the siege up to that date, and the F.O. cipher. *Abbas* was escorted by two of the larger steamers, *Safia* and *Mansura*, as far as Berber, and was accompanied by two sailing boats carrying some Greek and Syrian inhabitants of Khartum. The sailing boats could be used by the party for negotiating the cataracts between Berber and Dongola in case the river had fallen too far for *Abbas* to get over them.

It is convenient briefly to leave Khartum and to accompany

this convoy to its tragic end. It got safely past Berber, and *Safia* and *Mansura* returned to Khartum as planned. After they had left and returned upstream of Berber, the enemy at Berber sent the steamer *el-Fasher*, which they had captured when Berber fell, in pursuit of *Abbas* and the two sailing boats. The sailing boats were overtaken and captured, but *Abbas* managed to get over the Fifth Cataract, thus escaping from *el-Fasher* which was a larger steamer and unable to negotiate it. Then, after covering another 200 miles, *Abbas* struck a rock. Stewart and his party landed, unarmed, under a flag of truce, and he, Herbin and Power were treacherously murdered by a local Shaikh with whom Stewart had entered into negotiation for the hire of camels for their onward journey.

The place at which *Abbas* struck a rock, and where Stewart and his companions were murdered, was only about 100 miles upstream of el-Debbeh where, unbeknown to Stewart, Major Kitchener had recently arrived as the Egyptian Government's representative to the Mudir of Dongola and forward Intelligence Officer to the relief expedition. He was very nearly within the friendly territory controlled by Mustafa Pasha Yawir, Mudir of Dongola.

On the day Stewart left Khartum, Gordon sent, by another messenger, a letter for Baring, which he did not receive until November, telling him of Stewart's departure. "How many times have we written asking for reinforcements. . . . No answer at all has come to us . . . and the hearts of men have become weary at this delay. . . . The reason why I have now sent Col. Stewart is because you have been silent all this while and neglected us and lost time without doing any good. If troops were sent, as soon as they reach Berber this rebellion would cease and the inhabitants will return to their former occupations. It is therefore hoped that you listen to all that is told you by Stewart and the consuls[4] and send troops as we have asked without any delay."[5]

Stewart's departure about coincided with the end of the first and the beginning of the second phase of the siege. We are much better informed about the first stage of this second period since Gordon's Journals, covering the period from Stewart's departure to 14 December, have survived, Gordon having sent them down in batches by river, where they were eventually received by the relief force.

At the end of August, news of Mohamed Ali's victories over Abu Girgeh had been received at the Mahdi's camp at Rahad, in Kordofan. Slatin, the Governor of Darfur, who had recently surrendered to the Mahdi with the el-Fasher garrison, was a prisoner in the camp at the time and relates how the Khalifa Abdullahi, the Mahdi's second-in-command and destined successor, told him that Wad-el-Nejumi, one of the Mahdi's best commanders, was being sent to Khartum with reinforcements of men and artillery to take over the conduct of the siege.[6] Soon after this, the Mahdi himself, with the bulk of his army consisting, together with camp followers, of about 200,000 people, started advancing slowly across Kordofan towards Khartum.

The Mahdi apparently still hoped that Khartum would surrender. During the first half of September he sent several emissaries calling on the town to submit. The first was sent back with a negative answer on 9 September, just before Stewart left. On the following day, Cuzzi, who had been with the Mahdi in Kordofan, arrived with a second message, and, later the same day, two dervishes arrived with a letter to Gordon from the Mahdi, bearing a dervish outfit and inviting him to embrace Islam and join the Mahdi.

The river route to Sennaar was still open and, after Mohamed Ali's defeat, two steamers left Khartum for Sennaar, taking with them a letter from Gordon to Shaikh el-Obeid to be delivered on the way proposing that "we should mutually remain quiet in relation to one another, as we are rendering the country a desert". Later that month the steamers returned safely from Sennaar with cargoes of grain. After they returned, Gordon wrote on 27 September that "it is no use sending up to Sennaar again for durra [maize], for we have no money to pay for it and it is a risk with the Arab guns".[7] Since about the middle of September, the advance guard of the Mahdi's main army, under Wad-el-Nejumi, had been arriving with reinforcements of artillery. As early as 14 September Khartum was bombarded by cannon at a distance from the south. On the same day dervishes were reported to be massing near Halfaya.

A good deal of news about the enemy, some of it unreliable, was being obtained from deserters.

On 18 September there was a battle between the steamer *Taufiqia* and the enemy at Geraf, just outside Khartum. The enemy were closing in.

On 21 September messengers arrived at Khartum with dispatches from Cairo which Gordon could not decipher, as Stewart had taken the cipher book with him. They also brought a letter from Kitchener addressed to Stewart, written from Dongola, and one from Floyer, a British official of the Egyptian Posts and Telegraphs, both dispatched from el-Debbeh on 22 August, giving news of the relief expedition. This was the first news which Gordon had had that a relief expedition was being contemplated. Four days before, on 17 September, he had written in his Journal that he had "the strongest suspicions that these tales of troops at Dongola and Merowe are all gas-works and that, if you wanted to find H.M.'s forces, you would have to go to Shepheard's Hotel Cairo".[8] He was not far wrong, since Wolseley and his staff were still in Cairo and did not go south until the end of September.

On 22 September the steamers *Safia* and *Mansura* returned to Khartum with the report that *Abbas* and the two sailing boats had passed Berber safely. Also on 22 September two more messages arrived from Kitchener, written from el-Debbeh on 29 and 31 August. The first told Gordon that the 35th Regiment had been ordered to advance from Halfa to Dongola "at once", and that Wolseley was leaving London to take over the supreme command. The second told him that a column would probably be sent by land from el-Debbeh to Khartum and that another column would go by river to Berber. Kitchener added that "a few words about what you wish done would be very acceptable". There was also a cipher message from Egerton which Gordon could not read and a message from him in clear passed on by Kitchener telling him that "steamers are being passed over the Second Cataract" and that "we wish to be informed through Dongola exactly when you expect to be in difficulties as to provisions and ammunition". Gordon, in his Journal, commented sarcastically on this message: "It is as if a man on the bank, having seen his friend in river already bobbed down two or three times, hails, 'I say, old fellow, I know you have bobbed down two or three times, but it is a pity to throw you the lifebuoy until you are really *in extremis*.' "[9]

On 23 September the defenders drove an enemy force away from Halfaya in the north and a steamer successfully attacked a raiding party of fifty Arab horsemen at Buri in the south.

On 25 September the Arabs attacked in some force along the Blue Nile but were repulsed by fire from the steamer *Mansura*. On 26 September the steamers *Bordein* and *Tel el Hewein* arrived back from Sennaar with 2,000 ardebs of durra.[10] They had a stiff battle near Geraf on the way back and Gordon sent up the steamers *Mansura* and *Ismailia* to reinforce them. On 30 September, three steamers, *Tel el Hewein*, *Mansura* and *Safia*, left Khartum downstream, manned with Egyptian troops and bearing the first two volumes of Gordon's Journal. *Tel el Hewein* was to return to Khartum after escorting the other two steamers as far as Shendi (opposite Metemme), where *Safia* and *Mansura* were to await the expected relief force, which Gordon evidently believed to be farther advanced than it really was. (The main body was just beginning to negotiate the Second Cataract south of Wadi Halfa.)

During the second half of September enemy troops from Kordofan under the command of Wad-el-Nejumi had been continually arriving at the White Nile and were being ferried across to the Gezira at Kalakala, about five miles south of Khartum, to take position at the western end of the landward defences. Opposite the eastern, or Blue Nile, end were the forces of Abu Girgeh, whom Mohamed Ali had defeated in August. Shaikh el-Obeid and his men had crossed over to the east bank of the Blue Nile and were advancing northward towards Halfaya. The Mahdi himself was believed to be advancing northward along the west bank of the White Nile towards Omdurman. The besiegers now had a certain amount of artillery in the form of Krupp and mountain guns to which the steamers were vulnerable. The last convoy from Sennaar had come under heavy fire and Gordon decided to send no more expeditions so far up-river. But he sent *Bordein* for a short distance up the Blue Nile and *Taufiqia* up the White Nile to harass the enemy in the immediate vicinity of Khartum.

Bordein returned on 6 October with a shell hole just above the water line.

On 12 October Gordon sent *Taufiqia* downstream to join the other three steamers at Shendi and Metemme waiting for the expected relief expedition. Manned with Egyptian troops, it took with it Gordon's Journal up to 11 October. He also sent *Bordein,* which had just returned from a marauding expedition upstream, up the White Nile to Kalakala to attack the ferry there. At the same time he decided to evacuate Halfaya and to transfer the garrison there—consisting of the still loyal tribe of Shaggia who had occupied it since its recapture in August—to North Fort, on the east bank of the Blue Nile opposite Buri. On 13 October a detachment of these Shaggia made a cavalry sortie from Buri and "captured fifteen slaves and killed thirteen men who resisted".

On 16 October, Slatin, who had been taken prisoner in Darfur, arrived at Khartum as an emissary from the Mahdi, bringing Gordon the first news of the fate of Stewart and his companions. Gordon refused to see him as he took a harsh view of his apostacy. (Slatin had become a Moslem during the siege of el-Fasher in an attempt to retain the loyalty of his troops.) But Slatin apparently made a proposal to Hansel, the Austrian Consul in Khartum, that he should break his parole given to the Mahdi and rejoin Gordon. Gordon, advised of this by Hansel, refused the offer both on ethical grounds and because it would jeopardise the lives of other European prisoners in the Mahdi's hands.

On 17 October *Husainia,* a steamer newly assembled in the Khartum dockyard (and named after the Superintendent of the dockyard), was launched. Next day, in company with *Bordein,* it went on a raid up the White Nile, where the two steamers were heavily engaged by the enemy. After that Gordon finally stopped these steamer forays upstream, noting in his Journal: "I will never believe in ships against land batteries, unless troops are landed, for unless a steamer can get close alongside a battery, the battery will hold its own."[11]

On 19 October *Tel el Hewein* returned to Khartum from Shendi with news about the capture of the two sailing boats accompanying *Abbas.* (It had no news about the subsequent fate of *Abbas*; Gordon was still hoping that Slatin's news was untrue.) Two days later *Tel el Hewein* and *Bordein* left for Shendi bearing Gordon's Journals to date, with instructions from Gordon for *Tel el Hewein*, *Safia* and *Taufiqia* to go downstream from Shendi towards Berber in search of the relief expedition. *Mansura* was to stay at Shendi and *Bordein* was to return to Khartum from Shendi with any news it had been able to pick up. This left Gordon with only *Ismailia* and *Husainia* at Khartum.

On 19 October Gordon noted in his Journal details of the strength of the garrison and the amount of his remaining provisions. The garrison consisted of 2,316 regular Sudanese troops, 1,421 regular Egyptian troops, 1,906 "Cairo Bashi-bazouks", 2,330 Shaggia tribesmen and 692 enrolled townspeople, a total of 8,665. Of these he expressed the intention, several times repeated in his Journal, of evacuating the Egyptian troops to Berber "as soon as it is possible to find transport and as soon as you [i.e. the relief expedition] get to Berber". He noted that he had twelve guns and 21,141 rounds of artillery ammunition. There were also 2,165,000 rounds of rifle ammunition. With regard to provisions, he had 4,018 ardebs of durra (of which the garrison's consumption alone was 500 ardebs a week) and 349,000 okes of biscuit.[12]

A few days later, on 25 October, Gordon made an estimate of the enemy strength facing him. In the Gezira there were 600 men and two guns at Geraf on the Blue Nile under Abu Girgeh and 5,000 men and eight guns under Wad-el-Nejumi near Kalakala on the White Nile. On the west bank of the White Nile and approaching Omdurman was the Mahdi himself with 4,000 men and six guns. On the east bank of the Blue Nile near Halfaya were 4,000 men and one gun under Shaikh el-Obeid. The enemy in the Gezira were now well within sight of Khartum, and Gordon, in his Journal, writes frequently of the "church parades" he could see from the roof of the Palace, which he seems to have used as his command post.

On 22 October Gordon received a long letter from the Mahdi giving him full details of the fate which had overtaken Stewart and his party, and telling him that Lupton, the Governor of Bahr-al-Ghazal, had surrendered.

On 24 October Gordon, working on such information and rumours as he had heard, calculated that the relief expedition should have arrived at el-Debbeh on 12 October, would be at Shendi on 10 November, and that, by making use of the steamers he had sent downstream, the advance guard of the expedition should be in Khartum by 15 November.[13] He concluded: "If they do not come before 30 November the game is up and Rule Britannia."[14] In fact, Gordon's calculations were much too optimistic. On 24 October the main body of the relief force had still not reached Dongola. The Army and Navy were quarrelling about the best methods of hauling boats up the rapids and the build-up of supplies had been delayed because someone had neglected to lay down enough coal for the steamers plying between Aswan and Wadi Halfa.

On 1 November Gordon noted that there were six weeks' supplies of grain left in Khartum.

On 3 November *Bordein* arrived back in Khartum from Shendi with a message from Kitchener dated 14 October confirming what Gordon had heard already about the fate of Stewart and his party, and telling him that it was "expected the expedition will definitely start from Dongola on or about 1 November". There was also a message from Wolseley in code which Gordon was unable to decipher. The news about the expedition must have been a disappointment for Gordon, since it showed that it was about a month behind his previous calculations and could not be expected in Khartum before the end of the year.

On 4 November Gordon sent Wolseley a letter which he received on 17 November, when he was in Dongola, explaining that he no longer had the cipher,[15] and had been unable to read his message. He told him that five steamers and nine guns would be at Metemme awaiting the expedition and that he could hold out for "forty days with ease; after that it will be difficult". He advised the expedition to take the desert route from Um Bakul (near el-Debbeh) to Metemme.[16]

On 5 November *Bordein* was turned round again and sent downstream to Metemme with the next instalment of Gordon's Journal and instructions to return with the latest news.

On 8 November the enemy advanced on both sides of the

Blue Nile towards Buri and North Forts, but were driven off by fire from the steamers *Ismailia* and *Husainia.* As Gordon remarked in his Journal,[17] the enemy had found a weak point in the defence—the prolongation of the southern land front on the Blue Nile side as a result of the fall of the Blue Nile from its flood level, which exposed several hundred yards of unfortified front which had previously been covered by the flood water.

By this time Khartum was surrounded by the enemy on three sides. The Mahdi, with the main force, was on the west bank of the White Nile facing the fort of Omdurman; in the south, in the Gezira between the White and Blue Niles were Wad-el-Nejumi and Abu Girgeh; in the east, facing the North Fort, was Shaikh el-Obeid. Encirclement to the north was checked by the garrisons in Omdurman and North Forts (apparently rather ineffectively by the Shaggia in North Fort), and by fire from *Ismailia* and *Husainia.* Tuti Island was still in the defenders' possession and there was still regular communication across the river between the main garrison and the Egyptian troops in Omdurman and the Shaggia in North Fort. There had been no very determined enemy attacks on the town and only sporadic and not very lethal artillery bombardment. It seemed that, in spite of a growing superiority in men and armament, the Mahdi counted on starving the town out, and wished to avoid committing his troops to an expensive and possibly unsuccessful assault. At all events the enemy concentrated on completing the encirclement of the town by outflanking or taking Omdurman and crippling the two steamers.

On 12 November there was a relatively heavy attack on Omdurman Fort. Of the steamers coming to its aid, *Husainia* ran aground near the junction of the two Niles and *Ismailia* was hit by shell at least five times. Firing went on all day in what Gordon described as "the greatest battle (as yet) of our . . . blockade". The defenders fired eighty-four rounds of Krupp ammunition and forty-three rockets from Fort Mogren (situated within the perimeter near the junction of the Blue and White Niles) and the enemy were estimated to have fired 370 rounds of artillery ammunition at the steamers. Something like 50,000 rounds of small arms ammunition were estimated to have been fired by each side. Apart from damage to the steamers, casualties were light and the enemy made no attempt to press home their attacks on the ground. The day seems to have been saved by *Ismailia*, which continually attacked the enemy with musketry from its castellated turrets, passing and re-passing the enemy guns upwards of twenty times. Gordon commented in his Journal that "no Royal Navy vessels would have behaved better than *Ismailia* to-day".[18]

Next day, 13 November, the battle was renewed, with *Ismailia* trying to get off *Husainia* and the enemy artillery trying to disable both steamers. In the end the crew and guns of *Husainia* were taken off and *Ismailia* had to put into the dock-yard for repairs.

The enemy were now in possession of the west bank of the White Nile and Omdurman Fort was effectively cut off from Khartum, with one and a half months' supply of food and water. Henceforward there was only communication by flag and bugle-call, and by an occasional smuggled messenger. The situation of the defenders, who were now exposed to continuous, if rather ineffective, artillery fire, was becoming serious. Gordon commented in his Journal: "Certainly we have been left to almost the very last extremity."[19] On 15 November he calculated that there was enough food for another month and enough ammunition for fifty days.[20]

The main body of the relief expedition had not yet reached Dongola.

On 22 November Gordon noted that the defenders had lost between 1,800 and 1,900 killed since March and that there were 242 wounded in hospital.[21] By this time Khartum was nearly encircled. About 2,000 of the enemy had outflanked North Fort and were on the east bank of the river about five miles downstream of Khartum. Another 5,000 were on the east bank of the Blue Nile blockading North Fort, 3,000 enemy troops with two guns were on the Blue Nile side of the Gezira about five miles from Khartum, and 3,000 with four guns on the White Nile side at the same distance. The enemy's main force, with the Mahdi himself, consisting of 6,000 men and ten guns, was on the west bank of the White Nile surrounding Omdurman Fort.

On 24 November *Husainia*, which was still aground, sank, leaving Gordon with only one steamer—*Ismailia.* Another, which he named *Zubair*, was being assembled in Husain Bey's dockyard, and was launched on 27 November.

On 25 November *Bordein* returned to Khartum from Metemme, running the gauntlet of heavy enemy fire at Halfaya, from which point she was escorted into Khartum by *Ismailia.* She brought Gordon several enciphered messages from Cairo, which he was unable to read, a letter from Sir Samuel Baker praising Kitchener, and a delayed message from Kitchener (written previous to the one dated 14 October which he had already received). No fresh news about the relief expedition. There was also the message from the Khedive telling Gordon about the limitation of his authority,[22] which was apparently mistranslated, with the result that Gordon did not understand its purport.

At the end of November Omdurman was still holding out, but running short of food and ammunition. Its fall would complete the encirclement of Khartum and probably also enable the enemy to occupy Tuti Island. Gordon determined to try and relieve it. On 6 December, in what he described as a "last resource"[23] to save Khartum, he attacked the enemy surrounding Omdurman with gunfire from Mogren Fort and with small arms fire from *Bordein*, *Ismailia* and *Zubair*. But, in spite of having inflicted fairly heavy casualties, Gordon decided that he had not the ground troops to follow up this bombardment by a landing, and the attempt to relieve Omdurman was abandoned.

On 8 December the steamers were again in action, this time on the Blue Nile, to repel an enemy attack on Buri. They were hit by several shells.

By this time the town, and particularly the Palace, Gordon's headquarters, were under continual bombardment from the enemy artillery on the west bank of the White Nile. On 12 December Gordon estimated that over 2,000 shells had been fired into Khartum, but that only about three people had been killed by them. On the same day he recorded that provisions were down to 700 ardebs of grain and 110,000 okes of biscuit.

All sorts of stories were in circulation, but no exact information had been received, about the whereabouts of the relief force. There were rumours, which Gordon discounted, that it had taken Berber. In fact, by 12 December, it was beginning to assemble at Korti, near el-Debbeh. It was another three weeks before the desert column was to start its advance from Korti to Metemme and five weeks before this column was to arrive at Metemme. On 13 December Gordon noted: "If some effort is not made before ten days' time the town will fall."[24]

On 14 December Gordon recorded that supplies of durra had fallen to 546 ardebs and supplies of biscuit to 83,525 okes. He determined to send *Bordein* downriver once more with his Journal, which he concluded with the message: "If the expeditionary force, and I ask for no more than 200 men, does not come in ten days, the town may fall."[25] *Bordein* left on 15 December.

On 31 December Wolseley, at el-Debbeh, received a verbal message said to emanate from Gordon and apparently authenticated by a piece of paper the size of a postage stamp containing the handwritten message: "Khartum all right 14.12.84. C. G. Gordon." The verbal message was to the effect that Khartum was besieged on three sides, that it could hold out so long as food lasted, but that the enemy were very numerous and that Wolseley should bring plenty of troops. He was advised to take two routes, via Berber by river and to Metemme across the desert, and not to leave Berber in his rear. He was to send word to Khartum when Berber had been taken.[26] There is some doubt as to whether this message was authentic. Gordon made no reference to it in his Journal. Wolseley had his doubts, as he had been "counting on an expression which occurs more than once in Gordon's letters, that the whole attack on Khartum would collapse if he had a few hundred determined soldiers on whom he could depend".[27] Because of this, Wolseley had "determined on forcing my way into Khartum with about 1,500 of the finest men in our or any other army. Now this message from him tells me not to advance unless I am strong."[28] Wolseley decided to take the message seriously and to advance with more deliberation than he had intended. "I have therefore determined upon sending four Battalions to Metemme across the desert, one to be the garrison of that place, the other three to go on with the

Camel Corps, 19th Hussars and ten guns to Khartum. I shall have to hold the wells at Abu Klea, Gakdul and Hambuk as well as Korti. So, including Metemme and Korti, I shall have three Battalions on this desert line of communications, leaving only two Battalions and detachments of cavalry, artillery and Engineers for operations up the river towards Abu Hamed. This will be a safer plan of operations than I had previously determined upon, but it will take more time and prevent me perhaps from being in Khartum as I had hoped to be with a fighting force on January 31 at latest."[29]

In a telegram to Baring Wolseley explained that Gordon's message meant that he must "move by water and take Berber before I march on Khartum". He added that "meanwhile I shall have established a post at Metemme by men and stores sent across the desert. I shall be able to communicate with Gordon by steamer, learn his exact position and, if he is *in extremis* before infantry arrive by river, to push forward by Camel Corps to help him at all hazards."[30]

On the whole, it seems that the messenger, who also told Wolseley that Gordon had 18,000 soldiers at Khartum (he had less than half that number) was not authentic. There is nothing in Gordon's Journal to suggest that he would be urging caution on Wolseley. On the contrary, he complains constantly about slowness and delay. It is hardly conceivable that, on the very day he was writing in his Journal—"if the expeditionary force, and I ask for no more than 200 men, does not come in ten days the town may fall"—he should have sent a verbal message to Wolseley urging him, in effect, to advance cautiously and to bring plenty of troops.

At all events, the effect of the message was to slow down still further the somewhat leisurely tempo of Wolseley's advance. According to the information in Wolseley's possession, conveyed in Gordon's message of 4 November, in which he wrote that he could hold out for forty days "with ease"—that is to say, until mid-December—even his original plan to have 1,500 fighting men in Khartum by the end of January was based on rather optimistic assumptions. The truth seems to be that Wolseley was an extremely cautious commander, and that Gordon's supposed advice not to leave Berber in his rear chimed exactly with his own views. Coming, as it appeared to do, from Gordon himself, it seemed to justify a caution which concern for Gordon's safety would otherwise have induced him to neglect.

When *Bordein* left Khartum on 15 December she took with her Gordon's last messages. As well as the Journal, he sent (*a*) a message addressed to the Chief-of-Staff of the expeditionary force telling him that "one cannot foresee more than five to seven days, after which the town might at any time fall";[31] (*b*) a letter to his friend Watson in Cairo in similar terms: "I think the game is up. . . . We may expect a catastrophe in the town in or after ten days' time";[32] and (*c*) a letter to Nushi Pasha, in command of the steamers downstream, urging him to impress on the British Commander-in-Chief the need for haste, as Khartum was "in great straits".[33] The Captain of *Bordein* was instructed to go to Metemme with the other four steamers and to remain there until the arrival of British troops.

Gordon never seems to have thought that he was in serious danger until towards the end of October, when he commented in his Journal that, unless the relief force arrived by the end of November, "the game is up". By that time enemy reinforcements of men and, more important, of artillery, from Kordofan had prevented his foraging expeditions into the Gezira and so cut him off from replenishments of grain and cattle. It had become a race between starvation and the arrival of the relief force.

As we have seen, soon after his arrival in Khartum, Gordon asked both for Zubair and for the dispatch of a small British force to Berber as a means of getting Khartum evacuated. When, by 9 April, he had been given to understand that he would get neither the one nor the other, he began putting forward the idea of Turkish troops as a *pis aller*. Up to the beginning of September, although becoming progressively more irritated with the British Government's passive attitude (which he erroneously attributed to Baring), he seems to have been confident of his ability to hold on to Khartum indefinitely. He was holding his own against the enemy in battle, and the route to Sennaar was still open for replenishments of grain. But, early in September, things began to get worse. He lost about a third of his best troops as a result of Mohamed Ali's defeat in the Gezira. The enemy were being heavily reinforced with men and artillery from Kordofan, thus making it progressively more difficult to get in supplies. The Blue Nile was falling and rendering his landward front more vulnerable. Hence his sending Stewart downstream in *Abbas* to impress upon Cairo the seriousness of the situation.

On 21 September he received, in messages from Kitchener and Floyer, his first news that a relief expedition was being prepared. This immediately raised his spirits and, within a few days, he was busy making plans on the assumption that it would have arrived in a month's time. His idea was that the relief force, with the assistance of the steamers he was sending down, would capture Berber and then send "a fighting column up to Khartum on the steamers. This fighting column would be able to drive the enemy away from the immediate vicinity of Khartum."[34] Having relieved Khartum, he recommended that, instead of evacuating immediately, the relief force should stay for six months, install either Zubair or the Turks at Khartum, and "combinating with us, commence an attack upon Kordofan. . . . You will not be obliged to go 50 miles beyond Khartum. As for the Equator, give it to me and I will, DV, keep it from Zubair. It is a thousand pities to give up Khartum to the Mahdi when there is a chance of keeping it under Zubair."[35]

This euphoria was succeeded by second thoughts. He began to suspect, from the wording of Kitchener's and Floyer's messages, that the expedition was coming to relieve him and not the garrisons. He would not accept this. "I am not the rescued lamb and will not be."[36] He briefly toyed with the idea of resigning his commission as Governor-General into the hands of Abdul Qadir or some other suitable Egyptian as soon as the relief force arrived in order to avoid responsibility for whatever policy was adopted. But he soon rejected this and started making new plans for the expedition. Assuming that it would occupy Berber on 28 October (this was on 3 October) he estimated that there would be 1,000 British troops in Khartum by 5 November. On the assumption that 6,000 Turkish troops would be landed at Suakin and 4,000 at Massawa at the beginning of November to march to Khartum via Berber and Kassala respectively, he estimated that the British relief expedition, with the Egyptian garrisons and all those who wanted to leave, would be able to leave Khartum for Wadi Halfa towards the end of December, leaving the country to the Turks. "As for the slave trade, one cannot help it."[37] He was insistent that the country could not be left to the Mahdi, as, if "our programme is a skedaddle the consequences might be most disastrous".[38] He thought that the time had gone by for Zubair and that handing the country over to the Turks was the only practicable alternative.

The truth was that, even with a British relief expedition arriving in time, it would have been impossible to get away the 10,000 or so civilians in Khartum who wished to leave without, in effect, making a temporary reconquest of the eastern Sudan. The difficulty was that there was nobody available to reconquer it. The British Government would not; the Egyptian Government could not; the Ottoman Government neither would nor could. Even if the relief force had arrived in time, even if it had been able to drive off the enemy around Khartum as easily as Gordon thought it could, even if it had been willing and able to evacuate the garrisons of Khartum and Sennaar (which it might have been), there would still have remained the problem of the Egyptian civilians, who could not have been evacuated through a hostile country, whom Gordon would not have been prepared to leave, and who could not have been left without a garrison to defend them. Unless the Cabinet were prepared to reconquer the eastern Sudan, all that the relief force would have been able to do would be to fight its way to Khartum and then fight its way back again, leaving Gordon and the garrison and the Egyptian civilians there with a little more food and a little more ammunition to prolong their agony.

Since it was obvious that British public opinion would not allow this to happen, the sending of a relief expedition really represented a commitment to reconquer the eastern Sudan, so long as Khartum continued to hold out. In England, both opponents and supporters of sending a relief expedition—or most of them—realised this. It is probable that Gordon did not. He probably regarded the dispatch of Turkish troops as a practicable way out of the impasse. It is almost fantastic to suppose, as many members of the Cabinet did suppose, that he had deliberately manœuvred the British Government into sending an expedition as a means of accomplishing the reconquest of the Sudan by the British.

The arrival, on 3 November, of Kitchener's message advising him of Stewart's death and of the probability that the relief expedition could not reach Khartum until the end of December, marks the beginning of Gordon's final agony. He made no more plans for what the relief expedition would do when it arrived. He seems to have known that it would not arrive in time. He made no more proposals about Turkish troops, although he occasionally reverted to the possibility of Zubair being able to pacify the country and make an evacuation possible if he came up with the expedition. He wrote, with increasing bitterness, of what he regarded as the perfidy of the British Government, and of his own determination to "stay here and fall with the town and run all risks".[39]

Information about the last six weeks of the siege, after the departure of *Bordein* on 15 December with the last of Gordon's Journals, is fragmentary, and consists of accounts (*a*) by some of the survivors of the besieged and (*b*) by some of the European prisoners of the Mahdi who were in the besiegers' camp. Included in (*a*) are the reminiscences of Bordini Bey, a Khartum merchant, contained in Wingate's *Mahdism and the Egyptian Sudan; La Chute de Khartoum*, an account of evidence at a Court of Inquiry held in Cairo in 1887 and published in 1893 by Borelli Bey, a lawyer practising in Egypt; and *The Sudan under Gordon and Kitchener* published in 1891 in Arabic by Ibrahim Fauzi Bey, whom Gordon had taken to Khartum as his secretary and who survived the siege. Included in (*b*) are the reminiscences of Father Ohrwalder—*Ten Years' Captivity in the Mahdi's Camp*—and those of Slatin Pasha—*Fire and Sword in the Sudan*.

During December the food situation deteriorated as the result of foraging expeditions being no longer possible. The maize crop on Tuti Island was plucked before it was ripe and exposed on Khartum quays to ripen in the sun before being threshed. At the beginning of January, Gordon, in order to reduce the number of mouths to be fed, publicly announced that any townspeople wishing to join the Mahdi could leave the town. A great many did so, and Gordon sent a message to the Mahdi asking for them to be treated kindly.

On 15 January the fort of Omdurman, after Gordon had failed to relieve it by sorties from Khartum, and after its supplies of food and ammunition had been exhausted, surrendered, under Gordon's instructions, to the besieging force. This enabled the besiegers to complete the encirclement of Khartum and to mount guns along the banks of the White Nile opposite the town.

By mid-January supplies of grain and biscuit in Khartum were exhausted and the remaining inhabitants were reduced to eating horses, donkeys, rats, gum and the pith from date palms. Dysentery broke out and many of the garrison became too weak to man the fortifications. It was apparent that, reduced by starvation, the town would no longer be able to resist a determined assault. The Mahdi nevertheless seems not to have been anxious to mount an assault and was only persuaded to do so by news reaching his camp of the advance of the British relief force.

In accordance with Wolseley's changed plans after having received Gordon's supposed message of 14 December, the desert column had started its advance from Korti to Metemme and the river column was advancing upstream towards Abu Hamed. On 30 December an advance party of the desert column set out from Korti to occupy Hambuk and Gakdul wells, the first two of the three staging posts on the 150-mile route to Metemme. These having been garrisoned and provisioned, the commander of the desert column, Sir Herbert Stewart, left Korti on 8 January with the main body. His orders were to establish a third staging post at Abu Klea, to capture Metemme, to make contact with Gordon's steamers, establish communication with and send reinforcements to Khartum, and to co-operate with General Earle, the commander of the river column, in the capture of Berber. When this had been done it was Wolseley's intention to go himself to Berber in order to lead the final advance of the reunited columns to Khartum.

But Wolseley's leisurely advance had given the Dervish forces ample warning of his approach and the desert column met with unexpected resistance. Wolseley had expected Stewart to take

Metemme on 17 January, after having got there without being seriously resisted.[40] But, on 17 January, at the wells of Abu Klea, some three-quarters of the way between Korti and Metemme, Stewart was attacked by a strong force of the enemy. The column formed square, defeated the Dervishes with heavy losses and resumed its advance. The British losses were seventy-four killed, including Colonel Burnaby, whom Wolseley had designated to take command of the column in the event of Stewart becoming a casualty.

Between Abu Klea and Metemme the column was continually harassed by the enemy and, on 19 January, in another skirmish a few miles from Metemme, Sir Herbert Stewart was mortally wounded. The command then devolved on Sir Charles Wilson, the Intelligence Officer of the column, who had little experience of active warfare. After further fighting, during which Wilson captured Gubat, a village near the Nile, but failed to capture Metemme, the column reached the Nile on 21 January a little upstream of Metemme. Here they made contact with Gordon's four steamers—*Bordein*, *Tel el Hewein*, *Safia and Taufiqia* (*Mansura* had been sunk). From Nushi Pasha, commanding the steamers, Wilson received Gordon's Journals up to 14 December and the various letters dated 14 December, which have already been quoted and which had been carried downstream by *Bordein*.

It was obvious from these messages that Khartum was in desperate straits. But it was not until the morning of 24 January that Sir Charles Wilson, with two of the steamers—*Bordein* and *Tel el Hewein*—twenty British troops and some supplies of grain, set off upriver for Khartum. Wilson's delay was severely criticised at the time and has not been satisfactorily explained since. In the last entry in his Journal Gordon had written: "All that is necessary is for fifty of the Expeditionary Force to get on board a steamer and come up to Halfaya and thus let their presence be felt; this is not asking much, but it must happen at once, or it will as usual be too late." Wolseley's orders were that Lord Charles Beresford, of the Naval Brigade, who accompanied the desert column, should, on the arrival of the column at Metemme, "at once take over and man any steamer or, if you can, steamers, that are there or in the vicinity and you will use every means in your power to put one or more of the steamers that will, it is believed, be available into an efficient state. You will do this under the instructions of the senior military officer at the post and will take his instructions regarding the steamers when ready." Sir Charles Wilson, as Intelligence Officer to the column, had been instructed by Wolseley that "as soon as Lord Charles Beresford reports that he is ready to proceed with one or more steamers to Khartum, you will go to that place with him and deliver the enclosed letter to General Gordon. . . . Orders have been given to Sir Herbert Stewart to send a small detachment of infantry with you to Khartum. . . . You will only stay in Khartum long enough to confer with General Gordon. Having done so, you will return in the steamers to Metemme." He was further ordered by Wolseley to take with him three named British officers to Khartum who "will remain there to assist General Gordon until I am able to relieve that place".

Immediately after reading Gordon's messages, Wilson, now commanding the desert column, wrote to Wolseley expressing his intention to carry out his "original mission and proceed at once" to Khartum, handing over command of the column to Colonel Boscawen of the Coldstream Guards.[41]

In view of Wilson's expressed intention to proceed "at once", and in view of the obvious urgency, it is not clear why three days should have elapsed before turning round *Bordein* and *Tel el Hewein*, which appear to have been ready for the return journey, apart from being loaded with supplies and reinforcements. It has been surmised[42] that the principal reason was the advice of Lord Charles Beresford, who had been designated by Wolseley to command the steamers, and who thought it necessary to make reconnaisances up and down the river on 22 and 23 January before setting out for Khartum on 24 January.

The two steamers arrived off Khartum on 28 January to find that the town had fallen. As they passed along Tuti Island they were met with a furious cannonade from the enemy; after pushing their way up to the junction of the Blue and White Niles, Wilson realised that there was nothing to be done but to return by the way they had come. They had a desperate struggle getting back, running the gauntlet of enemy fire through the Shabluka gorge near Halfaya.

Khartum had fallen on 26 January, two days before the arrival of the steamers. The Mahdi's decision to attack seems to have been taken as a result of his having received news of the desert column's victory at Abu Klea on 17 January, with its indication that Gordon would soon be receiving reinforcements. Conditions were extremely favourable for an assault. The White Nile had fallen, necessitating the repair of the previously submerged fortifications along the landward approach south-west of the town for a distance of some 1,500 yards down the gentle slope. These repairs had to be carried out under harassing fire from the enemy, and weakness due to famine made it increasingly difficult for the soldiers to carry on with the work. The departure of most of the steamers and the loss of *Husainia* diminished the offensive fire power of the defenders. Morale in the town and among the garrison was becoming progressively lower as a result of shortage of food and a diminishing belief in Gordon's oft-repeated and over-optimistic promises about the arrival of a relief expedition. The enemy also seems to have been assisted by treachery on the part of one of Gordon's officers, who deserted to the Mahdi's camp during the last week of the siege and revealed details of a weak point in the fortifications.[43]

Throughout Sunday, 25 January, a stream of reinforcements crossed the White Nile at Kalakala ferry from the Mahdi's main camp to join Wad-el-Nejumi's force facing Khartum's south-west defences. If Gordon had had more steamers available he might have been able to impede their crossing. But *Ismailia* remained moored at Khartum, apparently in order to enable some civilians to evacuate the town. It is not clear what had happened to *Zubair*. At sundown on the 25th the Mahdi himself and his three Khalifa crossed over by the ferry to give Wad-el-Nejumi his final orders.

The attack started an hour after midnight, concentrating on the western, or White Nile, end of the defences, which had been exposed by the fall of the river and which Gordon endeavoured to protect by enfilading fire from three barges moored on the White Nile bank. Supported by artillery fire from the Omdurman bank of the White Nile, the attackers broke through the enfilading fire from the barges on their left and from the ramparts on their right, and soon pierced the weakened defences. By four o'clock they were in possession of the town.

There is no certain account of the manner of Gordon's end. According to Bordini Bey, Gordon was on the steps of the Palace when the Dervishes broke in, dressed in a white uniform, wearing a sword and with a pistol in his hand. He was standing in "a calm and dignified manner, his left hand resting on the hilt of his sword. Taha Shahin [one of the Dervish leaders], dashing forward with the curse 'Ya Malaoun, al-yom yomak' (O cursed one, your time has come), plunged his spear into his body. Gordon made a gesture of scorn with his right hand and turned his back, when he received another spear wound which caused him to fall forward and was most likely his mortal wound. The other three men closely following Shahin then rushed in and, cutting at the prostrate body with their swords, must have killed him in a few seconds. His death occurred just before sunrise. He made no resistance and neither drew his sword nor fired a shot from his revolver." A few hours later, Slatin, a prisoner at Omdurman, was approached by a group of Dervishes carrying something wrapped in a cloth. They undid the cloth and he saw before him the head of Gordon. "His blue eyes were half opened; the mouth was perfectly natural; the hair of his head, and his short whiskers, were almost quite white."

So Gordon found the death which he had sought for so long, and the fame which he craved and despised.

CHAPTER TEN

EPILOGUE

IT IS POSSIBLE that, if *Bordein* and *Tel el Hewein* had been turned round within twenty-four hours of their meeting the desert column, the fall of Khartum would have been averted. They would probably have reached Khartum on the morning of 25 January, before the final order for the assault had been given, and just as the reinforcements for Wad-el-Nejumi from the west bank were beginning to cross the ferry at Kalakala. The two steamers might have been able to disrupt the ferry. Or the Mahdi, recognising them as the advance guard of the relief expedition, might possibly have decided to raise the siege.

It is even more likely that the fall of Khartum might have been averted if Wolseley had ignored the supposed verbal message from Gordon, received on 31 December, urging caution on him, and had proceeded with his original plan to make a quick dash across the desert with 1,500 of his best troops.

But in either case the relief expedition would have had either to reconquer the eastern Sudan, or to withdraw after having provided Gordon with some temporary and limited supplies and reinforcements. For it would not have been able to evacuate the garrison and the civilians who wished to leave without reconquering the eastern Sudan and it is unlikely that Gordon would have consented to leave either to their fate.

At first it appeared that the virtual commitment to the reconquest of the eastern Sudan created by the dispatch of the relief expedition would not be liquidated by the fall of Khartum and the presumed death of Gordon. News of these events reached Wolseley on 4 February and was in the English newspapers on 6 February. There was a predictable outburst of public indignation, mainly directed against the Government, and a predictable popular demand for avenging Gordon by "smashing the Mahdi". Some of this, like the Queen's *en clair* telegram of rebuke to Gladstone, was genuine, evanescent emotionalism; but much of it was a calculated reaction from those who had, all along, pressed, first for Gordon's appointment, and then for a relief expedition, with the objects of consolidating the British hold on Egypt and of opening a British-controlled route into Central Africa. For this powerful body of opinion, Gordon's presumed death and the fall of Khartum were incidents to be used as a means of imposing on the Government a policy of reconquest.

The Cabinet's first reaction to the news was unexpectedly robust. On 7 February, in reply to a request from Wolseley for guidance as to future policy, Hartington told him that the Government's policy aimed at overthrowing the power of the Mahdi at Khartum and that he was to decide when to attack and when and where reinforcements would be required.[1] The Government were already, with Wolseley's somewhat dubious concurrence, arranging for the dispatch of an expedition to Suakin, once more under the command of General Graham, with the object of engaging Osman Digna's forces and so facilitating Wolseley's capture of Berber. They were also once more thinking in terms of the construction of a railway between Suakin and Berber with the ostensible object of facilitating the evacuation of Khartum. In fact, the hopes on one side and the fears on the other that the dispatch of a relief expedition would lead to a reconquest of the Sudan were already on the way to being fulfilled. For it was idle to suppose that the Government would abandon the Sudan after having built an expensive railway there. But officially, the Government's policy was to smash the power of the Mahdi at Khartum in order to scotch the menace which he was now believed to present to Egypt proper, and then to withdraw. In the House of Commons four reasons were given by the Government for their decision to advance on Khartum. (1) That there were people in Khartum to whom Gordon was bound in honour, and that it was the Government's duty to go to their assistance; (2) that an advance to Khartum would make it possible to establish there an ordered government friendly to Egypt; (3) that it would check the slave trade; (4) that the possession of Khartum would, without any further extension of operations, help to relieve the garrisons still holding out. These four reasons represented a rationalisation of two unacknowledged motives which temporarily dictated British policy in the Sudan; (*a*) to appease public opinion which was clamouring for Gordon to be avenged; (*b*) to prevent what was believed to be the serious possibility of an invasion of Egypt proper by the victorious Mahdist armies.

Wolseley, on hearing of Sir Herbert Stewart's wound, had sent his Chief-of-Staff, Buller, to Metemme to take command of the desert column. When he heard of the fall of Khartum, he sent orders to Buller and to Earle, commanding the river column, not to undertake further offensive operations pending a decision by the Government about the future of the campaign. When he received the Cabinet's decision to "smash the Mahdi" his reaction was ambivalent. On the one hand he was officially pleased at what appeared to be a vindication of the policy he had advocated, and conventionally delighted, as a soldier was expected to be, at the prospect of an offensive campaign. On the other hand, he was unofficially depressed at the prospective difficulties of such a campaign, which he fully realised and even tended to exaggerate. He made plans for a converging advance on Berber by Earle from upstream and by Buller from downstream after the latter had captured Metemme. Earle resumed his advance up-river; but Buller, reporting on the strength of the enemy and the difficulties of his supply situation, told Wolseley that he was using the discretion given him to withdraw his force back across the desert to Korti. Wolseley accepted this, scrapped his plans for a converging attack on Berber, and decided to pull the river column back to Merowe in preparation for an up-river advance on Berber and Khartum by his whole force the following autumn. Before the river column received the order to withdraw, it had advanced to within about thirty miles of Abu Hamed, and had fought an engagement at Kirbekan in which Earle, the commander of the force, had been killed.

By this time Wolseley was privately tired of the whole Sudanese business and would have liked nothing better than to receive an order to withdraw his force from the Sudan entirely. He was conscious, perhaps over-conscious, of the fact that a campaign for the recapture of Khartum was a much more formidable affair than one for the relief of Khartum, since the Mahdi's capture of Khartum had strengthened the enemy both materially and psychologically. He was sickened by his failure to relieve Gordon, apprehensive of the effect of a Sudanese summer on the health of his troops, and generally anxious about the whole future of the campaign. He voiced his official thoughts in his dispatches to the Government, and his unofficial thoughts in his letters to his friends. Inevitably, the Cabinet got to know of the latter, and this, together with other factors, hastened the reversal of policy which they were already contemplating. Public demands for the avenging of Gordon were dying down. The danger of a Mahdist invasion of Egypt were seen to have been exaggerated, if not altogether without foundation. Wolseley's dispatches were impressing them disagreeably with the cost in money and lives, and the uncertain outcome, of a campaign to "smash the Mahdi". Baring was advocating the abandonment of offensive operations and the retention of Suakin and Dongola.

The advocates of reconquest soon came to realise that they were no longer supported by the General on the spot and, just as they had previously under-estimated the strength of the Dervishes, so now they over-estimated it. The advocates of evacuation in the Cabinet soon found that they were pushing at an open door. A crisis in relations with Russia which arose on the North-West Frontier of India was the excuse rather than the reason for a reversal of policy in the Sudan.

At the end of March Hartington suggested to Wolseley that he should go via Cairo to Suakin, where active operations were proceeding against Osman Digna. By this time, the relief force in the Nile valley had been pulled back into Dongola, where the enemy showed no signs of following them. Active operations were at an end for the time being, but preparations were going forward and supplies being delivered for an autumn campaign which would have as its object the recapture of Khartum. When Wolseley reached Cairo in mid-April he received a private telegram from Hartington warning him that a change of policy, involving the evacuation of the Sudan, was imminent. On 21 April this change of policy was announced in the House of Commons. It was not intended to advance on Khartum or to undertake any further offensive operations in the Sudan. Suakin and its immediate surroundings were to be held, but the

Suakin–Berber railway would not be built, and Graham's force was to be withdrawn except for such part of it as might be necessary to secure Suakin.

The only question which remained to be settled was the extent of withdrawal down the Nile valley. Was Dongola to be held, or was the frontier between the Sudan and "Egypt proper" to be established at Wadi Halfa in accordance with the original plan? Most military opinion was in favour of retaining Dongola, but it was clear that those expressing it still had in view an eventual advance on Khartum, and naturally regarded Dongola as a better jumping-off point for this than Wadi Halfa. But the Cabinet, and Baring, were only interested in making the best arrangements for the defence of "Egypt proper". From this point of view, Baring was in favour of retaining Dongola under some kind of indirect Anglo-Egyptian administration. On 14 April Wolseley expressed the opinion that "if our position is to be exclusively one of defence, I would hold Wadi Halfa and Korosko as outposts, with a strong Brigade at Aswan". He reversed this opinion next day and advocated retaining Dongola, but Hartington, on 8 May, told him that the Government, "after considering all reports received, adhered to the decision to adopt the proposal for the defence of Egypt at Wadi Halfa and Aswan contained in your telegram of April 14".

On 8 June the Liberal Government was defeated in the House of Commons and resigned office. By this time the evacuation of Dongola was under way. The new Conservative Government, of which Lord Salisbury was Prime Minister, after consulting Wolseley, decided to adhere to the policy of evacuating Dongola. On 7 July Wolseley left Alexandria for England. The Gordon relief campaign was at an end. Three weeks earlier, on 22 June, Mohamed Ahmed, the Mahdi, and *de facto* ruler of most of the Sudan, had died at Omdurman, where he had established his capital after the fall of Khartum, following the usual fashion of Oriental potentates, who are reluctant to establish themselves in the capital cities of their defeated predecessors. He was succeeded by the Khalifa Abdullah al-Taashi, who ruled the Sudan for the next thirteen years, until he was defeated at the battle of Omdurman by an Anglo-Egyptian force commanded by Sir Herbert Kitchener.

APPENDIX

GORDON'S STEAMERS

BORDEIN. Made several journeys downstream with mail and eventually sent to Metemme to meet the relief force.

TEL EL HEWEIN. Sent to Metemme to meet the relief force.

SAFIA. Escorted Stewart's party in *Abbas* as far as Berber. Eventually sent down to Metemme to meet the relief force.

MANSURA. Escorted Stewart's party in *Abbas* as far as Berber. Sunk on the way to meet the relief force.

MESSALAMIA. Captured by the Dervishes at Berber in May 1884.

TAUFIQIA. Sent down to Metemme to meet the relief force.

ISMAILIA. Remained at Khartum throughout the siege.

MOHAMED ALI. Captured by Dervishes on the Blue Nile in April 1884.

ABBAS. Left Khartum with Stewart and party in September 1884 and wrecked below Berber in September 1884.

EL FASHER. Captured by the Dervishes at Berber in May 1884. Sent by the Dervishes in pursuit of *Abbas* in September 1884.

In addition to these, Gordon had two steamers assembled at Khartum during the siege:

HUSAINIA. Sunk by enemy action in November 1884 soon after being launched.

ZUBAIR. Launched towards the end of the siege.

BIBLIOGRAPHY

I. GENERAL BIOGRAPHY

BERNARD M. ALLEN, *Gordon and the Sudan*, 1931.

BERNARD M. ALLEN, *Gordon in China*, 1933.

BERNARD M. ALLEN, *Gordon*, 1935.

C. H. ALLEN, *Life of Chinese Gordon*, 1884.

"ANON", *A Woman's Memories of Gordon*, 1885. Author of *Our Queen, Life of General Gordon*, 1885.

CHARLES BEATTY, *His Country Was the World; A Study of Gordon of Khartoum*, 1954.

A. BIOVES, *Un Grand Aventurier du 19me Siècle*, 1907.

D. C. BOULGER, *Life of Gordon*, 1896.

W. F. BUTLER, *Charles G. Gordon*, 1889.

S. CHURCHILL, *General Gordon*, 1890.

C. C. COE, *General Gordon in a New Light*, 1885.

LORD ELTON, *General Gordon*, 1954.

G. R. EMERSON, *General Gordon* (Eminent Men of Action Series), 1885.

ARCHIBALD FORBES, *Chinese Gordon*, 1884.

MRS FREESE, *More About Gordon*, 1894.

HON. GERALD FRENCH, *Gordon Pacha of the Sudan; The Life Story of an Ill-requited Soldier*, 1958.

H. W. GORDON, *Events in the Life of General Gordon*, 1886.

SIR G. GRAHAM, *Last Words with Gordon*, 1887.

F. GRIN, *Charles Gordon, Un Héros*, 1885.

C. R. HAINES, *General Gordon, A Sketch*, 1902.

A. E. HAKE, *Gordon in China and the Sudan*, 1896.

LAWRENCE and ELIZABETH HANSON, *Gordon, the Story of a Hero*, 1953.

J. MACAULAY, *Gordon Anecdotes*, 1888.

ANTHONY NUTTING, *Gordon: Martyr and Misfit*, 1966.

"S.O.", *The Hero Sacrificed*, 1885.

J. W. G. SPARROW, *Gordon: Mandarin and Pasha*, 1962.

W. G. STABLES, *For Honour not Honours*, 1896.

LYTTON STRACHEY, "The End of General Gordon", essay in *Eminent Victorians*, 1918.

L. P. STUBBS, *Gordon Memorials*, 1885.

S. A. SWAINE, *General Gordon*, 1885.

M. B. SYNGE, *Life of General Charles Gordon*, 1900.

MARIE TABARIE, *Charles Gordon, Le Defenseur de Khartoum*, 1886.

E. VIZETELLY, *Gordon and the Mahdi*, 1885.

2. PUBLISHED LETTERS, ETC.

R. H. BARNES and C. E. BROWN, *C. G. Gordon; A Sketch with Facsimile Letters*, 1885.

D. C. BOULGER (ed.), *Letters from the Crimea, the Danube and Armenia 1854–58*, 1884.

LORD ELTON (ed.), *General Gordon's Khartoum Journals*, 1961.

C. G. GORDON, *Reflections in Palestine, 1883; 1884.*

M. A. GORDON (ed.), *Letters from General Gordon to his Sister*, 1888.

A. E. HAKE (ed.), *Journals of Major-General C. G. Gordon, C.B., at Khartum*, 1885.

G. B. HILL (ed.), *Colonel Gordon in Central Africa*, 1874–79. *Letters etc.*, 1881.

A. MACDONALD (ed.), *Too Late. Unpublished letters from General Gordon*, 1887.

3. PUBLISHED WORKS ABOUT GORDON DEALING WITH PARTICULAR PERIODS OF HIS CAREER

(*a*) *China*

A. E. HAKE (ed.), *Events in the Taiping Rebellion*, MSS. Reports, 1891.

S. T. LYSTER (ed.), *With Gordon in China*. Letters, 1891.

S. MOSSMAN, *Gordon in China. The Ever Victorious Army*, 1875.

A. WILSON, *The Ever Victorious Army. China Campaign with Gordon*, 1868.

(*b*) *Gravesend*

W. E. LILLEY, *Life and Works of Gordon at Gravesend*, 1885.

H. C. WILSON, *General Gordon at Gravesend*, 1885.

(*c*) *Sudan, 1874–9*

P. CRABITES, *Gordon, the Sudan and Slavery*, 1933.

(*d*) *Khartoum, 1884–5*

"A WAR CORRESPONDENT", *Why Gordon Perished*, 1896.

JOHN BUCHAN, *Gordon at Khartum*, 1934.

J. DELBECQUE, *Gordon et Le Drame de Khartoum*, 1935.

A. A. NOSKOV, *Ein Mann erhüttert Afrika; Kampf um den Soudan*, 1937.

4. HISTORICAL, AUTOBIOGRAPHICAL & BIOGRAPHICAL PUBLISHED WORKS THROWING LIGHT ON GORDON AT PARTICULAR PERIODS OF HIS CAREER

(*a*) *China*

D. C. BOULGER, *Life of Sir Halliday Macartney*, 1908.

JULIET BREDON, *Life of Sir Robert Hart*, 1909.

J. W. FOSTER (tr. and ed.), *Memoirs of Li Hung Chang*, 1913.

(*b*) *Sudan 1874–9*

C. CHAILLE-LONG, *Central Africa*, 1876.

C. CHAILLE-LONG, *The Three Prophets 1884* (New York).

C. CHAILLE-LONG, *L'Egypte et Sa Province Perdue*, 1892.

C. CHAILLE-LONG, *My Life in Four Continents*, 1912.

G. DOUIN, *Règne de Khedive Ismail*, Vol. IV, 1938.

R. W. FELKIN and C. T. WILSON, *Uganda and the Egyptian Sudan*, 1882.

R. GESSI, *Seven Years in the Sudan*, 1892.

VITA HASSAN, *La Verité sur Emin Pasha*, 1893.

R. L. HILL, *Egypt and the Sudan, 1820–1881*, 1959.

E. B. MALET, *Shifting Scenes*, 1901.

E. MARNO, *Reisen in den Aegyptischen Aquatorial-Provinz*, 1878.

S. LANE POOLE, *Watson Pasha*, 1919.

M. SABRY, *L'Empire Egyptien sous Ismail et L'Ingérence Anglo-Française*, Livre 3 (1863–79), 1933.

G. SCHWEINFURTH, (tr. Mrs Felkin), *Emin Pasha in Central Africa*, 1888.

MOHD. FUAD SHUKRI, *Al Hukm al Misri fi'il Sudan*, 1945 (Cairo).

(*c*) *Palestine 1883*

L. OLIPHANT, *Haifa*, 1887.

5. KHARTUM, 1884–5

G. C. A. ARTHUR, *Lord Kitchener*, 1920.

G. C. A. ARTHUR, *The Letters of Lord and Lady Wolseley*, 1922.

E. H. C. M. BELL, *The Life and Letters of C. F. Moberly Bell*, 1927.

BORELLI BEY, *La Chute de Khartoum*, 1893.

IBRAHIM FAUZI BEY, *The Sudan Under Gordon and Kitchener* (in Arabic), 1891.
W. S. BLUNT, *Gordon at Khartum*, 1911.
F. BRACKENBURY, *The River Column*, 1885.
G. E. BUCKLE (ed.), *Queen Victoria; Life and Letters*, Vol. 3, 1928.
W. F. BUTLER, *The Campaign of the Cataracts, 1884–85*, 1887.
E. S. C. CHILDERS, *Life of the Rt. Hon. Hugh C. E. Childers*, 1901.
COL. H. E. COLVILLE, *History of the Sudan Campaign*, 1889.
LORD CROMER, *Modern Egypt*, 2 vols., 1908.
C. CUZZI, *Funfzehn Jahre Gefangenen des Falschen Propheten*, 1900.
G. DUBARRIE, *L'Etat Mahdiste de Soudan*, 1901.
VISCOUNT ESHER, *Extracts from Journals*, 1908.
BYRON E. FARWELL, *Prisoners of the Mahdi*, 1967.
E. G. P. FITZMAURICE, *Life of Earl Granville*, 2 vols., 1905.
A. G. GARDINER, *Sir William Harcourt*, 1923.
R. L. HILL, *Slatin Pasha (1857–1932)*, 1965.
P. M. HOLT, *The Mahdist State in the Sudan, 1881–98*, 1958.
B. H. HOLLAND, *Life of Spencer Compton, 8th Duke of Devonshire*, 2 vols., 1915.
ROY JENKINS, *Sir Charles Dilke*, 1958.
A. C. LYALL, *Life of Lord Dufferin*, 1909.
JOHN MORLEY, *Rt. Hon. W. E. Gladstone*, Vol. 3, 1903.
SIR B. MALLET, *Thomas George, Earl of Northbrook*, 1908.
PHILIP MAGNUS, *Kitchener; Portrait of an Imperialist*, 1958.
F. D. MAURICE and G. C. A. ARTHUR, *Lord Wolseley*, 1924.
F. OHRWALDER, *Ten Years' Captivity in the Mahdi's Camp* (tr.), 1903.
ROUNDELL PALMER, EARL OF SELBORNE, *Memorials*, Vol. 2, 1896–98.
ADRIAN PRESTON (ed.). *In Relief of Gordon; Lord Wolseley's Campaign Journal of the Gordon Relief Expedition, 1884–85*, 1967.
F. POWER, *Letters from Khartum During the Siege*, 1885.
C. ROYLE, *The Egyptian Campaigns, 1882–85*, 1900.
COL. E. W. C. SANDES, *Royal Engineers in Egypt and the Sudan*, 1937.
A. H. SAYCE, *Reminiscences*, 1923.
MEKKI SHIBEIKA, *British Policy in the Sudan, 1882–1902*, 1952.
RUDOLF SLATIN, *Fire and Sword in the Sudan*, 1906.
JULIAN SYMONS, *England's Pride; the Story of the Gordon Relief Expedition*, 1965.

A. B. THEOBALD, *The Mahdiya; A History of the Anglo-Egyptian Sudan, 1881–1899*, 1951.

S. L. GWYN and GERTRUDE M. TUCKWELL, *Sir Charles Dilke*, 2 vols., 1917.

R. H. VETCH, *Sir G. Graham. Life, Letters and Diaries*, 1901.

R. H. VETCH, *Life of Sir Andrew Clarke*, 1905.

C. M. WATSON, *Sir Charles Wilson*, 1909.

F. WAYTE, *W. T. Stead*, 1925.

C. W. WILSON, *From Korti to Khartum*, 1886.

F. R. WINGATE, *Mahdism in the Egyptian Sudan*, 1891.

SIR EVELYN WOOD, *From Midshipman to Field Marshal*, 1906.

A. B. WYLDE, *'83 to '87 in the Sudan*, 1888.

6. MISCELLANEOUS PUBLICATIONS

Durham University Journal, Vol. XLVII, No. 3, June 1955, R. L. Hill, "The Gordon Literature".

Pall Mall Gazette, Extra No. 14, 1885 (London Library, p. 2891).

Revue Politique et Litteraire, February 1884, J. Reinach, "Account of Conversations with Gordon in January 1880".

Royal Engineers Journal, June 1892, Watson Pasha, "How Gordon Was Lost".

Royal Engineers' Journal, October 1885, "Watson Pasha. The Campaigns of Gordon's Steamers".

C. RIVERS WILSON, *Chapters from My Official Life*, 1926.

Sudan Notes and Records, Vol. X, 1927, "Unpublished Letters from Gordon to Colonel Stanton, 1874–79".

Sudan Notes and Records, Vol. XIII, 1930, "Account of last days of siege of Khartum".

7. BLUE BOOKS (Available at Foreign Office Library, Cornwall House, Stamford St., London, S.E.1.)

China, No. 3 (1864).

Egypt, Nos. 11 and 22 (1883).

Egypt, Nos. 2, 6, 7, 8, 9, 12, 13, 16 and 19 (1884).

Egypt, Nos. 2 and 9 (1885).

8. HANSARD

Parliamentary Debates, Lords and Commons, February 1884 to June 1885.

9. DAILY JOURNALS. (Available at British Museum Newspaper Library, Colindale.)

Pall Mall Gazette, December 1883–end February 1885.
The Times, Ditto.

10. UNPUBLISHED MATERIAL AVAILABLE FOR PUBLIC INSPECTION

(*a*) *British Museum*

Gladstone Papers, B.M. Add. MS. 44132 to 44769.
Letters from Gordon to Sir Charles Watson (Morrow Bequest).
Original MS. of Gordon's Khartum Journals.
Originals of Gordon's correspondence with members of his family (Moffit Papers).

(*b*) *Public Record Office* Chancery Lane

Cromer Papers, F.O. 633, Vol. 4.
Granville Papers, P.R.O. 30/29.
F.O. 17/371–412 (for Gordon's career in China).
F.O. 78 and F.O. 141 series from October 1882 to May 1885.
W.O. 32 series from August 1884 to May 1885.

(*c*) *Institute of Royal Engineers, Chatham*

C. G. GORDON, "Notes on Operations round Shanghai".

(*d*) *Rhodes House Library, Oxford*

Maund Papers, Miscellaneous letters from General Gordon.
Waller Papers, Letters from General Gordon to Rev. Horace Waller.

11. UNPUBLISHED MATERIAL BELIEVED TO BE IN PRIVATE HANDS

Barnes Papers, Letters from Gordon to Rev. R. H. Barnes.
Blunt Papers, Letters from Gordon to W. S. Blunt.
Bredin Papers, Miscellaneous letters from Gordon.
Donnelly Papers, Letters from Gordon to Major-Gen. Sir J. Donnelly.
Freese Papers, Letters from Gordon to Mrs Freese.
Gordon's Diary of Events in Equatoria Province, 1874–76.

NOTES

INTRODUCTION: THE GORDON LITERATURE AND LEGEND

1. By B. M. Allen in his book *Gordon and the Sudan* published in 1931.

CHAPTER ONE: THE MISSIONARY

1. H. E. Wortham: *Gordon: An Intimate Portrait*, p. 22.
2. The expression Gordon used for his young protégés at Gravesend.
3. R. Hill: *Egypt in the Sudan, 1820–1881*, p. 139.
4. For text of this memorandum, see *The Times* of 24/9/85, when it was first published; also Boulger: *Life of Gordon*, pp. 204–7.
5. Boulger, op. cit., p. 225.
6. See Granville Papers, dated 18/11/82, in P.R.O. 30/29/168 memo.
7. *Gordon at Khartum*, p. 11.
8. If Blunt's recollection is correct, Gordon must have derived this impression from his interview with Granville. The British Government had certainly intervened to prevent Arabi and his associates from being executed, but there was no question, so far as the British Government were concerned, of Arabi's restoration to office, although they might have been prepared to contemplate his eventual return to Egypt as a private citizen.
9. Oliphant: *Haifa*, p. 277.

CHAPTER TWO: THE BACKGROUND TO THE MISSION

1. Note by Sir C. Wilson to Malet enclosed with Malet–Granville 659, 2/10/82, F.O. 78/3442.
2. Report by Wilson enclosed in Malet–Granville 744, 28/10/82, F.O. 78/3442. Gordon had left Cape Town on 14 October and, at the time Wilson wrote his report, was on his way to England.
3. Granville–Malet 404, 7/11/82, F.O. 78/3443.
4. Ibid. 387, 30/10/82, ibid.
5. Malet–Granville, 1/11/82, F.O. 78/3443.
6. Granville–Malet 393, 2/11/82, ibid.
7. Memo by Alison encl. with Malet–Granville 787, 4/11/82, ibid.
8. Malet-Granville 788, 4/11/82, ibid.
9. Memo by Granville dated 18/11/82 in 30/29/168.
10. Granville–Dufferin, 3/11/82, F.O. 141/167.
11. Dufferin–Granville, 21/11/82 and 25/11/82, 30/29/166.
12. Stewart–Dufferin, 13/3/83, F.O. 141/168.
13. Malet–Granville 32, 11/6/83, F.O. 78/3561.
14. Granville–Malet 32, 11/5/83, F.O. 78/3561.
15. Cromer: *Modern Egypt*, Vol. I, p. 367.
16. Baring–Granville 43, 28/9/83, F.O. 78/3557.
17. Granville–Baring 247, 3/10/83, F.O. 78/3561.
18. Baring-Granville, 19/11/83, F.O. 78/3559.
19. Granville–Baring, 20/11/83, F.O. 78/3561.

20. Cromer, op. cit., Vol. I, p. 401.
21. Ibid., p. 402.
22. Ibid., p. 403.
23. Gladstone–Granville, 24/12/83, 30/29/127.
24. Northbrook–Granville, 24/12/83, 30/29/139.
25. Granville–Hartington, 28/12/83, 30/29/135.
26. Note by Granville, 29/12/83 in 30/29/146.
27. Cromer: *Modern Egypt*, Vol. I, p. 382.
28. A. B. Theobald: *The Mahdiya*, p. 78.
29. 30/29/162.
30. Baring-Granville, 21/1/84, F.O. 78/3666.

CHAPTER THREE: THE SELECTION OF THE MISSIONARY

1. Gwyn and Tuckwell: *Sir Charles Dilke*, Vol. I, p. 552.
2. E. S. C. Childers: *Life of Rt. Hon. Hugh C. E. Childers*, Vol. II, p. 180.
3. See memo. Wolseley–Hartington, 23/11/83 which was communicated to Granville by Hartington. 30/29/133.
4. Northbrook-Granville, 23/11/82, 30/29/138.
5. Ponsonby–Granville, 24/12/82, 30/29/41.
6. See Childers, op. cit., Vol. II, p. 176.
7. Granville–Gladstone, 27/11/83, B.M. Add. M.S. 44176.
8. Cromer: *Modern Egypt*, Vol. I, p. 423.
9. E. H. C. M. Bell: *The Life and Letters of C. F. Moberly Bell*, p. 91.
10. R. H. Vetch: *Life of Sir Andrew Clarke*, p. 264.
11. Holland: *Life of Devonshire*, Vol. I, p. 415.
12. See Blunt: *Gordon at Khartum*, pp. 160–9.
13. Holland, op. cit., p. 414: Gordon had made some favourable references to Nubar in the *Pall Mall Gazette* interview and in various private letters. But the two were not friends. Their personal relations, when Gordon had been in the Sudan, were bad. Gordon had regarded Nubar as a typical representative of Pashadom. He had once challenged him to a duel. Nubar once described Gordon as a man who spent the morning praying and then went out and hanged somebody in the afternoon.
14. Holland, op. cit., p. 416.
15. Buckle: *Letters of Queen Victoria*, Vol. 3, p. 469. Baring had made one request, which was not repeated and which was apparently repented, for one British officer.
16. Cromer: *Modern Egypt*, Vol. I, pp. 424–5.
17. Holland, op. cit., p. 416.
18. 30/29/128.
19. From a letter from Wolseley to Sir Henry Gordon dated 6/9/85.
20. Holland, op. cit., p. 419.
21. Baring–Granville 28, 15/1/84, F.O. 78/3662.
22. See Morley: *Life of Gladstone*, Vol. 3, p. 150.
23. See B. M. Allen: *Gordon in the Sudan*, pp. 225–6 for an elucidation of the times of these telegrams.
24. Telegram No. 44a, F.O. 78/3865.
25. 30/29/128.

CHAPTER FOUR: THE OBJECT OF THE MISSION

1. Fitzmaurice: *Life of Granville*, Vol. II, p. 401.
2. Jenkins: *Dilke*, p. 179.
3. Gwyn and Tuckwell, op. cit., p. 29.
4. Cromer, op. cit., Vol. 1, p. 429 note.
5. Granville–Baring, 18/1/84, F.O. 78/3696.
6. Ibid., 30/29/162.
7. Gwyn and Tuckwell, op. cit., pp. 29–30; Jenkins, op. cit., p. 180.
8. Hartington–Granville, 18/1/84, 30/29/134.
9. Holland, op. cit., p. 418.
10. See 30/29/128 telegrams of 18 and 19/1/84. Gladstone's reply, translated from Gladstonese, indicated a very limited measure of approval.
11. Sayce: *Reminiscences*, pp. 229–30.
12. Baring–Granville 30/29/162.
13. Between Suakin and Berber.
14. Governor of Bahr-al-Ghazal.
15. Morley, op. cit., Vol. 3, p. 151.
16. 30/29/122.
17. Gordon–Granville, 19/1/84, F.O. 75/3696.
18. Tuckwell, op. cit., p. 30.
19. Granville–Baring, 22/1/84, F.O. 78/3662.
20. 30/29/139.
21. Cromer, op. cit., Vol. I, p. 433.
22. Ibid., p. 434.
23. Gordon–Baring, 22/1/84, F.O. 78/3696.
24. Vetch: *Life of Sir Gerald Graham*, p. 253.
25. See encl. to Baring–Granville 171, 11/2/84, F.O. 78/3667.
26. See Baring–Gordon, 25/1/84, F.O. 78/3666.
27. Baring had obviously inserted this in view of Gordon's publicly-expressed opinions in opposition to evacuation. He recorded that, on reading the instructions over to him, Gordon not only concurred, but insisted on adding "you think it should on no account be changed".
28. Gordon–Baring, 28/1/84, encl. with Baring–Granville 119, 4/2/84, F.O. 78/3666.
29. For texts and English translations of these see encl. A1, A2, B1 and B2 to Baring–Granville, 1/2/84, F.O. 78/3666. An Arabic scholar, P. M. Holt, who has examined the Arabic texts of these documents, is of the opinion that "the phraseology suggests that they were not intended as alternatives but to authorise two successive stages in Gordon's mission".
30. Baring–Granville, 1/2/84, F.O. 78/3666.
31. Cromer, op. cit., Vol. I, pp. 447–8.
32. P. M. Holt: *The Mahdist State in the Sudan*, p. 80.
33. Cromer, op. cit., Vol. I, pp. 455–7.
34. Ibid., p. 459.
35. Described in detail by Baring in *Egypt*, No. 12 (1884), pp. 38–41.
36. Cromer, op. cit., Vol. I, pp. 458–9.
37. Ibid.
38. Allen, op. cit., p. 251 note 4.

39. 30/29/162.
40. Vetch, op. cit., pp. 254–5.
41. *Pall Mall Gazette*, 6/2/84.
42. Ibid., 15/2/84.
43. A tribe inhabiting the Eastern Sudan.
44. Baring–Granville, 1/2/84, F.O. 78/3666.
45. Cromer, op. cit., Vol. I, p. 563.
46. Ibid., p. 567.
47. Ibid., p. 570.
48. Morley, op. cit., Vol. 3, p. 558.
49. Ibid., p. 169.
50. Fitzmaurice: *Life of Granville*, Vol. 2, p. 400.
51. Mallet: *Life of Northbrook*, p. 184.
52. Gwyn and Tuckwell, op. cit., Vol. II, p. 35.
53. Ibid., p. 37.
54. Ibid., p. 41.
55. Holland, op. cit., Vol. I, p. 492.
56. Selborne: *Memorials*, Vol. 2, p. 349.

CHAPTER FIVE: THE OUTSET OF THE MISSION

1. This, and most of the other information about the journey to Khartum, is derived from Colonel Stewart's diaries, the first instalments of which were sent by him to Baring and by Baring to London. See F.O. 78/3666.
2. Gordon–Baring, 31/1/84, F.O. 78/3666.
3. Baring–Granville, 5/2/84, F.O. 73/3666.
4. Baring–Granville, 10/2/84, F.O. 78/3666.
5. Gordon–Baring, 31/1/84, ibid.
6. Baring–Granville and enclosures, 9/2/84, F.O. 78/3666.
7. Which the F.O. were at that time trying to negotiate. See F.O. 78/3666.
8. Vetch, op. cit., pp. 259–60.
9. Ibid.
10. Gordon–Baring, 8/2/84, F.O. 78/3667.
11. See F.O. 78/3667.
12. Whom Stewart suspected of being a secret adherent of the Mahdi.
13. This was the Anglo-Egyptian Anti-Slavery Convention of 1877.
14. Cuzzi: *Funfzehn Jahre Gefangener des falschen Propheten*, p. 75 et seq.
15. See F.O. 78/3666.
16. Baring–Granville, 12/2/84, F.O. 73/3666.
17. Power: *Letters from Khartum.*
18. Shibeika: *Anglo-Egyptian Policy in the Sudan, 1882–1902*, p. 213. Apparently only the first Firman was published in Khartum and not the second Firman authorising Gordon to conduct the evacuation.
19. Holland, op. cit., Vol. I, p. 425.
20. The only "British troops" in Suakin at that time were some Marines who had been landed to help defend the town.
21. Holland, op. cit., Vol. I, p. 425.
22. B.M. Add. MS. 44547.
23. Allen, op. cit., p. 466.

24. Gordon had not said anything of the kind.
25. See *inter alia* Tuckwell, op. cit., Vol. 2, p. 37.
26. Granville–Baring, 15/2/84, 30/29/100.
27. Gladstone on 12 February.
28. Hartington on 19 February.
29. Lord Edmond Fitzmaurice, Under-Secretary of State for Foreign Affairs on 15 February.
30. Cromer, op. cit., Vol. I, p. 412.
31. Baring–Granville, 3/3/84, F.O. 78/3668.
32. Vetch, op. cit., pp. 277–8.

CHAPTER SIX: THE CONDUCT OF THE MISSION

1. Gordon–Baring encl. with Baring–Granville, 19/2/84, F.O. 78/4194.
2. Gladstone–Granville, 20/2/84, B.M. Add. MS. 44547.
3. Granville–Baring, 21/2/84, 30/29/200; Tuckwell, op. cit., Vol. 2, p. 33.
4. Granville–Baring, 22/2/84, F.O. 78/4194.
5. Gordon–Cuzzi, 27/2/84, F.O. 78/3744.
6. Baring–Granville, 27/2/84, F.O. 78/3667.
7. Gordon–Baring, 26/2/84, encl. in Baring–Granville, 28/2/84, F.O. 78/3667.
8. This was incorrect; they were drawn out by Granville in London and by Baring in Cairo.
9. Tuckwell, op. cit., Vol. II, p. 40.
10. Tuckwell, op. cit., Vol. II, p. 40.
11. Ibid.
12. Baring–Granville, 28/2/84, F.O. 78/4194.
13. Tuckwell, op. cit., p. 40.
14. See enclosures to Baring-Granville, 2/3/84, F.O. 78/3667.
15. Granville–Baring, 1/3/84, F.O. 78/3662.
16. Baring–Gordon, 2/3/84, F.O. 78/3667.
17. Stewart–Baring, 4/3/84, encl. with Baring–Granville, 4/3/84, F.O. 78/4194.
18. Cromer, op. cit., p. 504.
19. Ibid., p. 505.
20. Ibid., p. 506.
21. Granville–Baring, 5/3/84, F.O. 78/4194.
22. Cromer, op. cit., pp. 510–11.
23. Encl. with Baring–Granville, 9/3/84, F.O. 78/4194.
24. Baring–Granville, 9/3/84, F.O. 78/4194.
25. Cromer, op. cit., p. 515.
26. Tuckwell, op. cit., pp. 42–3.
27. Morley, op. cit., Vol. 3, p. 159.
28. Cromer, op. cit., p. 520.
29. Tuckwell, op. cit., p. 43.
30. Morley, op. cit., Vol. 3, p. 169.
31. Mallet, op. cit., p. 181.
32. Which was not a "slave trade" but a "slave owning" Proclamation.
33. Cromer, op. cit., p. 522 n.

34. See F.O. 78/3668.
35. Encl. to Baring–Granville, 13/3/84, F.O. 78/3668.
36. Cromer, op. cit., p. 521.
37. Ibid., p. 522.
38. Granville–Baring, 13/3/84, F.O. 78/4194.
39. Baring–Granville, 14/3/84, F.O. 78/4194.
40. Granville–Baring, 16/3/84, F.O. 78/4194.
41. Encl. to Baring–Granville, 18/3/84, F.O. 78/4194.
42. Baring–Granville, 16/3/84, F.O. 78/3668.
43. Granville–Baring, 16/3/84, F.O. 78/3669.
44. Ibid., 21/3/84, F.O. 78/3662.
45. Baring–Granville, 22/3/84, with Hewett–Baring, 22/3/84, encl. F.O. 78/3669.
46. Baring–Granville, 24/3/84, F.O. 78/3669.
47. Ibid., 30/29/162.
48. Granville–Baring, 25/3/84, F.O. 78/3662.
49. Allen, op. cit., pp. 306–7.
50. Tuckwell, op. cit., p. 44.
51. Cromer, op. cit., p. 545.
52. Baring–Granville, 26/3/84, F.O. 78/3669.
53. This, like many of Coetlogon's military views, was unduly pessimistic.
54. Granville–Baring, 29/3/84, 30/29/200.
55. Ibid., 28/3/84, F.O. 78/3662.
56. Tuckwell, op. cit., p. 44.
57. Granville–Baring, 28/3/84, F.O. 78/3662.
58. Cromer, op. cit., p. 447.
59. Ibid., p. 547.
60. Tuckwell, op. cit., p. 48.
61. Dilke omits Childers, the Chancellor of the Exchequer, who was one of those most strongly against an expedition.
62. Holland, op. cit., p. 435.
63. Tuckwell, op. cit., p. 5.
64. Ibid.

CHAPTER SEVEN: THE FAILURE OF THE MISSION

1. This was not correct since the defeat at Halfaya was not known to H.M.G. until after Graham's force had left the Sudan.
2. Holland, op. cit., pp. 439–40.
3. Ibid., p. 440.
4. Ibid., pp. 440–1.
5. Ibid., p. 441 et seq.
6. 30/29/134.
7. Baring–Granville, 14/4/84, F.O. 78/3671.
8. Encl. with Baring–Granville, 16/4/84, F.O. 78/3671.
9. Encl. in Baring–Granville, 18/4/84, F.O. 78/3671.
10. Holland, op. cit., p. 447.
11. Granville–Egerton, 23/4/84, F.O. 78/3663.
12. Holland, op. cit., p. 448.

13. Ibid., p. 450.
14. Ibid., pp. 451–2.
15. Ibid., p. 453.
16. Egerton–Granville, 25/4/84, F.O. 78/3671.
17. Gladstone–Granville, 8/5/84, 30/29/128.
18. Blunt, op. cit., p. 221.
19. Ibid., p. 223.
20. Ibid., p. 231.
21. *Egypt*, Nos. 12 and 13 (1884).
22. *Egypt*, Nos. 15 and 16 (1884).
23. Blunt, op. cit., p. 232.
24. This is debatable, although Stewart certainly regarded the two proposals as interlinked.
25. Granville–Egerton, 17/5/84, F.O. 78/3663.
26. Holland, op. cit., p. 458.
27. Tuckwell, op. cit., p. 53.
28. Ibid., pp. 53–4.
29. Holland, op. cit., p. 464.
30. Ibid., pp. 460–1.
31. Ibid., p. 460.
32. Tuckwell, op. cit., p. 60.
33. Holland, op. cit., pp. 464–5.
34. At this time a controversial Government Bill for extending the franchise was the principal preoccupation both of the Cabinet and of Parliament.
35. Holland, op. cit., p. 467.
36. Tuckwell, op. cit., p. 60.
37. According to another account by Gladstone—Cabinet Memoranda B.M. Add. MS. 44645—a Nile expedition was favoured by Hartington and Selborne, with Northbrook, Dodson, Granville and Carlingford lukewarm. Gladstone recorded that he was "disappointed", presumably with the growing trend of opinion in favour of an expedition.
38. Egerton–Granville, 20/7/84, F.O. 78/3696.
39. Tuckwell, op. cit., p. 60.
40. Granville–Egerton, 24/7/84, F.O. 78/3664.
41. Fitzmaurice, op. cit., Vol. 2, p. 393.
42. Tuckwell, op. cit., p. 61.
43. Holland, op. cit., p. 472.
44. Selborne: *Memorials*, Vol. 2, p. 349.
45. Holland, op. cit., p. 476.
46. Ibid., pp. 476–7.
47. Ibid., p. 477.
48. Ibid.

CHAPTER EIGHT: THE RELIEF EXPEDITION

1. Hartington-Granville, 22/8/84, Holland, op. cit., p. 483.
2. Ibid.
3. Tuckwell, op. cit., p. 61.

4. Holland, op. cit., p. 487.
5. Ibid., pp. 480–1.
6. Ibid., p. 483.
7. Ibid., pp. 483–4.
8. W. S. Blunt wrote that the reason for Granville's subservience to Gladstone in this, and in other, matters, was that "he was poor and in debt and dependent on Gladstone for his continuance in office". Blunt, op. cit., p. 168.
9. Holland, op. cit., pp. 489–91.
10. Hartington–Gladstone, 12/9/84, B.M. Add. MS. 44147.
11. Hartington–Granville, 16/9/84, 30/29/134.
12. Ibid.
13. Encl. to Baring-Granville, 21/9/84, F.O. 78/3678.
14. Granville–Baring, 20/9/84, F.O. 141/198.
15. Encl. to Baring-Granville, 21/9/84, F.O. 78/3678.
16. Egerton–Granville, 29/7/84, F.O. 78/3678.
17. Kitchener–Wood, 3/8/84, F.O. 141/199.
18. Egerton–Granville, 29/8/84, F.O. 141/200. Granville, idiotically, replied to this telegram asking for an explanation for the delay in the receipt of these messages!
19. Baring–Granville, 17/9/84, F.O. 141/200.
20. This almost certainly should have read 2,000.
21. In fact he had not.
22. This message was not received until later.
23. One of his military commanders.
24. Baring–Granville, 18/9/84, F.O. 141/200.
25. In considering the somewhat incoherent phraseology of these two messages to the Khedive, it must be remembered that they had first been translated from Gordon's English into Arabic in Khartum and then retranslated from Arabic into English in Cairo.
26. Gladstone–Granville, 19/9/84, 30/29/128.
27. Holland, op. cit., p. 492.
28. *Dundee Advertiser*, 18/9/84.
29. Encls. to Baring–Granville, 20/9/84, F.O. 78/3678.
30. "Mutamahdi" means, in Arabic "the so-called Mahdi".
31. Encl. to Baring–Granville, 21/9/84, F.O. 78/3678.
32. Baring–Granville, 22/9/84, ibid.
33. Ibid.
34. Ibid., 28/9/84, F.O. 78/3678.
35. Ibid., 5/10/84, F.O. 78/3679.
36. Ibid., 5/10/84, 30/29/30.
37. *The Letters of Lord and Lady Wolseley*, p. 119.
38. Egerton–Sanderson, 31/8/84, F.O. 78/3677.
39. See *Wolseley's Campaign Journal*, ed. Adrian Preston, p. 46.
40. See 30/29/140.
41. Mallet, op. cit., p. 184.
42. Ibid., pp. 194–5.
43. Preston, op. cit., p. 57.

44. Ibid., pp. 98–9.
45. Ibid., p. 103.
46. Ibid., p. 57.
47. Ibid., p. xxxiv.
48. Ibid., p. xxxii.

CHAPTER NINE: THE AGONY OF THE MISSIONARY

1. Allen, op. cit., p. 355.
2. See Appendix "Gordon's Steamers" for details of his "fleet".
3. Journal, p. 8. (Journal reference from A. E. Hake's 1885 edition.) It is not clear whether this includes the garrison.
4. Power had been appointed British Consular Agent at Khartum in December 1883.
5. Allen, op. cit., p. 365.
6. R. Slatin: *Fire and Sword in the Sudan*, p. 301.
7. Journal, p. 104.
8. Ibid., p. 38.
9. Ibid., p. 74.
10. An ardeb is about $5\frac{1}{2}$ bushels.
11. Journal, p. 204.
12. Ibid., pp. 206–7 An oke is about $2\frac{3}{4}$ lb.
13. Ibid., p. 225.
14. Ibid., p. 227.
15. Wolseley commented in his diary "That any man could have been so idiotic is to me a puzzle. If, as he says, he did not consider it safe to keep cipher any longer in Khartum why not have burnt it?" Preston, op. cit., p. 67.
16. Gordon–Wolseley, 4/11/84, encl. in Baring–Granville, 15/11/84, F.O. 78/3680.
17. Journal, p. 301.
18. Ibid., p. 319.
19. Ibid., p. 324.
20. Ibid., p. 331.
21. Ibid., p. 351.
22. Ibid., p. 255.
23. Ibid., p. 384.
24. Ibid., p. 394.
25. Ibid., p. 395.
26. See Preston, op. cit., p. 102.
27. Ibid., p. 103.
28. Ibid.
29. Ibid., pp. 103–4.
30. Colville: *History of the Sudan Campaign*, Part 1, p. 139.
31. W.O. 32/265.
32. Lane Poole: *Watson Pasha*, p. 163.
33. Sir H. Gordon: *Events in the Life of C. G. Gordon*, p. 390.
34. Journal, p. 85.
35. Ibid., pp. 86–7.
36. Ibid., p. 93.

37. Ibid., pp. 136–7.
38. Ibid., p. 138.
39. Ibid., p. 307.
40. Preston, op. cit., p. 118.
41. For text of dispatches containing the above orders, etc., see W.O. 32/127.
42. See Allen, op. cit., Appendix D.
43. Allen, op. cit., pp. 429–30.

CHAPTER TEN: EPILOGUE

1. Hartington–Wolseley, 7/2/85, W.O. 33/34.

INDEX